THE IRONIC HUME

The Ironic Hume

by John Valdimir Price

UNIVERSITY OF TEXAS PRESS, AUSTIN

Printed by The University of Texas Printing Division, Austin
Bound by Universal Bookbindery, Inc., San Antonio

To
N H P
A K P

PREFACE

Of books about irony, or of irony itself, there is no end, nor is there likely to be, so long as men have a sense of humor. Of books about David Hume, no end is yet in sight. Having wondered what impact the ironic mode in England during the eighteenth century had on David Hume, I attended to a close study of his texts, his life, and, most important, the intellectual milieu in which he lived. A feeling that many of Hume's concessions to religion were ironic led me to correlate his writings with his life and his intellectual milieu. Consequently, one of the assumptions of this book is that the text alone is not enough in determining an author's meaning. With this in mind, I have used Professor Mossner's biography of Hume as something of a guidebook, and I should like to think that my work supplements our understanding of Hume's life and thought. Indeed, much of what I say may be puzzling to the reader unfamiliar with *The Life of David Hume,* but scholarship stands to gain little by the repetition of more than the essential facts.

I have resisted, not always successfully, the temptation to correlate Hume's ironic mode with other examples from the eighteenth century. Such a digression would have been interesting but beyond my intention in writing this book, as contrasted to a hypothetical book I *might* have written. As for other excursions the book does not contain—I have not enumerated every manifestation of Hume's irony; some of those I have omitted are mentioned in other books and articles on Hume listed in the secondary sources. Hume's lesser-known works, such as the *Account of Stewart,* receive disproportionate attention simply because they illuminate the mode and methodology of irony in Hume's better-known writings, such as the two *Enquiries.*

I have tried in most places to avoid "explicating" the irony of a particular passage, except when it must serve as prologue to an explanation of one of Hume's ideas or to the intellectual, cultural, and social background against which the irony must be seen. Were lengthy titles in vogue today, I should probably have subtitled this book *An Inquiry into the Intellectual Background of Irony as a Developing Mode of Thought in David Hume's Life and Writings.* But lengthy subtitles, like Pinocchio's nose, can go on forever.

One is never quite certain how a study of this kind will turn out until the research and writing have been completed. I was able to find most of the materials I needed in The University of Texas library and the Henry E. Huntington library, whose librarians were courteous and helpful. I am particularly grateful for the aid I received outside of this country from the National Library of Scotland, from Mr. R. Burnet and Miss Margaret Deal of that library; and from Mr. R. O. MacKenna of the University Library, Glasgow. Mr. MacKenna was instrumental in helping me locate copies of the *Bellmen's Petition* and the *Account of Stewart.*

While libraries, indispensable for research, are usually accessible to the scholar, financial support for projects in the "humanities" (to accept for a moment the artificial distinction between "scientists" and "humanists") is not so accessible. It is a pleasure to thank the Committee on Research of the University of California, Riverside, for a grant that considerably lessened some of the tedious work that would otherwise have been necessary.

I am indebted to a number of people for their aid in reading the manuscript in its various stages. Professors Thomas M. Cranfill, Daniel Kading, and Gordon H. Mills, all of The University of Texas, were kind enough to read the manuscript in its early stages with great care and to make numerous useful comments, which I very much appreciate. Professor Ralph Cohen of the University of California, Los Angeles, also read the manuscript and made some particularly acute suggestions. My good friend Jack Gilbert of Louisiana State University, Baton Rouge, has given me much help by reading various drafts of the manuscript, and our numerous conversations about Hume have always been instructive to me. I am indebted to no one so much as Professor Ernest Campbell Mossner, whose scholarship on Hume must be the starting point for anyone writing on Hume. His seemingly unlimited knowledge of Hume and Humeana more than once kept me from foolish errors. His encouragement and his similar interest in Hume kept my enthusiasm high, and his meticulous reading and subsequent suggestions for improvement of the manuscript were an invaluable aid in writing. Among my colleagues at the University of California, Riverside, I should like to express my appreciation to Frederick J. Hoffman for reading the manuscript and for other kindnesses too numerous to count, and to Stanley Stewart, whose encouragement, friendship, and example made the writing of the manuscript seem, at the very least, much easier. Finally, it is a commonplace in acknowledgments to thank one's wife, and I would be more than remiss in my duties did I not so thank my wife, Sylvia, for continual aid in proofreading, in checking footnotes, and in spotting logical inconsistencies.

All this help, of course, does not relieve me of the responsibility for any remaining errors. In accord with convention, then, I add the assertion, not likely to be challenged, that I alone am guilty of any errors of fact or judgment that may be committed in the ensuing pages.

J. V. P.

Riverside, California

CONTENTS

Preface vii

Abbreviations xiii

Bibliographical Note xv

Permissions xvi

1. The Formation of a Literary Mode 3

2. A Mode of Living and Writing 36

3. The Expansion of a Literary Mode 74

4. The Culmination of a Literary Mode 121

Appendixes

    A. *Account of Stewart* 153

    B. *Bellmen's Petition* 173

Authorities Cited 177

Index 181

ABBREVIATIONS

In order to eliminate excessive footnoting, I have used throughout the following abbreviations:

Texts for works of David Hume:

Dialogues = *Dialogues concerning Natural Religion*, ed. by Norman Kemp Smith.

ECHU = *An Inquiry concerning Human Understanding*, ed. by Charles W. Hendel.

ECPM = *An Inquiry concerning the Principles of Morals*, ed. by Charles W. Hendel.

History = *The History of England from the Invasion of Julius Caesar to the Revolution in 1688.*

HL = *The Letters of David Hume*, ed. by J. Y. T. Greig.

NHL = *New Letters of David Hume*, ed. by Raymond Klibansky and Ernest Campbell Mossner.

THN = *A Treatise of Human Nature*, ed. by L. A. Selby-Bigge.

Works = *The Philosophical Works of David Hume*, ed. by T. H. Green and T. H. Grose.

Life = *The Life of David Hume*, Ernest Campbell Mossner.

A BIBLIOGRAPHICAL NOTE

In many instances I have been able to include the reference within the text and have done so. In other instances, where the material referred to would clarify the discussion for the reader unfamiliar with Hume, the reference has been footnoted. In other words, sources for quotations are usually cited in the text, while explanatory material, even from the source, is cited in a footnote.

For the most part, quotations from Hume's literary and philosophical works have been taken from the Green and Grose edition; the *Dialogues concerning Natural Religion* is the major exception. The references to material from the *Treatise of Human Nature* and the two *Enquiries* also include a page reference to other editions of those works, since the Green and Grose is not always available, even in university libraries. The reader who compares the other editions to Green and Grose will no doubt discover a number of errors, as I did, in the Hendel and, especially, in the Selby-Bigge texts. The problem in regard to the *History of England* is even greater, since this work is more often ignored than consulted in any study of Hume. Quotations from it include in Roman numerals the chapter source, for example, *History*, V, Chap. XL, 160–161. All quotations are reproduced exactly as they appear in the text; no "modernization" has been attempted in reproducing Hume's letters or the *History*. Readers checking quotations from the *History* will encounter some difficulties: textual corruption is a constant companion to each successive reprint of the *History*. Even editions labelled "with the author's last corrections and improvements, to which is prefixed a short account of his life, written by himself" cannot be trusted. I have used an edition printed in Hume's lifetime because it would seem to obviate most of the errors, although it does not incorporate the "last corrections." I hope that I have introduced no further errors.

PERMISSIONS

Permission to quote from the following publications is gratefully acknowledged:

Boswell, James. *Life of Johnson*, ed. by G. B. Hill, rev. and enlarged by L. F. Powell. 6 vols. Oxford: Clarendon Press, 1934–1950.

Boswell, James. *Private Papers of James Boswell from Malahide Castle*, ed. by F. A. Pottle. 18 vols. New York: Privately Printed, 1928–1934.

Broad, C. D. *Five Types of Ethical Theory*. London: Routledge and Kegan Paul, Ltd., 1956.

Hume, David. *Letters of David Hume*, ed. by J. Y. T. Greig. 2 vols. Oxford: Clarendon Press, 1932.

Hume, David. *New Letters of David Hume*, ed. by Raymond Klibansky and Ernest Campbell Mossner, Oxford: Clarendon Press, 1954.

Mandeville, Bernard. *The Fable of the Bees*, ed. by F. B. Kaye. 2 vols. Oxford: Clarendon Press, 1924.

Mossner, Ernest Campbell. *The Life of David Hume*. Austin: University of Texas Press, 1954.

THE IRONIC HUME

1. The Formation of a Literary Mode

"The first Success of most of my writings was not such as to be an Object of Vanity."

David Hume was born on 26 April 1711 (O.S.), at the very apogee of the Augustan Age, when, among countless other works, *Absalom and Achitophel* (1681), *The Shortest Way with Dissenters* (1702), and *A Tale of a Tub* (1704), had been widely read and discussed. For the next twenty-five years, during which Hume, by his own admission, was reading through the family library, such important works of English literature as the *Essay on Criticism* (1711) and the *Essay on Man* (1733–1734), *Gulliver's Travels* (1726), *A Modest Proposal* (1729), to name only a few, were published; and Hume undoubtedly read them. In addition, papers from the *Tatler* and the *Spectator* were part of his reading; yet classical authors were not neglected as he admits in his autobiography: "while [my family] fancyed I was poring over Voet and Vinnius, Cicero and Virgil were the Authors which I was secretly devouring." In short, Hume had refined the process of self-education as well as any young man born into the eighteenth century could.[1]

These formative years cast the mold for mental attitudes that were to persist throughout his life. For example, in an early essay, written as a school exercise, entitled "An Historical Essay on Chivalry and modern Honour,"[2] Hume argued that the Dark Ages were responsible

[1] For an extensive and useful discussion of Hume's education and reading, consult the first five chapters of Professor Mossner's *Life*.

[2] Reprinted, with an introduction by Ernest Campbell Mossner, "David Hume's 'An Historical Essay on Chivalry and modern Honour'," in *Modern Philology*, **XLV** (1947), 54–60.

for the degeneration of classical virtue and gave birth to the spurious Gothic reverence for chivalry; this unfavorable opinion of the Dark Ages continued throughout his life. His religious scepticism had a similar beginning and a similar persistence in his life and thought; by 1725 or 1726 he was the religious sceptic that he remained during the rest of his life.[3]

While Hume shares many of the virtues and vices of his age, he was certain about his superior abilities, though modest enough about them in his relations with other people. The age into which he was born took as its ruling literary modes satire and irony; few will deny that some of the greatest masterpieces of irony and satire come from what is called the Augustan Age. Yet it is also an age of contradictions and paradoxes. Despite its insistence upon liberty, a great deal of conformity in thought was required, as Hobbes had earlier found out. One was free to inquire, to discuss, to dispute, to doubt, but only within certain boundaries; beyond them was a cultural and intellectual no man's land that only the foolish, the ignorant, or the brave entered. As an essentially irreligious man Hume was prejudged by that large part of society which equates religious scepticism with moral degradation. I would like to suggest that this initial religious scepticism combined with the predominantly satiric-ironic mode in literature to lead Hume to seek irony as a method for expressing himself.

When a man was under the intellectual and cultural pressure which Hume experienced he could not respond easily by denunciations, by shouting, or by threats. As a civilized man, Hume would not have responded that way under any circumstance. His method of dealing with those who would persecute him or ostracize him simply because of his religious or philosophical or moral opinions was subtle and effective. Irony gave him a method of operating in a world that found his ideas both strange and shocking: strange because most people were simply unable to handle them, shocking because his scepticism dared to attack

---

[3] See *Life*, pp. 51, 64; also *HL*, I, 48, a letter to Francis Hutcheson (1694–1746), about Hutcheson's *Philosophiae Moralis Institutio Compendiaria* (1742), in which Hume concludes: "I must own I am pleas'd to see such Philosophy & such instructive Morals to have once set their Foot in the Schools. I hope they will next get into the World, & then into the Churches." His continuingly unfavorable opinion of chivalry is reflected in Appendix II of the history of the Anglo-Saxons; see *History*, II, 102–144.

the citadel of religion. New ways of thinking about man's place in nature, especially if they do not reassure one's blind faith, are often difficult for the "vulgar," as Hume called them, to tolerate. Irony could at least create artificial tolerance.

In a very real sense, Hume was intellectually isolated from the cultural milieu in which he found himself. Locke had died in 1704, and even the impact of his thought had not created a climate receptive to Hume's scepticism. With the religious intellects of his time—Bishop George Berkeley (1685–1753), Bishop Joseph Butler (1692–1752) —he had little in common, and he had less in common with the religionists. He was out of step with the philosophers of his age; the new philosophical roads he opened up were not those that the less intrepid of them wished to enter, and few were bold enough or clever enough to follow the road even when Hume had pointed it out. Worse still, he had to endure the gratuitous insults of the rigidly righteous; and even someone as intellectually respectable as Bishop Butler was perhaps incapable of assimilating Hume's ways of thinking about the problems presented by the traditional approach to religion or the traditional approach to philosophy. If Bishop Butler was unable to perceive the logic of Hume's new approach to the problems of life and philosophy, then the less intellectual religionists, such as Beattie, could not possibly reply to Hume intellectually; consequently, they resorted to sarcasm and slander. The "good people" of his Scottish community, too, would be inclined to take the side of the religionists rather than Hume's without the necessity of hearing what Hume had to say. In daily contact with these people and in need of getting along with them simply because he was another human being, he handled them ironically when possible. And if that did not work, he would simply ignore them as best he could. Fortunately for him, his ironic treatment of their importunities turned them away more often than it egged them on.

In any circumstance where religion would play an important role, Hume knew that his viewpoints would be unwelcome, and their reception could range from mild to explosive. Since some of his best friends, however, were clergymen, it was obvious that unpleasant impasses might arise even among them, if religion was the topic of conversation. Although he was prepared to pursue any religious discussion as far as intelligence and reason would lead, he was unwilling to accept any dogma, especially from a friend. When that stage of the discussion was reached—if ever it was—in which reason was overcome by emotion, and dogmatism prevailed, Hume turned aside the hopefully heuristic piety of his clerical friends with irony. He had no desire to alienate them from his life, although they probably exceeded the boundaries of discretion more than they suspected.[4] If they did insult his intelligence, as I imagine they unknowingly did, Hume was not the sort of philosopher to brood about it for days on end. The philosopher, finding relations between human beings more important than supernatural certitude, could avoid those dangerous areas whenever necessary, passing off an importunate question with an ironic answer. The irony in these interchanges was friendly, even if it did often remind those friends that they had presumed too much. And they usually responded by accepting his scepticism as the product of an intelligent, reasoning mind, and not as just the whimsy sprung from perverse human nature.

Hume's friends learned, as I think we shall see, that irony was a constant, yet varied mode of expression in his life. In his first extant letter, to his college friend Michael Ramsay, dated 4 July 1727, Hume begins on a semi-ironic note:

I receivd all the Books you writ of & your Milton among the rest; when I saw it I perceivd there was a difference betwixt preaching & practizing; You accuse me of niceness & yet practize it most egregiously your self; What was the Necessity of sending your Milton wch I knew you were so fond of? Why! I lent yours & can't get it. But would you not in the same manner have lent your own? Yes. Then Why this Ceremony & Goodbreeding? (*HL*, I, 9)

That passage is typical of one of the many forms that Hume's ironic mode assumes. In this instance it is humorous, but suggests a puzzling or curious disproportion between the ideal and the actual, or between what is and what was. This letter represents Hume's early awareness of a duality, although not a Cartesian one, in human nature. The rhetorical consequences of applying reason to this duality create Hume's

---

[4] See letter to Hugh Blair, written in 1761 (below, Chap. Four), also *HL*, I, 348–351.

irony. This sample is, of course, juvenile, but good enough for a teen-ager (Hume was then sixteen); it is a token of what is to come: the observation and recording of disproportions and anomalies in human life. Coleridge has observed that the writer often notes this dispropor-tion and permits the reader to add the ironic tone himself; in the above letter Hume implies an irony which he encourages Ramsay to infer. Irony is, after all, different from what is superficially said or done; it is a projection of ambiguity into a rhetorical mode with two polarizing levels of meaning, usually a literal one and a symbolic one. Naturally, this rhetorical mode can be employed in diverse ways. Hume uses predominantly two forms: (a) that which is usually called "cosmic irony," but which asks the reader to add the ironic tone himself; and (b) that which means the opposite of what one says. Of these two, the former is characteristic of the "light touch" that he frequently gives to his serious writings, while the latter is used as a literary device.

In Hume's philosophical writings irony becomes an adjunct to his scepticism, both of which can and should be of mutual benefit to the other. On the one hand, scepticism, not accepting the authority of dogma or the privilege of tradition, can treat revered concepts with irony, while pointing out the fallacies in logic or reason in a given position. On the other hand, irony, in its two mutually exclusive levels of meaning can, in its nonliteral level, express doubt, disapproval, or dissatisfaction with the implication of the superficial level of meaning. The level of meaning which best represents the author's feelings is, in other words, sceptical about the surface meaning of the words simply interpreted. The scepticism functions on the symbolic level in order to achieve a criticism of the superficial meaning; this scepticism is ex-pressed in the two polarized levels of meaning. It is really a product of the two levels considered together, since neither is complete without the other.

Hume's use of irony in this particular way is not easy to pinpoint, for it is part of the tone of his writing, less frequently a part of the arguments. Occasionally it breaks out into the open, but it more often makes its presence felt by the shape it gives to the piece of writing as a whole. This ironic tone is, in a familiar phrase, greater than the sum total of its various parts. In Hume's philosophical works, it is estheti-cally integrated into various parts of his philosophy, appearing, one

might say, as one of the components we usually associate with belles-
lettres.

The ironic tone—phraseology that encourages the reader to infer
a disproportion in man's activities—presents itself in Hume's first
published work, to give its full title, *A Treatise of Human Nature:
Being An Attempt to introduce the experimental Method of Reasoning into* MORAL SUBJECTS (1739–1741). Sometimes this disproportion is amusing, sometimes curious, sometimes distressing. Generally
speaking, we expect an ironic tone to be mocking; or we expect irony to
be a structural, primarily literary device. Yet I think the perception of
the irony in life may legitimately be called an ironic use of language.
While the modern preference in writing is to elucidate as much as possible for the reader, the eighteenth century frequently demanded as
much of the reader as the reader demanded of the writer. Hume was
certainly not the first to perceive the ironic juxtaposition of events,
which is a by-product of the reflective life, but he did have the virtue
of calling this irony of life—in manifestations personally experienced
—to the attention of his readers, friends, and detractors.

In the *Treatise* Hume shares with the reader his recognition of the
ironic in life, hoping that he will see some of the difficulties involved
in philosophical inquiries. In Book I of the *Treatise* Hume has examined the foundations for epistemology, and his sceptical doubts are
not always reassuring, even to the sceptic. Having written at length
about the uncertainty that besets life and not finding any certainty in
the events of life, Hume here suggests that despair and abandon would
seem to be the natural product of his philosophy. Since the certainty
of any matter of fact cannot be established, how can one choose a
criterion for truth, other than custom or habit? In the last part of
Book I Hume is personal and concrete, asking himself if these speculations about the nature of reality leave man with nothing solid to
cling to. And he answers himself in this manner:

Most fortunately it happens, that since reason is incapable of dispelling
these clouds, nature herself suffices to that purpose, and cures me of this philosophical melancholy and delirium, either by relaxing this bent of mind, or
by some avocation, and lively impression of my senses, which obliterate all
these chimeras. I dine, I play a game of backgammon, I converse, and am
merry with my friends; and when after three or four hours' amusement, I

wou'd return to these speculations, they appear so cold, and strain'd, and ridiculous, that I cannot find in my heart to enter into them any farther. (*Works*, I, 548–549; *THN*, p. 269)

In other words, as a man ("Be a philosopher; but amidst all your philosophy be still a man.") Hume cannot always succumb to the sceptical temperament. He yields, as he says, to the "current of Nature," and drops those doubts which would leave a person without a means of dealing with the world. Too, the last sentence is ironic in that Hume was quite capable of re-entering into those "cold, and strain'd" speculations.

From this egocentric insight into the irony of certain philosophical problems, one might think that Hume morosely feared that many problems in philosophy, in ethics, and in human behavior were insoluble. To those looking for absolute answers, Hume's statement of the problems would leave little room for comfort. His scepticism, however, was not likely to lead to solipsism and he involved himself in contemporary ethical and social problems to a much larger degree than the two men with whom his name is usually linked in the eighteenth century, Locke and Berkeley.[5] In the *Treatise,* for example, he has some sceptical doubts about the role of woman in a sexually selective society, under the frank title "Of Chastity and Modesty." Here he argues that if either of the species should practice marital fidelity it is the female, because of her position as child bearer. Since the male in the marriage agreement wants to be assured that the child he raises is his, society properly

[5] Since the publication of Norman Kemp Smith's book, *The Philosophy of David Hume,* Francis Hutcheson must be assigned a place of importance in eighteenth-century thought. Chapters 2 and 14 of Kemp Smith's book leave little doubt about Hutcheson's effect on Hume. Hutcheson apparently read Book III of the *Treatise* (see *HL,* I, 32). In September 1739, Hume wrote to Hutcheson: "I have many other Reflections to communicate to you; but wou'd be troublesome. I shall therefore conclude with telling you, that I intend to follow your Advice in altering most of those Passages you have remarkt as defective in Point of Prudence; tho' I must own, I think you a little too delicate. Except a Man be in Orders, or be immediately concern'd in the Instruction of Youth, I do not think his Character depends upon his philosophical Speculations, as the World is now model'd; & a little Liberty seems requisite to bring into the public Notice a Book that is calculated for so few Readers. I hope you will allow me the Freedom of consulting you when I am in any Difficulty . . ." (*HL,* I, 34). Hume's four extant letters to Hutcheson are among his most philosophically interesting.

inculcates sexual exclusiveness in the female and punishes, by obloquy or ostracism, those who go astray. So argue the first five paragraphs of the section, and it would seem that Hume emphatically accepted the double standard of sexual morality. But there is more to it than that:

> Such wou'd be the reasonings of our speculative philosopher: But I am persuaded, that if he had not a perfect knowledge of human nature, he wou'd be apt to regard them as mere chimerical speculations, and wou'd consider the infamy attending infidelity, and backwardness to all its approaches, as principles that were rather to be wish'd than hop'd for in the world. For what means, wou'd he say, of persuading mankind, that the transgressions of conjugal duty are more infamous than any other kind of injustice, when 'tis evident they are more excusable, upon account of the greatness of the temptation? And what possibility of giving a backwardness to the approaches of a pleasure, to which nature has inspir'd so strong a propensity; and a propensity that 'tis absolutely necessary in the end to comply with, for the support of the species? (*Works,* II, 332; *THN,* p. 572)

In this passage Hume, whose feelings about speculative philosophy were not cordial, is gently mocking the speculative philosophers for their lack of insight into the human condition. Lacking experience, they would be apt to think society would forgive transgressions—especially such harmless ones—when the provocation toward them is so great, and the very performance of which is necessary for the continuation of the race. The paragraph immediately following clarifies Hume's meaning: "But speculative reasonings, which cost so much pains to philosophers, are often form'd by the world naturally, and without reflection: As difficulties, which seem unsurmountable in theory, are easily got over in practice" (*Works,* II, 332–333; *THN,* p. 572). That is, by attention to experience and not to speculative reasoning, the philosopher can arrive at a true estimate of the proper behavior of the sexes. The speculative philosopher is essentially wasting time that he could spend on more profitable reasonings. Women, having provoked this jest at empty speculation, are now seen to be the victims of an ironic doubleness in human nature:

And tho' all these maxims have a plain reference to generation, yet women past child-bearing have no more privilege in this respect, than those who are in the flower of their youth and beauty. Men have undoubtedly an implicit notion, that all those ideas of modesty and decency have a regard to generation; since they impose not the same laws, *with the same force*, on the male sex, where that reason takes not place. The exception is there obvious and extensive, and founded on a remarkable difference, which produces a clear separation and disjunction of ideas. But as the case is not the same with regard to the different ages of women, for this reason, tho' men know, that these notions are founded on the public interest, yet the general rule carries us beyond the original principle, and makes us extend the notions of modesty over the whole sex, from their earliest infancy to their extremest old-age and infirmity. (*Works*, II, 333; *THN*, pp. 572–573)

If possible conception from someone other than one's husband is the reason we deny sexual promiscuity to women, it would seem fatuous to apply the rules to females incapable of conception. In fact, given the conditions which established the rules, exactly how would these rules apply to women incapable of bearing children? As a matter of logic, they could not. Consequently, man's enthusiasm for what seems an excellent reason to oppose unrestricted sexual congress for women breaks down when we discover that he applies this rule to those least in need of it. The irony takes the form of the disparity between man's "reasoned" (in reality, emotive) generalizations about the actions of women and the actual extent to which the rules are applied. This hesitation on Hume's part to apply the double standard at any time to those incapable of bearing children also implies a distaste for the double standard in any of its applications. We cannot be sure about this, however, for the last paragraph of this particular section of the *Treatise* is slightly confused. The reader will see, I hope, what I mean:

As to the obligations which the male sex lie under, with regard to chastity, we may observe, that according to the general notions of the world, they bear nearly the same proportion to the obligations of women, as the obligations of the law of nations do to those of the law of nature. 'Tis contrary to the interest of civil society, that men shou'd have an *entire* liberty of indulging their appetites in venereal enjoyment: But as this interest is weaker than in the case of the female sex, the moral obligation, arising from it, must be proportionably weaker. And to prove this we need only appeal to the practice and sentiments of all nations and ages. (*Works*, II, 333; *THN*, p .573)

The first sentence of this section would seem to reject the logic behind the double standard, if we know what the relationship between the "law of nations" and the "law of nature" is. Apparently the law of nations and the law of nature have little relationship, coextensive only in so far as the law of nations obviously cannot violate a law of nature, but must adapt its law to the laws of nature.[6] This interpretation is supported by the second sentence, which limits any freewheeling incontinence on the part of the male sex. The sentence coming immediately after the colon, however, offers interpretational difficulties. What is the antecedent of "this interest"? Is it the interest that men have in indulging their venereal appetites? Or the lesser interest of women? Or is it the interest of civil society? Perhaps since the same two words are repeated, the references of the second "this interest" is to the first. If we accept this view, then we might rewrite that sentence as follows: "But as the interests of civil society in preventing complete venereal indulgence is weaker with the male sex than it is in the case of the female sex, the moral obligation arising from this interest of civil society must be proportionably weaker." I think this is a correct interpretation of the last paragraph. If it is, it is not a stunning endorsement of the double standard, but a carefully—even precisely—qualified admission of its existence. Its existence serves one useful function: it is a substantial basis for raising a family, but it has no other purpose than that. Hume recognized that if men observed the strictures they so generously applied to women, and were themselves as continent as they wished the female sex to be, then the reason advanced in support of the double standard would be illogical. For if they were as continent as women were supposed to be, then they would never have to worry that the children they raised were anybody's but their own. Without any marital infidelity at all, no doubt could arise about paternity, unless another divine conception was in the making.[7]

The section "Of Chastity and Modesty" would seem to exhibit most

---

[6] Hume does not accept the law of nature in any a priori sense, but does accept the law of nature when empirically discovered. Hence the law of nations is not obliged to follow the law of nature any more than males are obliged to follow feminine rules of chastity.

[7] For a contrasting interpretation, see Sir Leslie Stephen, *English Thought in the Eighteenth Century*, IX, 100–101. (These references are to chapter and paragraph number, in accordance with the arrangement of his two volumes.) Also, Hume's attitude in the *Enquiry concerning Human Understanding* seems different, although uncertain.

of the shortcomings of the age, since it is concerned primarily with female continence and very little with male continence. The irony of the discussions hinges upon the transitional sentence that begins "Such wou'd be the reasonings of our speculative philosopher . . ." Prior to that, Hume had discussed the "ideal" rules which would govern sexual behavior. To make clear that he doesn't think these rules are ideal, he then treats them to a series of ironic objections. And he is plainly ironic in a sentence about sanctimonious bachelors who perpetuate the unfairness of the double standard: "Thus batchelors, however debauch'd, cannot chuse but be shock'd with any instance of lewdness or impudence in women." But of course they can! To be shocked at "lewdness or impudence" in other people and not in oneself is hypocritical, though typical behavior in human beings, who give curiously flustered reasons for it. Once man recognizes the hypocrisy of his sexual ethic, perhaps he will do something about it, Hume implies.

Hume's ironic handling of ethical problems is often similar to the procedure just outlined. Three or four sentences in several paragraphs will give the reader the clue to the ironic solution he offers to problems which wouldn't be problems if men were capable of thinking reasonably. In a sentence one word may be sufficient to give an ironic cast to the entire sentence. Hume, writing for an audience accustomed to subtle irony, would expect his reader to be aware of his methods; the least a modern reader can do is to be on guard for them. As Hume's thoughts and writing develop, it becomes clear that he is often distressed by an ethic which condemns certain action only when it is performed by other people; in oneself it is excusable. A double standard not only of sexual morality, but of ethics in general, was to Hume no solution to the problem of leading a moral life.

The discussion "Of Chastity and Modesty" (in women) is perhaps the outgrowth of the juvenile essay "An Historical Essay on Chivalry and modern Honour." Whatever its origins, Hume was to return to the topic of the "weak, pious sex," in an essay entitled "Of Love and Marriage," published in 1741, two years after the failure of the *Treatise*. It is possible that the irony of the *Treatise* had been too subtle for most of his readers, and Hume attempts to write in an Addisonian vein. Consider the opening lines of the essay:

I know not whence it proceeds, that women are so apt to take amiss every thing which is said in disparagement of the married state; and always consider a satyr upon matrimony as a satyr upon themselves. Do they mean, that they are the parties principally concerned, and that if a backwardness to enter into that state should prevail in the world, they would be the greatest sufferers? Or, are they sensible, that misfortunes and miscarriages of the married state are owing more to their sex than to ours? I hope they do not intend to confess either of these two particulars, or to give such an advantage to their adversaries, the men, as even to allow them to suspect it.

I have often had thoughts of complying with this humour of the fair sex, and of writing a panegyric upon marriage: But, in looking around for materials, they seemed to be of so mixed a nature, that at the conclusion of my reflections, I found that I was as much disposed to write a satyr, which might be placed on the opposite pages of the panegyric: And I am afraid, that as satyr is, on most occasions, thought to contain more truth than panegyric, I should have done their cause more harm than good by this expedient. To misrepresent facts is what, I know, they will not require of me. I must be more a friend to truth, than even to them, where their interests are opposite. (*Works*, IV, 383–384)

Hume knows quite well, of course, why women consider satire upon matrimony a satire upon themselves: for the satires on marriage in the eighteenth century were always so expressed that the blame for cacophony in marriage fell upon the females. Later in the essay, after a description of the Scythian women's Lysistratan plan for subduing their men, he remarks about marriage that there should be "no pretensions to authority on either side; but that every thing was carried on with perfect equality, as between two equal members of the same body." The irony of the opening paragraphs now becomes clear. Although he joshed women for petulance over satirical mistreatment of their role in marriage, it is plain that Hume felt the disturbances of married life are the fault of those who would dominate, even though he has accused women of "love of dominion" in marriage. The example of the Scythian women's dominion over their men is one of very few in history; and Hume was well aware that the male figure in the household was all too frequently domineering, cruel, and unsparingly critical, as he admits in these lines: "to lay the blame more equally, I am afraid it is the fault of our sex, if the women be so fond of rule, and that if we did not abuse our authority, they would never think it worth while to dispute it." I do not wish to imply that Hume is an eighteenth-century feminist, but to emphasize his impatience with spurious distinctions over the abilities of the two sexes. The distinctions and differences actually present were enough to cope with, and to invent more was foolhardy.

An essay which began with apparent jibes at women is now ironic, for Hume is seen to sympathize with their plight. It is an irony of understanding, and is an oblique criticism of the unfair and sometimes inhumane treatment women received in a marriage agreement. He could not have begun by poking fun at the male sex in the same manner; he was too much of a traditionalist (where literary genres were concerned) to do that, and he knew the role of the male writer was not to diparage, but to take his proper side in the so-called battle of the sexes. But Hume was not one to take much relish in winning battles in which the odds were so unfairly weighted against his opponents. What victory is it to crush a defenseless opponent? His point in this essay is not to take an easy victory. By charting one course at the beginning of the essay and then changing directions before he has a full wind in his sails, he is able to direct criticism at both sexes for not seeking to live in harmony. The subject of the rest of the essay is an allegorical account, extended from Plato's *Symposium,* of the search for the perfect mate. The account of Plato, whom Hume denotes "that fanciful philosopher," relates that mankind was not at the beginning divided into male and female, but existed as a compound of both sexes: "This union, no doubt, was very intire, and the parts very well adjusted together, since there resulted a perfect harmony betwixt the male and female, altho' they were obliged to be inseparable companions." This happy state of affairs could not long exist, and Jupiter divided them, making two imperfect creatures. Since, argues Plato, we are still capable of remembering the happiness we enjoyed in that unbroken state, we spend our lives searching for our "better halves." Hume's continuation of this "fiction" of Plato presents Jupiter repenting of his cruelty and sending down "Love and Hymen, to collect the broken halves of human kind, and piece them together in the best manner possible." Their work went well, until Care, the counselor and favorite of Hymen, had a falling out with Pleasure, the favorite of Love. Soon, they were undoing the work of their masters until Jupiter called them back, ordered a reconciliation between Love and Hymen as the only way to give happiness to mankind; they were then to consult Care and Pleasure before uniting the broken halves, and when they had reunited the separated parts, the union formed one "perfect and happy creature."

The above summary is no substitute for a reading of the essay, but it will give the reader an idea of Hume's ironic playfulness in dealing with matters that human beings often take too seriously. As a man who never married, and who was not likely to make any precipitous arrangement, Hume could afford to poke fun at an institution which was not nearly so ideal as it was thought to be. The essay was published in 1741, twenty-three years before his frustrating affair with the Comtesse de Boufflers.[8] It is one of the few places in his published writings that he mentions women as a sex. But he is reluctant to accept any of the masculine notions about the general inferiority of women to men. Instead, he uses an opening jest at the "fair sex" to lead into an ironic comment about the exaggerated opinion the male has of his importance in the marriage contract. In addition to this essay, and the other examples of irony bearing upon the distaff side, Hume mentions and discusses women as a sex elsewhere but almost always with an ironic twinge; his form of irony, however, is removed from that of any misogynist. Bachelor he may have been, but hater of women he was not.

That Hume was a favorite of many women is well established; and we have little reason to disbelieve the statement in his autobiography that he "took a particular Pleasure in the Company of modest women . . . [having] no Reason to be displeased with the Reception I met with from them." He had no Boswellian impulses to frequent sexual conquests, or at least none that his biographers have been able to discover, which, in an age accepting the double standard, is remarkable. Yet, he was not inclined to marriage, and his feminine admirers would have been greatly surprised had he married, although they thought he was the sort of man who should marry.[9] Considering this and his ironical

---

[8] In 1748, while in Turin, Hume was infatuated with an Italian woman, the Countess of [Duvernan?], to whom he was introduced by James Caulfield, later Lord Charlemont; the episode is discussed in *Life,* pp. 212–217. However, his friendship with the Comtesse de Boufflers (below, Chap. Three) had a greater emotional impact upon him.

[9] In 1700 he considered marrying Miss Nancy Orde, whose affection for him is undoubted. See *Life,* pp. 566–567.

treatment of women as a sex, we may wonder if he had any particular, specialized, or idiosyncratic notions about women. I think, considering the age in which he lived, he did, although we would not perhaps consider such notions so unusual today. He had the great misfortune of considering (rightly) women to be the social, moral, and intellectual equivalents of men. Nothing in the physiological differences between the two sexes would logically imply any potential moral inequality between men and women, and Hume did not feel that his sex was the superior one intellectually, or that men were due any special social or moral prerogatives merely because of an accident of sexual selection. This attitude toward women was not unfortunate because it was an incorrect view, but because it was so universally discredited at his time. Consequently, when he tried to treat the Comtesse de Boufflers as an equal intellectually and morally, and she initially responded as he hoped she might, her behavior augured well for any great expectations he might have had. But the Comtesse de Boufflers, if I may get ahead of myself for a minute, was aware of the inferior position—legally, morally, and intellectually—which women were forced to bear, and she was determined to do as much as she could by marrying well when her first husband died. Hume, the sceptic who argued that reason should be the guide to the passions, found her reason either failing to guide her passions, or guiding them in so chimerical a manner as to degrade the name of reason. When he writes of women ironically or calls attention to the irony which shrouds the behavior expected of them, he is implying their equality with men, a notion the eighteenth century was not ready to accept. To him it was unreasonable that women were not accepted as equals to men when it was certainly reasonable that they should be. The Comtesse de Boufflers was shrewd enough to realize the anomalous position women held, while her lessers—scrub women, maids, and ordinary housewives—had been assiduously convinced since birth of their inferior position and did nothing to challenge that view. Hume felt that he could treat them ironically without their receiving it as a personal insult; but because of the position forced on them by the times, the invariable reaction of women so treated was dismay, frustration, or—worst of all—acceptance of the status quo. Hume was willing to accept them as equals, but as equals they would have to accept his good-natured irony in the amiable spirit he intended it. Under the weight of tradition, it was not surprising that they mis-understood Hume's acceptance of them as equals. And even if he were prepared to support their equality with enthusiasm, that still did not change the rest of the world. When they could not or would not ac-cept the offer of equality, there was little Hume could do but return to the sidelines, a spectator to a battle he believed should never have been fought.

"Of Love and Marriage" was originally published in the two-volume set *Essays, Moral and Political* (1741–1742), which is sometimes re-garded as an attempt to recast the unsuccessful *Treatise*. Actually, the *Essays* are not a "recasting" of the *Treatise,* but an application of some of the ideas in the *Treatise* to practical affairs, embodied in a practical essay form that could be understood by any literate person. During the time between the publication of the *Treatise* and the *Essays, Moral and Political,* Hume was making every effort to establish for himself a literary reputation.[10] He was learning various ways to shield himself against both the hostility and the indifference of the public. While he was taking pleasure in some of his ironic treatment of various philo-sophical problems, he was also developing irony as a mode of living. For example, he was plainly disappointed by the failure of the *Treatise*; in a letter dated 1 July 1739 he wrote his good friend Henry Home (later Lord Kames), "I am not much in the humour of such compo-sitions at present, having received news from London of the success of my Philosophy, which is but indifferent, if I may judge by the sale of the book, and if I may believe my bookseller" (*HL,* I, 30). But he had recovered his good spirits enough to write his friend again, on 13 June 1742, about the *Essays, Moral and Political*:

The Essays are all sold in London; as I am inform'd by two Letters from English Gentlemen of my Acquaintance. There is a Demand for them; & as one of them tells me, Innys the great Bookseller in Paul's Church Yard wonders there is not a new Edition, for that he cannot find Copies for his Customers. I am also told that Dr Butler has every where recommended them. So that I hope they will have some Success. They may prove like Dung with Marle, & bring forward the rest of my Philosophy, which is of a more

---

[10] Ernest Campbell Mossner, in "Philosophy and Biography: The Case of David Hume," *Philosophical Review,* LIX (1950), 184–201, has disposed of the notion that Hume craved mere vulgar success.

durable, tho of a harder & more stubborn Nature. You see, I can talk to you in your own Style. (*NHL*, p. 10)

This light-hearted approach, with its scatological overtones, to his writings is more typical of the philosopher than the self-recriminations briefly indulged in after the publication of the *Treatise*. But the success of the *Essays* had put Hume into better spirits. Obviously he felt that the origin of his philosophy was a little more exalted than the above quotation might imply. Henry Home would have especially appreciated this allusion, since he was an ardent farmer who introduced modern methods into Scotland. By giving another application to Home's farming methods and placing them in a different context, Hume conveys his delight at the success of his *Essays*.

Successful as they may have been, it was just as well that he could treat himself and his writings ironically, since he was to withstand some of the most reckless abuse ever inflicted on a philosopher. I suspect that he was capable of taking in stride all the epithets he heard applied to his *Treatise* or to the various editions of his essays, and that he could use them ironically, no mean accomplishment for an author who hoped that posterity would find his philosophy useful and instructive. His friends may not have found his philosophy useful or instructive, but they must have found his letters entertaining. Hume's letters are remarkable in the way that they provide a backdrop for the ironic frame of his mind. Among other virtues, they exhibit his ability to enjoy a joke on himself. They are full of ironic suggestions to his friends, ironic comments about their writings or their lives, and an ironic approach to the problems of the world. A letter to William Mure, written 14 November 1742, is a good example (and I quote the entire first paragraph since any explanation for the reader would be as long as the letter):

I am surpriz'd you shou'd find Fault with my Letter [not extant]. For my Part I esteem it the best I ever wrote. There is neither Barbarism, Solecism, Equivoque, Redundancy, nor Transgression of one single Rule of Grammar or Rhetoric thro the Whole. The Words were chosen with an exact Propriety to the Sense, & the Sense was full of masculine Strength & Energy. In short it comes up fully to the Duke of Buckingham's Description of fine Writing. *Exact Propriety of Words & Thought*. This is more than what can be said of most Compositions. But I shall not be redundant in the Praise of Brevity, tho much might be said on that Subject. To conclude all, I shall venture to affirm, that my last Letter will be equal in Bulk to all the Orations you shall deliver during the two first Sessions of Parliament. For let all the Letters of my Epistle be regularly divided, they will be found equivalent to a dozen of *No's* & as Many *Ay's*. There will be found a *No* for the Triennial Bill, for the Pension Bill, for the Bill about regulating Elections, for the Bill of Pains & Penalties against L. Orford &c. There will also be found an *Ay* for the Standing Army, for Votes of Credit, for the Approbation of Treaties &c. As to the last *No* I mention'd with regard to Lord Orford, I beg it of you as a particular Favour. For having publish'd to all Britain my Sentiments on that Affair, it will be thought by all Britain, that I have no Influence on you, if your Sentiments be not conformable to mine. Beside, as you are my Disciple in Religion & Morals, why shou'd you not be so in Politics? I entreat you to get the Bill about Witches repeal'd, & to move for some new Bill to secure the Christian Religion, by burning Deists, Socinians, Moralists, & Hutchinsonians. (*HL*, I, 43–44)

The intricacy of the irony in this letter is evidence of the subtlety of Hume's thought, and it is perhaps worth a careful examination for that reason. Because Mure was a lifelong friend—described by Hume as his "oldest and best friend"—I should think that Hume had written some hasty note about a matter deemed more important by Mure. He playfully suggests that much could be said about brevity, knowing full well that observations on brevity are vitiated unless they are brief. The irony is more purposeful, however, when he suggests the votes that could be cast for or against particular bills. He is certainly being ironic in his suggestion of a "No" for the bill against Lord Orford, Sir Robert Walpole. An earlier essay, "A Character of Sir Robert Walpole," was a dispassionate analysis of that politician's chicanery and possibly helped in removing him from office. At the time he wrote the letter to Mure, then, he would probably have been in favor of the bill against Walpole; and his suggestion of a "No" is ironic. I should imagine that he was also in favor of all the bills for which he suggests a "No." It is generally an easier task to determine a thinker's position where abstract problems are concerned than it is in specific, concrete occasions of the abstraction. Since it is unlikely that he would really have been opposed to the bill against Sir Robert, we would infer that he was also in favor of the other bills in this particular series.

If the ironic position in Mure's suggested votes on certain specific bills is difficult to determine, the irony is more transparent when Hume moves from politics to religion and morals. If Mure agrees with Hume about religion and morals—and Hume implies that he does—why not politics? It is a mild understatement here to say that Hume is not representing accurately his relations with the Mures. None of them approved of his notions on religion and morals, and told him so. When Hume was on his deathbed, Mrs. Mure, commenting about a copy of the *History of England* he had inscribed to her, said, "O David, that's a book you may weel be proud o, but before ye dee, ye should burn a' your wee bookies [which were, of course, his philosophical writings collected in *Essays and Treatises on Several Subjects*]." Their disapproval of Hume's religious views was openly acknowledged throughout their relationship, but it is always the delight of the sceptic to take his religious scepticism with his more orthodox friends in a genial manner, even giving them credit for being as perspicacious as he is, as Hume does in the above letter. Most of Hume's religiously inclined friends would not, however, wish to be "perspicacious" in the same capacity that he was, preferring the citadel of security proffered by orthodoxy to the uncertainty of a life guided by scepticism. If they did not appreciate having Hume's views imputed to them, even by such a good friend as he, they were made the objects of an irony having both a social purpose and an esthetic purpose. Esthetically, the irony in the above letter is much more satisfying than any long harangue about Hume's right *not to believe* would be. His right not to believe is the social purpose of the irony. By ironically implying that Mure's opinions on religion are the same as his, he reminds the Mures that his beliefs are as important—and inviolable—to him as theirs are to them.

If Hume was not certain about the existence and immutability of God, he was much less sure about the existence of witches. Mure, enlightened man of what is called the "Age of Reason," or sometimes the "Age of Enlightenment," was not apt to be a believer in witches or witchcraft. Although the act making witchcraft a capital offense had been repealed in 1736, Hume ironically suggests that Mure should use his position in Parliament to establish the Christian religion. Since the more bigoted Presbyterians in Scotland, and later such Englishmen as John Wesley, regarded this repeal of the witchcraft act as a sign of the impious immorality of the time, they probably would have cheered any suggestion to reinstate burning at the stake for nonbelievers. Mure, naturally, was highly unlikely to make such a suggestion to Parliament, and Hume knew it; but, in conjunction with his own religious scepticism, he did not resist the temptation to sport with his friend about Mure's recent election to Parliament. Since he would have been one of the first to go to the stake, the conjunction is appropriate. It is another example of the form Hume's scepticism assumed. He took life seriously, but he recognized the importance of levity. As a sceptic he held little sacred or immutable; when one of his friends made the philosophical mistake of accepting the immutability or inviolate sacredness of some concept, his reaction was characteristic: Hume reminded him with a smile, to be sure, that the world was not so perfect as he thought.

The world in which Hume lived was one that responded to irony and satire because it felt that they were accurate representations of life, life seen through a two-way mirror. A perfect world would be unreliable or unreasonable because it would be inhabited by people forever expecting the imperfect. Hume enjoyed a joke with his friends about subjects of disagreement, but he also enjoyed poking fun at classical, rationalistic philosophies; and he could be fairly sure that his readers would understand his intent. In recasting (that word is somewhat inaccurate, as we shall see in a later chapter) the *Treatise,* he composed four essays designed to explain the tenets of various philosophical systems: "The Epicurean," "The Stoic," "The Platonist," "The Sceptic." However, we need to be careful when reading pronouncements from Hume about the attractiveness of Epicureanism or Platonism. In reading "The Epicurean," for example, we should proceed with caution, especially when Hume tells us, in a footnote to the title of the essay, "The intention of this and the three following essays is not so much to explain accurately the sentiments of the ancient sects of philosophy, as to deliver the sentiments of sects, that naturally form themselves in the world, and entertain different ideas of human life and of happiness." The essay begins innocuously enough, and Hume's description of an Epicurean seems to be straightforward and literal. But the rhetoric has a curiously musical organization. It begins with the quiet, uncluttered prose that is characteristic of Hume, and then crescendos into a Carlylese that we would almost never expect from

Hume. When we do find it, we may suspect that Hume is doing more than needlessly squirting rosewater. In a man whose habits of thought and habits of life were practical and judicious, seldom if ever extreme, what is the purpose of rhetoric such as this:

> But see, propitious to my wishes, the divine, the amiable PLEASURE, the supreme love of GODS and men, advances towards me. At her approach, my heart beats with genial heat, and every sense and every faculty is dissolved in joy; while she pours around me all the embellishments of the spring, and all the treasure of the autumn. The melody of her voice charms my ears with the softest music, as she invites me to partake of those delicious fruits, which, with a smile that diffuses a glory on the heavens and the earth, she presents to me. The sportive CUPIDS, who attend her, or fan me with their odoriferous wings, or pour on my head the most fragrant oils, or offer me their sparkling nectar in golden goblets. O! for ever let me spread my limbs on this bed of roses, and thus, thus feel the delicious moments, with soft and downy steps, glide along. But cruel chance! Whither do you fly so fast? Why do my ardent wishes, and that load of pleasures, under which you labour, rather hasten than retard your unrelenting pace? Suffer me to enjoy this soft repose, after all my fatigues in search of happiness. Suffer me to satiate myself with these delicacies, after the pains of so long and so foolish an abstinence. (*Works*, III, 199–200)

This rhapsodic strain is pursued in subsequent paragraphs, much, I fear, to the detriment of Epicureanism as far as the eighteenth century, as well as the twentieth, is concerned. But what an expeditious way for a philosopher to sound out the emptiness of a certain philosophical system! Nothing could be more devastatingly ironic to a philosophy— or a philosopher—than to have its own words so effectively used as adversaries. In "The Epicurean" the deliberate hyperbole creates the irony, because the words ultimately mean something quite different from what an Epicurean would like to think they mean. (Indeed, a Freudian could have a field day with them.) To Hume, the extravagant expostulations of the Epicurean could be adequately demolished by using his own verbal flatulence against him. The irony has the twofold purpose of poking fun at those who pretend to knowledge as Epicureans and of exposing the logical emptiness of an Epicurean philosophy.

The Epicurean, however, is not the only one to suffer the sting of

Hume's irony, for that superb rationalist, "The Platonist," is the subject of something less than wholehearted approbation. The development, though not quite so detailed, is exactly the same as it was in "The Epicurean," although the pace is quicker. Hume begins calmly enough by stating, "To some philosophers it appears matter of surprize, that all mankind, possessing the same nature, and being endowed with the same faculties, should yet differ so widely in their pursuits and inclinations, and that one should utterly condemn what is fondly sought after by another." Yet this tranquil beginning soon develops into something approaching a sermon that Wordsworth might have preached:

> O philosopher! thy wisdom is vain, and thy virtue unprofitable. Thou seekest the ignorant applauses of men, not the solid reflections of thy own conscience, or the more solid approbation of that being, who, with one regard of his all-seeing eye, penetrates the universe. Thou surely art conscious of the hollowness of thy pretended probity, whilst calling thyself a citizen, a son, a friend, thou forgettest thy higher sovereign, thy true father, thy greatest benefactor. Where is the adoration due to infinite perfection, whence every thing good and valuable is derived? Where is the gratitude, owing to thy creator, who called thee forth from nothing, who placed thee in all these relations to thy fellow-creatures, and requiring thee to fulfil the duty of each relation, forbids thee to neglect what thou owest to himself, the most perfect being, to whom thou art connected by the closest tye? (*Works*, III, 212)

We would probably agree that Hume has not been entirely fair to either the Epicurean or to the Platonist, but I do not think he intended to be. By overstating their arguments, after a plausible introduction, he could easily poke the greatest amount of fun at them. Since he was not primarily interested in a detailed account or explanation of the philosophical structure of Epicureanism or Platonism, he could take the arguments—or what passed for arguments—of these philosophers and, with a straight face, introduce this extravagant rhetoric as an accurate summary of their respective philosophies. We know that he was not enthusiastic about perpetuating either philosophical system; so his ironic treatment of them comes as no great surprise. We recognize the irony in the treatment by the language he uses—language which has no parallel in his other writings, but which reflects his good humor.

The inevitable purpose of the irony is, of course, to lessen the importance of Epicureanism and Platonism. After reading Hume's devastating extension of their arguments into humorously absurd ones, I should think most reasonable men would be a little bit wary about any enthusiasm for their respective philosophies. And reasonable men would be especially wary if they should find themselves lunching with a notorious eighteenth-century sceptic some day.

These examples of "philosophical irony" which we have just considered exhibit the primary, expected characteristic of Humean irony: to deride, if not to discourage, a certain philosophy, or a certain habit of mind. As Hume uses it, it is effective, especially in the essays on the Epicurean and the Platonist. One's delight in reading them stems from the unfamiliar language Hume uses, but the language does not obscure the neatness with which he disposes of philosophies he thinks are grandiose in their pretensions, abysmally meager in their productions. His ironic commentaries succeed in showing up the a priori philosopher's inability to come to grips in any satisfying fashion with the problems of the world. An ironic treatment of philosophical problems is not common in philosophers, with the notable contemporary exception of Bertrand Russell. Socratic irony was a form of pretended ignorance, different from Hume's ironic observations about philosophy and philosophers who gather to themselves more knowledge than a human being can achieve. As a result, at the hands of a good-humored sceptic, they receive an ironic welcome. If philosophers are going to make fools of themselves in one way or another, or if human beings are going to imagine that their philosophy has all the answers, Hume will let them, as he ironically comments on the mistakes they call philosophies.

To treat philosophies ironically and yet remain a cogent philosopher is no small task. Irony, however, is not only a concept, it is a way of dealing with concepts. When one does not sympathize with certain concepts, he may handle them ironically, and the clever ironist will then receive a double satisfaction from his irony. The perspicacious or those in on the secret will recognize the irony; the rest, uninformed, will take the ironist's statements at face value and be self-deceived. He will have accomplished two purposes: those to whom he wished his real meaning to be known will be aware of it; those whom he does not wish to know may be dense enough to take his sentiments at face value. Religious concepts especially seem to invite irony of the sort that would be recognized by the perspicacious few and unperceived by the multitude. David Hume, as a great sceptic, was not one to let an opportunity like this pass by unnoticed.

Hume's religious position, although it is yet to be fully discussed,[11] is no longer a matter of dispute, the recent apocryphal story of the Sorbonne lecturer who died of a heart attack after announcing a lecture on David Hume as Christian perhaps serving as an example to theists who would draw him into their fold. Hume did take religious matters seriously, but he was also a great believer in the dictum that nothing was too sacred for spoofing. Religion was not to escape. The serious interest that he had in religion, however, was mitigated by his scepticism, and it was the sceptic as man of letters who had the last word in any of Hume's writings about religion. Even so, he was good friends with many of the moderate clergy of Edinburgh, and it was perhaps through irony that he was able to retain their friendship, in spite of his scepticism.

At the beginning of his career Hume was cautious about the ways in which he used religious irony. He would not, for example, ask Bishop Butler to read his *Treatise,* for fear the treatment of religion would offend him. In the *Treatise* what Hume has to say about religion is not at all extensive, but he gives an inkling of what to expect in his later works. In completing this work and preparing it for the press, Hume exercised, for the reading of Butler and at the advice of his friends, a certain amount of discretion by omitting the early version of what probably became the essay "Of Miracles." The omission does not constitute reason for believing that his position toward the church softened in later life. Even so, his analysis of certain religious propositions in the *Treatise* is unsympathetic. In Book I, Part IV, Section 5, Hume discusses the "immateriality of the soul." With the same perspicuous logic that becomes brilliant in the late *Dialogues concerning*

---

[11] André-Louis Leroy, in *La Critique et la Religion chez David Hume,* has discussed, perhaps more fully than any one else, Hume's religious convictions, but no real attempt to collate and to judge all of Hume's thoughts on religion has been made. Since Hume's agnosticism is generally taken for granted, few scholars are interested in an inquiry to determine Hume's contributions to religious thought.

Natural Religion, he demolishes neatly the ideas advanced in support of the immateriality of the soul. Assuming that one accepts Hume's antirationalistic attack on the supernaturalism of religion, then his arguments against the existence of an eternal soul leave only shreds of what theists claimed was a substantial fabric. His whole empirical approach,[12] for that matter, did not leave much room for any religion based on a priori tenets, and it is not surprising to the modern scholar that the church was his aversion, as he said in a letter to Henry Home in June 1747. This particular section of the *Treatise* would have been enough to convince any theologian who was wise enough to understand that the church needed to close up many gaps in logic and reason in its theology, if the appeal to reason instead of blind faith was to be convincing. If this section from the *Treatise* left Hume's theologically inclined readers angered, perhaps the last two paragraphs would have pacified them:

There is only one occasion, when philosophy will think it necessary and even honourable to justify herself, and that is, when religion may seem to be in the least offended; whose rights are as dear to her as her own, and are indeed the same. If any one, therefore, shou'd imagine that the foregoing arguments are any ways dangerous to religion, I hope the following apology will remove his apprehensions.

There is no foundation for any conclusion *a priori,* either concerning the operations or duration of any object, of which 'tis possible for the human mind to form a conception. Any object may be imagin'd to become entirely inactive, or to be annihilated in a moment; and 'tis an evident principle, *that whatever we can imagine, is possible.* Now this is no more true of matter, than of spirit; of an extended compounded substance, than of a simple and unextended. In both cases the metaphysical arguments for the immortality of the soul are equally inconclusive; and in both cases the moral arguments and those deriv'd from the analogy of nature are equally strong and convincing. If my philosophy, therefore, makes no addition to the arguments for religion, I have at least the satisfaction to think it takes nothing from them,

---

12 Although Hume's *general* position as empiricist is incontestable, Immanuel Kant's valuable insight into the difficulties of synthetic a priori propositions is, I think, a legitimate criticism of Hume's empiricism. The argument that no matter of fact in the world is certain is, in effect, a synthetic a priori proposition. See *Critique of Pure Reason,* tr. by Norman Kemp Smith, pp. 606–612 (A760/B788 to A769/B797).

but that everything remains precisely as before. (*Works,* I, 532–533; *THN,* pp. 250–251)

The apology given by Hume in that last paragraph would by no means remove my apprehensions were I an a priori theologian of the eighteenth century. In the sentence immediately following the promise of the apology, he simply restates his position with respect to a priori arguments given in support of religion. He admits that his philosophy makes no addition to the arguments for religion, but surely he cannot be serious when he says that he has the satisfaction of knowing that it takes nothing away from them. The arguments for the support of religion that were dearest to the hearts of every threepenny theologian are precisely those which Hume will not accept and which he has pretty well demolished in the preceding part of that section. In fact, *everything* has been taken away from the arguments of the metaphysical theologian, and *nothing* remains exactly as before. If the metaphysician is to justify his pronouncements and propositions by reasoning in the light of experience, then he must begin digging in new ground. Before Hume he could use the dizzying speculations derived from a priori arguments, but he cannot now, if he is at all aware of the force of Hume's criticism.[13] To justify propositions about the immateriality of the soul or the existence of God by appeals to metaphysical theorizing is not enough. Instead, the arguments proceeding from supernatural allegations of causes must be replaced by arguments proceeding from man's experience of "natural" causes. If these do not suffice, then (as Hume later says) faith is the only basis for religion.

The irony here is of the most obvious and enjoyable sort; having stabbed metaphysical arguments in all the vital places, Hume now twists the knife. It is the sort of religious irony which Hume practiced with the greatest ease. But its importance cannot be diminished, since no concession is in fact made to the religionist. Its brevity, I should think, increases the insult to the theologian, who had often enough insulted Hume and would even more frequently repeat the offense.

---

[13] Bishop Butler would undoubtedly agree with these principles, but the philosophical-religious speculations of Butler were considerably less repugnant to Hume than those of William Warburton (below, Chap. Three), to choose an extreme example.

Having spent approximately eighteen pages dissecting and discarding the arguments for the immateriality of the soul, Hume now devotes less than a page to a defense of religion against the incursions of philosophy. And the one sentence that supposedly finds everything exactly as it was before is hardly a counterbalance to the previous eighteen pages. Even interpreted literally, it would be the barest sop to the religionists; as it is, it is the "most unkindest cut of all."

Most irony in Hume's writings is good-natured, not venomous. It is not necessarily better as a result of its good humor, but good humor is a characteristic of Humean irony. The good humor does not, however, eliminate the possibility of dismay over human performances; and Hume is, in his early writings, occasionally cynical in his sceptical irony concerning the knowledge of which human beings are capable. This cynical irony will continue to develop throughout his life as he becomes more certain of his ability to persuade, to withstand criticism, and to write more cogently than any British philosopher preceding him, and, with the possible exception of Bertrand Russell, better than any British philosopher following him.

Several reasons account for the ironic mode in Hume's writings, some of which may be explored here. Living in an age in which irony-satire was the dominant literary form, Hume would naturally adopt this form, as any writer employs the forms of his age, even though he may react against them. Hume was not a literary innovator, except that he paid more attention to style than philosophers usually did.[14] What is typical of his style is typical of the eighteenth century. Yet, in using irony as a mode of writing he was able to strike off in a direction essentially different from that found in other ironists. The objects of his irony were different from those of, say, Pope and Swift, but his purpose was probably the same.

Hume, in common with other writers of his age, was interested in reforming some human idiosyncrasies and anomalies; and if they couldn't be reformed then perhaps they could be replaced. Swift, in

[14] Hume did make a list of "Scotticisms" that were to be avoided in writing English; it was prefixed to some copies of the *Political Discourses* of 1752. Boswell informed Johnson of Hume's collection of Scotticisms, to which Johnson replied "I wonder that *he* should find them." But Hume's Scotticisms were not nearly so many as Dr. Johnson imagined.

Gulliver's Travels, had mocked many human failings, but sought always to improve human nature. Hume, I think, had the same idea in mind, although he took aim at institutions and practices that were often sacrosanct. The result was that irony sometimes became a mask for the advanced and iconoclastic ideas in his writings. As a man accused (wrongly) all his life of being an atheist and insulted for his honest scepticism, he could expect ecclesiastics to distort his philosophy and to belittle his accomplishments.[15] Since Hume was not given to acrimonious rebuttal and had resolved never to reply directly to any criticism of his life or of his writings, irony was clearly one of the ways he eased the internal pressure created by extravagant and distorted charges.

No single idea is likely to explain all the various ironic discussions of religious concepts; some of the reasons must have been conscious and precise, others subconscious and vague. And, above all, he was circumspect: even as late as 1770, a man could be hanged for asking some of the questions about religion that Hume either implied or actually asked. It was necessary, consequently, to make his religious reservations discreet; a man frequently called an atheist could not afford to tempt fate at every opportunity when a lynching party—with appropriate legal trappings—could be organized to deal with heretics.

---

[15] That "silly, bigoted fellow, Beattie" said of Hume, among other things: "But this idea [of free will] has had the misfortune to come under the examination of Mr. HUME, who, according to custom, has found means so to darken and disfigure it, that, till we have cleared it of his misrepresentations, we cannot proceed any further in the present subject. And we are the more inclined to digress on this occasion, that he has made the theory of power the ground of some atheistical inferences, which we should not scruple at any time to step out of our way to overturn.—Perhaps these frequent digressions are offensive to the reader: they are equally so to the writer. To remove rubbish is neither an elegant nor a pleasant work, but it is often necessary. It is peculiarly necessary in the philosophy of human nature" (James Beattie, *An Essay on the Nature and Immutability of* TRUTH, *in Opposition to Sophistry and Scepticism,* p. 295). It is worthwhile to contrast Kant's judgment of Beattie: "I should think that Hume might fairly have laid as much claim to common sense as Beattie, and in addition to a critical reason (such as the latter did not possess), which keeps common sense in check and prevents it from speculating, or, if speculations are under discussion, restrains the desire to decide because it cannot satisfy itself concerning its own arguments" (Immanuel Kant, *Prolegomena to Any Future Metaphysics,* ed. and tr. by Paul Carus, p. 6).

He was an unflinchingly honest man and would have answered any serious or intelligent questions about his belief with candor and conviction. Unlike soapbox orators or would-be dictators, however, he was aware of two facts: (1) that, in the minds of a great majority, the mere profession of doubt was enough to suggest lechery, dishonesty, malevolence, or what-have-you; and (2) that if he was eager to convince reasonable men of the validity of his reasonings and the truth of his convictions, he should operate in a dialectical yet prudential manner. Men were more likely to be convinced of the sceptic's position, Hume felt, by calm reason than by declamation, and calm reason had immense advantages when coupled with irony. In Hume's age it was more effective than declamation simply because of its contrast to the so-called intellectual positions, whose only claim to recognition was a highly vocal but highly dubious authority. Thus, the ultimate function of Humean irony in dealing with religious concepts can be tentatively identified as that of most irony: to change, in some desirable manner, men's ways of thinking about the world.

To change men's ways of thinking about ideas that they had long cherished can be both a pleasant and an unrewarding task: pleasant if one feels certain of his position and unrewarding if he is misunderstood and vilified. The early version of the essay "Of Miracles," which Hume was working on in 1737 but did not publish until 1748, had as its object the changing of thought about miracles. In 1737, as a young man of twenty-seven, Hume was eager to publish, but he was also circumspect. Still, he could think, in humorous terms, of the difficulties in getting the essay published and of the altercations it would raise. His letters to friends about the essay provide a background that will be useful to have when a discussion of the essay comes later. His correspondence also gives a clue to Hume's mental attitude at this time and helps account for the formation of the ironic mode in his writings. In a letter to his good friend Henry Home, dated 2 December 1737, he wrote:

Having a frankt Letter I was resolv'd to make Use of it, & accordingly enclose some Reasonings concerning Miracles. . . . I beg of you show it to no Body, except to Mr Hamilton, if he pleases; & let me know at your Leizure that you have receiv'd it, read it, & burnt it. I wou'd not even have you make another nameless Use of it, to which it wou'd not be improper, for fear of Accidents.

Your Thoughts & mine agree with Respect to Dr Butler, & I wou'd be glad to be introduc'd to him. I am at present castrating my Work, that is, cutting off its noble Parts, that is, endeavouring it shall give as little Offence as possible; before which I cou'd not pretend to put it into the Drs hands. This is a Piece of Cowardice, for which I blame myself; tho I believe none of my Friends will blame me. But I was resolv'd not be an Enthusiast, in Philosophy, while I was blaming other Enthusiasms. If ever I indulge any 'twill be when I tell you that I am

                                         Dear Sir Yours.
December 2. 1737   David Hume (*NHL*, pp. 2–3)

This combination of scatological and sexual humor is not typical of the Hume we find in the philosophy books. But it tells us that the man was not the long-faced bookworm that is an unfortunate stereotype of philosophers in the literature written for the Yahoos. I should like to anticipate the reader now, for he is probably asking what is ironic about the quotation. It seems to be nothing but raillery and jesting, which are not remarkable in any letter. However, I am persuaded that there are two forms of irony in the letter, one quantitative, the other tonic, but both giving an insight into the attitudes that went into Hume's earliest writings.

The sentence in which Hume instructs Lord Kames (I call him that so we will not confuse Hume and Home, which are pronounced alike) to burn his essay is the most obvious irony. Since the two were close friends, it is unlikely that Kames would have burned the essay, even though he had some philosophical differences with the line of reasoning in it. David is humorously anticipating or mocking the re- action he expects from Kames, who, though he may not think much of the arguments in the essay, would be unlikely to commit it to the flames. The irony here is subtle enough to be overlooked, since we might think that Hume meant for Kames to destroy the essay before some crusading evangelist found it and used it as evidence against Hume. No author, however, is apt to send any of his writings to one of his best friends with instructions to burn it when that friend has finished with the article. Kames may have wanted to burn the essay, mistakenly thinking he would thus protect his friend or thinking it unphilosophical and loosely reasoned, but his friendship for Hume was such that he would not destroy the essay, even when issued an ironic invitation to do so.

Following this subtle irony is a form just as abrupt, the sentence in which Lord Kames is cautioned against making a "nameless Use" of Hume's essay, "for fear of Accidents." It is easy to guess that "nameless Use" against which Kames is cautioned, and the result is laughable enough. More than likely, the religionists who read Hume's essay would be happy to make just that use of it, if they could not think of a coarser way of expressing their displeasure. The scatological analogy created between such a use of Hume's work and the opinion of the religionists is now clearer. Throughout the history of literature and art we find references to this method of critical opinion, if we can dignify it with such a name. Hume was probably aware that the religionists would like nothing better than to make that "nameless Use" of his manuscript; if not, they would be likely to think that the reasoning in the essay was the intellectual equivalent of excrement and say so. By advising his friend of the potential danger in the misuse of his essay, Hume could poke fun at himself and must have enjoyed it. In reading the letter ourselves, we see Hume implying this sly question: Would Lord Kames or Hume's essay run the greater risk? The answer to that question must be left to other speculators.

The manifestations of irony that we have been considering represent only partially the various instances of irony in Hume's early life and writings; most of them are drawn from the period surrounding the publication of the *Treatise* and the *Essays, Moral and Political*. Both the letters and the published works create a milieu for Hume that he found adaptable to his life and thought. His life at this time was financially uncertain; in the same letter to Lord Kames he mentions "a certain Shamefacedness I have to appear among you at my Years without having yet a Settlement or so much as having attempted any. How happens it that we Philosophers cannot as heartily despise the World as it despises us? I think in my Conscience the Contempt were as well founded on our Side as on the other." Incidentally, this "Shamefacedness" at his financial plight was to continue until 1748, when Hume was, as he states in his autobiography, "Master of near a thousand Pound." Without financial security, however, he could not permit

himself the luxury of permanently offending the religious power structure of Great Britain. Nor would he advance his arguments with the
certitude of a zealot, when the very point of his philosophy dealt with
the uncertainty of events as well as the frailty of human behavior.

Personal uncertainty helps account for the ironic deference that he
assumes with his friends. Usually, this deference is assumed when one
of his friends has not understood Hume's argument in a philosophical
investigation and has made a stereotyped or ignorant criticism of it. Although he had the kindly failing of overestimating his friends' abilities, he seldom found their substantive suggestions useful in revising
his works; their comments on style, however, may have been instructive, even if few would credit Hugh Blair or Henry Home with
having incomparable styles. Occasionally the irony at this time of his
life is a defense against misunderstanding and chagrin at his lack of
success. By referring to himself and to his writings (he frequently
labels himself "Philosopher" with a tone of implied irony, as in the
letter to Kames), he partially concealed his embarrassment and partially atoned for his "failure."

Even at this age, I think we can see a note of cynicism creeping into
Hume's thoughts. In the *Treatise* he is obviously sceptical about the
limits of human knowledge, and he is sceptical about the exalted
opinion man has of himself. In writing of man's foibles and shortcomings, he is often content only to suggest the irony inherent in
certain situations. It is possible now to account for this practice. A
mind as subtle and as well ordered as Hume's quickly perceived the
salient points in any argument. Just as quickly, it saw through pretense, pettifogging, and intellectual chicanery. His correspondence
fairly overflows with examples of his quickness of mind, in contrast
to perspicacity of friends, who, undeniably bright though they may
have been, did not think with that luminous clarity that is typical of
Hume. Much of what we read in Swift and Pope today is ironic to the
most solitary bird watcher, while it may not have been apparent to
more than a few of their contemporaries. The same is true of Hume,
except that he merely sets up the ironic situation and requires the reader
to draw out the ironic conclusion.

Finally, if the irony in his religious writings of this early period
seems too cautious, this caution is justifiable. At the very least, he had

to pay lip service to the social strength of the Christian religion; at the very most, he could afford only a few ironic sentences, which were as likely as not to be overlooked. It is possible that the *Treatise* would not have fallen *"dead-born from the Press"* had he been less cautious in his analyses of the evidence for religion; he might then have achieved literary success, but not the kind he desired. Religious irony is the most important irony in his writings, and it gives a key to his real attitudes and beliefs. This irony will become more and more apparent as his mind matures. Some of the good humor is likely to disappear, for the young are never pleased with the way their world turns out. Or, if they are pleased, they haven't made any contribution to it. Hume's contributions to philosophy, to ethics, to politics, to history, and to religion were not all that he may have wished them; his ironic mode draws attention to what was not accomplished, both by himself and by others.

2. A Mode of Living and Writing

*"These Symptoms of a rising Reputation gave
me Encouragement as I was ever more disposed
to see the favourable than the unfavourable Side
of things."*

The years between the publication of the
Essays, Moral and Political (1741–1742)
and the first publication of *Philosophical Essays concerning Human
Understanding* (1748), later entitled *An Enquiry concerning Human
Understanding,* were busy ones for Hume. He had the opportunity to
succeed Dr. John Pringle as Professor of Ethics and Pneumatical Philosophy at Edinburgh University in 1744; the professorship was denied
the author of the *Treatise of Human Nature* on the grounds of religious
heterodoxy (certainly an accurate charge). He was tutor to the Marquess of Annandale, who was unfortunately insane, from which position he resigned in April 1746. Later in 1746 he served as secretary
to Lieutenant-General James St. Clair in a projected military expedi-
tion to America, which ended in an invasion on the coast of France.
In 1747 his good friend Archibald Stewart, Provost of Edinburgh,
was accused of conspiring with the Jacobites, and Hume came to his
defense with a pamphlet entitled *A True Account of the Behaviour and
Conduct of Archibald Stewart, Esq: late Lord Provost of Edinburgh,
In a Letter to a Friend* (reprinted in the Appendix). In the latter part
of 1747 he accepted an invitation to accompany, again as secretary or
"Aide-de-Camp" as he calls himself in his autobiography, General St.
Clair on a military embassy to Vienna and Turin. These were sometimes disappointing, sometimes exciting years for Hume, but they

helped establish his financial security.[1] After 1748 he was able to devote himself almost exclusively to writing, though writing was never far from his thoughts at any time during the 1740's. The result was a series of new works with a purpose as serious and enlightening as the *Treatise,* but with a maturity which that work, however vigorous, lacked.

The kind of irony one finds in Hume's writings of this period enters most often into the conduct of the argument, although some of the other forms of irony, for example, both-and irony,[2] irony as a reversible vehicle, blame-by-praise irony,[3] are present. The ironic tone sometimes exists latently in the writing, and the reader must draw it out himself. It is a "shotgun irony," scattered throughout the argument but nevertheless part of the whole. In fact, one of Hume's favorite phrases may be used to describe his ironic approach: "on the whole," a passage will be ironic, but the ironic features of the language cannot be excised and codified. Most of the irony is subtle; some is blatant; the subtlety is usually more effective than the blatancy.

To be an effective writer was one of Hume's desires; but it must not be thought that he, eager for recognition, would sacrifice his empirical principles for expedient critical acclaim. Nor would he desert a

---

[1] See Mossner, *Life,* pp. 219–220. Hume was more successful than as depicted in Carl L. Becker's account in *The Heavenly City of the Eighteenth-Century Philosophers*: "Besides, the lonely man, tucked away in a provincial corner of the world, craved the applause of his fellows; and the disconcerting fact was that his speculative books not only did not sell, but were not well received by his friends" (p. 77).

[2] By this term I refer to statements that are both literally true and ironic; they are often intended by the author to be taken in this double sense. These statements function in the writings of an author to make the reader aware of the difficulty of simple ironic judgments. A good account of this kind of irony can be found in Professor Rebecca Price Parkin's book, *The Poetic Workmanship of Alexander Pope,* pp. 31–32, 47–48.

[3] By this term I mean statements that ostensibly praise a person or event but which in fact criticize the person or event. One frequently must have more than the text to determine if seeming praise is actual blame, and Hume's praise of certain people (like the Stoics) must be considered in light of all other pronouncements about them. A useful discussion of blame-by-praise irony may be found in Professor Ronald Knox's book, *The Word* IRONY *and its Context, 1500–1755,* pp. 45–76.

friend who had been wrongly accused of treachery, as in the case of Archibald Stewart. When Stewart was attacked and tried for supposedly collaborating with the Jacobites, Hume defended him in a pamphlet, which was mentioned above, the *Account of Stewart*[4] (to give it a manageable title), published in 1748. It is worth examining here because it combines three of Hume's great virtues as a writer: his philosophical acuteness, his historical procedure, and his ironic treatment of discrepancies between man's principles and his behavior.

On 17 September 1745 Prince Charles Edward Stuart, the Young Pretender, attacked and took Edinburgh with little or no resistance. Stewart did not cooperate with the Young Pretender, who had demanded surrender of the city, and was consequently jailed by him. Later, when the government reasserted its power in the city, Stewart was jailed for having given up the city. A trial for his neglect of office as Lord Provost of Edinburgh began on 24 March 1747; it ended, after several delays, on 2 November 1747 with the acquittal. (A full report can be found in Mossner's *Life,* pp. 177–186.) As a political pamphlet, the *Account of Stewart* is unique in Hume, an *ad hoc* piece of writing to defend a friend. It is of interest to the student of Hume's ideas as well as to the literary critic; to us, its use of irony should be particularly worthwhile, since it is the single best example of Hume's wit and urbanity in political controversy.

The "friend" to whom the letter is addressed apparently was misinformed about the nature of Stewart's "crime," and Hume proceeds to straighten him out, informing him, for example, of the size and quality of the militia that attacked Stewart:

> The Highlanders are altogether as ignorant of Discipline as the Low-Country Ploughmen, and know as little the Nature of Encampments, Marches, Ranks, Evolutions, Firing, and all the other Parts of military Exercise, which preserves [*sic*] order in an Army, and render it so formidable. They advance to Battle in a confused Heap, which some People have been pleased to call a Column: They can use no Weapon but the Broad-Sword, which gives not one Wound in ten that is mortal, and obliges each Combatant to occupy double the Ground that would suffice, did he employ the

---

[4] I quote from a Xerox copy of the original, published anonymously in London in 1748; cited hereafter in text as *Account of Stewart.* The *Account of Stewart* is reprinted in the Appendix.

Pushing-Sword or the Bayonet. And they become weaker by their Victories; while they disperse to their Homes, in order to secure the Plunder they have acquired ... (*Account of Stewart*, pp. 7–8)

Hume's ironic treatment of the militia is intended to show that the Young Pretender, even if his forces had been very bad, would have encountered little resistance in taking Edinburgh. The casual under-statement about the Highlanders' avarice as the result of small gain indicates one of the ironies about the troops: the more they win, the weaker they become, because of their subsequent devotion to the spoils of the victor rather than the duty of the soldier. His opinion of the adequacy of the defense troops employed by the government becomes sarcastic later:

I wish his Majesty would be pleased to honour me with the Command of either of the *Highland* Battalions, and that I had some honest *Jesuitical* Clergyman to lay my Scruples; I should think it a very easy Exploit to march them from *Dover* to *Inverness*, rob the Bank of *England* in my way, and carry my Spoils, without Interruption, thro' the whole Nation; provided the Army were disposed to continue mere Spectators of my Prowess. (*Account of Stewart*, p. 13)

This is the sort of force, the rebellious Highlanders (who constituted only one-fifth, Hume says, of all the other Highlander troops), that Stewart had to contend with. Imbued with a strong military back-ground, they were not the easiest forces to subdue. Even though Hume treats them ironically because he did not approve of Jacobitism, he nevertheless respects their might. He treats them with this biting irony to demonstrate, or so I should guess, his opposition to the rebellion.

The Highlanders may have been formidable; the forces Stewart commanded were a little less awesome:

Let us enumerate that Force, in order to judge the better of it, and deter-mine whether it was likely to resist the Rebels. We shall surely find a List of Heroes equal to those of which *Homer* has given us a Catalogue, if not in his *Illiad*, at least in his *Batrachomyomachia*, or Battle of the Frogs and Mice.

There were of the Town Guards ninety six Men, augmented at that time to 126. These are rather elderly Men, but pretty well disciplined; and in-deed, the only real Force the Provost was Master of. The rest were, in a

Word, undisciplined *Britons*, which implies just as formidable an Idea as undisciplined *Romans*, or undisciplined *Indians*. . . .

. . . I am told, that their Appearance resembled very much that of *Falstaff's* Tatterdemallion Company, which his Friend supposed he had levied by unloading the Gibbets and pressing the dead Bodies. But the merry Knight defended his Company, by saying, *Tut, mortal Men, mortal Men, good enough to toss, Food for Powder.* Tho' it is my humble Opinion, that had the Mortality of the Regiment abovementioned depended on their being Food for Powder, they would have deserved the Epithet of the *immortal Body,* as much as the King of *Persia's* Guards, who, as *Herodotus* tells us, were dignified with that Appellation. (*Account of Stewart,* pp. 14, 16)

These impressive forces surely must have struck terror into the hearts of their enemies. Although Hume has not been gentle with the forces of the Highlanders, he is even less so with the forces at Stewart's command. Though not quite so biting, the irony is much more insulting, for it implies a complete absence of the martial spirit necessary for victory; it implies instead a sort of haphazard collection of men who would much rather be elsewhere.

Insipid as these forces may be, perhaps they would have been stronger had they been equipped with the proper instruments of war:

I remember *Cardinal de Retz* says, that a great Prince made very merry with the new levied troops of *Paris,* during the Civil Wars; and when he mentioned the Defence that might be expected from the City against the King's Troops, usually called it, *La guerra des pots de chambre,* The War of the Chamber-pots. As it is well known, that a Chamber-pot is a very formidable Machine in *Edinburgh,* I wonder it has not been comprized amongst Provost *Stewart's* forces; at least, amongst his Auxiliaries, in Conjunction with the rest above mentioned.

Having thus given a faithful account of the Garrison, let us now bestow some Considerations on the Place . . . (*Account of Stewart,* pp. 18–19)

Exaggeration is the keynote of the irony here, and the exaggeration is the product of some farfetched analogies between the troops and various objects. Particularly appropriate in the above example, it illustrates with subtle humor the inadequacy of Stewart's troops and supplies. Any army forced to defend its city with chamber pots would be at the most laughable. This ironic caricature of their armament is particularly effective as a defense of Stewart, for it delineates the contrast between the appearance of Stewart's actions and the reality that forced him to lose the battle.

That is not all for these hapless defenders of mother, God, and country. In addition to Provost Stewart's Auxiliaries were two Regiments of Dragoons commanded, not by him, but by a Brigadier-General Fowke. Apparently they were the most skilled soldiers:

> Brigadier *Fowke* (whose Conduct in this whole Affair is too remarkable to be forgot), tho' he had only two Regiments of Dragoons, and a very few Infantry, was still a formidable Enemy to the Rebels. . . .
>
> But before the Rebels came within Sight of the King's Forces [commanded by Fowke], before they came within three Miles distance of them, Orders were issued to the Dragoons to wheel; which they immediately did, with the greatest Order and Regularity imaginable. As 'tis known, nothing is more beautiful than the Evolutions and Motions of Cavalry, the Spectators stood in Expectation what fine warlike *Manoeuvre* this might terminate in; when new Orders were immediately issued to retreat. . . .
>
> I have seen an *Italian* Opera called *Caesare in Egitto*, or *Caesar in Egypt*; where in the first Scene *Caesar* is introduced in a great Hurry, giving Orders to his Soldiers, *Fugge, fugge: a'llo scampo*. Fly, fly: to your Heels. This is a Proof, that the Commander at the *Colt-Bridge* is not the first Hero that gave such Orders to his Troops.
>
> 'Twas in Consideration of such great Example, I suppose, that he has been so honourably acquitted (Upon his Trial, he justified himself at *Mr. Stewart's* Expence, and threw much Blame upon the Provost) . . . (*Account of Stewart*, pp. 23–24, 26)

By treating such absurd troops as if they were the most dignified of soldiers, Hume achieves an ironic commentary by one of the most familiar forms of irony: blame-by-praise. When the "fine warlike Manoeuvre" turns out to be nothing more than a hasty retreat, we begin to suspect that the Regiments of Dragoons are more amusing than laudable. When an analogy between them and a scene in an Italian opera, which Hume disliked in general, is drawn, the picture is even more laughable. To a large number of men in the eighteenth century, opera was nothing but pointless when it tried to duplicate great battles, and most readers would have inferred the ridiculous posture of Fowke from this reference, although it ostensibly is given as historical "proof" that Fowke's command had a precedent. It is not a "great Example" at all, but a burlesque of heroic behavior.

The purpose of the letter is to dramatize the injustice of Stewart's being convicted for developments that were clearly beyond his control. Considered another way, it must have been "ironic" to Hume that one who had served his city as well as had Archibald Stewart would be accused of neglect of duty, when obviously the facts did not corroborate the charge. Since the facts did not convict Stewart, Hume could treat the charge ironically. By doing so, he was using an ironic tone to cast discredit on the grimmer irony of the charge against Stewart, and its use was successful esthetically.

Political irony must, of course, be fairly obvious, so that the unlettered reader will not mistake the author's intentions. I should imagine this is the reason why Hume's tone in the *Account of Stewart* is less subtle than it might have been, pasquinading as it does the various opposing military forces. Although we cannot measure its effectiveness against public opinion—since it was published after Stewart's acquittal —it is soundly argued. The ironic portions I quoted come from the first of the letter and set the reader up for a sharp legal defense of Stewart. The irony creates the proper atmosphere, since it implies that the whole proceedings are a bit silly anyway and that anyone who would believe the charges against Stewart was not aware of the facts or was too biased to care.

It is evident that the pamphlet was written for a reading public somewhat different from the kind to whom Hume usually tried to appeal. For one thing, he translates the phrases and titles in foreign languages, which he does not do in his other writings, those aimed at a highly literate readership. In the *Account of Stewart* Hume comes closer to the traditional ironic mode of writing in the eighteenth century than he does in any of his previous works. Even in the works that will come after this, Hume is more subtle and indirect. It is not a work of genius, for no author always writes at white heat, and the accidents in which occasional pieces turn out to be masterpieces instead are few indeed. But the kind of audience to whom this pamphlet would appeal was the type that needed to have its public "image" of Provost Stewart changed. Consequently, Hume makes a deliberate effort to insure that the writing and conduct of the argument will appeal to the "average" reader of the eighteenth century, one who might not understand the precise legal defense that occupies the latter half of the pamphlet, but who would respond favorably to the ironic discussion of Stewart's guilt.

In case we are inclined to think that Hume was unqualified to judge military affairs, let us remember the occasions when he served General St. Clair. Although the first occasion (described above) provided little success for General St. Clair, who was less to blame than the British Ministry (a complete account will be found in Mossner's *Life,* pp. 187–204), Hume had firsthand experience of civil and military war; he had seen how bureaucrats were capable of bungling even the most easily obtainable goals. The conduct and behavior of military men, or men with responsibility, under stress came before the careful eye of the observer of human nature, and certainly qualified him to judge the conduct and behavior of Stewart when he had been accused. So we cannot dismiss the *Account of Stewart* as meaningless because it involves the defense of a friend and, therefore, incorporates a distortion of the facts. Hume's regard for truth was as great as his regard for friends, and the *Account of Stewart* is humorous, precise, and learned.

In order to see more clearly the virtues of this pamphlet, we may compare it to another occasioned by a matter as concrete and specific as the one involving Stewart. (Hume's irony is almost always concrete and specific, seldom abstract and general.) This second pamphlet was directed against James Fraser, a "hot-headed Highlander and a rabid Jacobite" (*Life,* p. 236). In Hume's letters Fraser is sometimes the object of jests about his too ardent Jacobitism. Hume's ironic treatment of him, however, becomes more exact in a letter of 1751 to Colonel James Abercromby. In it he encloses a manuscript hopefully designed to cure Fraser of his political leanings. It is addressed "To THE RIGHT HONble the LORD-CHIEF REASON and the HONble the JUDGES, DIS-CRETION, PRUDENCE, RESERVE, and DELIBERATION, THE PETITION OF THE PATIENTS of WESTMINSTER against JAMES FRASER, apothecary."[5] Its form is an allegory alleging Fraser to be a good apothecary

---

[5] Reprinted in *HL,* II, 340–342.

whose cheerful disposition and exemplary practice of medicine had cured many sick people:

THAT there are many disconsolate Widows among your Petitioners, who believ'd themselves, & and were believ'd by all their Neighbours, to be dying of Grief; but as soon as the said James Fraser apply'd Lenitives, & proper topical Medicines, they were observ'd to recover wonderfully.

That in all hypocondriacal Cases he was Sovereign, insomuch that his very Presence dispell'd the Malady, cheering the Sight, exciting a gentle Agitation of the Muscles of the Lungs & Thorax, & thereby promoting Expectoration, Exhileration, Circulation, and Digestion.

These phrases laud Fraser, but they have a purpose other than mere praise:

That the said James Fraser associating himself with ———— Carey Surgeon, & William Guthrey Esqr & other evil intention'd Persons, not having the Fear of God before their Eyes, had given himself entirely up to the Care of Dame PUBLIC, and had utterly neglected your Petitioners.

That the Lady abovementioned was of a most admirable CONSTITUTION, envy'd by all who had ever seen her or heard of her; & was only afflicted sometimes with Vapours, & sometimes with a Looseness or Flux, which, not being of the bloody kind, those about her were rather pleas'd with it.

That, notwithstanding this, the said James Fraser uses all Diligence & Art to perswade the said Lady, that she is in the most desperate Case imaginable, & that nothing will recover her but a Medicine he has prepard, being a Composition of *Pulvis pyrius*, along with a Decoction of northern Steel, and an Infusion of southern *Aqua sacra* or holy Water.

That this Medicine or rather Poyson was at first wrapt up under a Wafer, markt Patriotism; but had since been attempted to be administrated without any Cover or Disguise.

That a Doze of it had secretly been pour'd down the Throat of the said Dame Public, while she was asleep, & had been attended with the most dismal Symptoms, visibly heightening her Vapours, & encreasing her Flux, & even producing some Symptoms of the bloody kind. And had she not thrown it up with great Violence, it had certainly prov'd fatal to her.

Hume concludes by asking that it "please your Worships to discharge the said James Fraser from any farther Attendance on the said Dame Public, & to order him to return to the Care & Inspection of your Petitioners & their Families."

If Hume succeeded we have no record of it, but his burlesque may not have been published at all, since the discretion of publishing it was left to Abercromby. Whatever its publishing fate, it is pleasant enough as a skit, its irony deriving, as before, from the legalistic jargon used. To Hume it is ironic that Fraser is trying to force down the throat of the public something it does not want and something that would bring bloodshed. Apparently he does not recognize Fraser as a really serious threat to the safety of "Dame Public," since the ironic treatment is, for the most part, good-natured. Its purpose, of course, is philosophical, not political: by means of an elaborate metaphor Hume hopes to convince Fraser that he is wasting his time on something he is not really qualified for, when he could be making another, much better use of his talents.

The emphasis on some of the body's more unpleasant functions has a Swiftian attitude about it, which is not surprising in view of Hume's professed desire to imitate Swift (*HL,* I, 153). These two examples, however, illustrate the primary function of irony in Hume's political writings: to persuade and to convince by tacitly assuming that the question under argument is almost too ridiculous to deserve serious treatment. But Hume treats the different situations both seriously and ironically. In the *Account of Stewart* he hoped, if it were necessary, to shed light on a predicament that involved a good friend. In the parody of Fraser's efforts he hoped to achieve, at least in Fraser, a recognition of the foolishness of his ardent Jacobitism. On a larger scale, perhaps it would have been an argument to the effect that the majority of Britishers were not inclined to accept Jacobitism as their political philosophy. The *Account of Stewart* reveals Hume's irony at its most caustic, matched only by his discussions of "true" religion. The "Petition" mocks an acquaintance and is more friendly than caustic. By employing irony to effect certain purposes, he was doing no more than following the tradition of his day, for the "Petition" is certainly no masterpiece of satire. But the *Account of Stewart* creates a fine defense of Archibald Stewart, first preparing the reader by the ironic treatment of Stewart's forces compared to those arrayed against him. In that example the irony works to a good purpose; in the other it falls flat.

Notwithstanding the weaknesses of Hume's ironic mode, irony, as a literary and philosophical device, is more surely and more subtly used in the works of this period than in the previous period. Irony is by definition subtle, and as Hume becomes confident of his literary talents his writing becomes more subtle. He writes in his autobiography that he had "always entertained a Notion, that my want of Success, in publishing the Treatise of human Nature, had proceeded more from the manner than the matter; and that I had been guilty of a very usual Indiscretion, in going to the Press too early." The result was, in reworking the ideas of the *Treatise,* that some of the obstreperous passages were toned down, usually with an emphasis, in the *Enquiries,* more convincing than the exuberance of the *Treatise.* As we might expect, he was determined not to alter the "matter" but the "manner" of his presentation; he was not abandoning principles, as a letter to James Oswald in October 1747 sufficiently illustrates: "But in the first place, I think I am too deep engaged to think of a retreat. In the second place, I see not what bad consequences follow, in the present age, from the character of an infidel; especially if a man's conduct be in other respects irreproachable" (*HL,* I, 106). Hume's conduct in "other respects" was irreproachable; few men have led such exemplary moral lives, although the religious bigot was quick to equate his scepticism with amorality or immorality.[6] Hume, at least, was not offered a cup of hemlock.

The *Enquiry concerning Human Understanding* exhibits an ironic approach toward many of the traditional problems of philosophy. By way of preparation for the reader, I would ask him to remember that irony is hard to isolate in any given work. In Hume's writings, the irony is frequently the result of an interpretation that conflicts with the intended one. And the ironic tone assumes many guises: rhetorical extravagance, overstatement, understatement, ambiguity, and naïveté. Hume, eager to cultivate a distinguished literary style, adopts much of the manner of the dominant literary form of the eighteenth century, although the method is sometimes different.

It is commonly thought (and, indeed, I have, for convenience, referred to it as such) that the *Enquiry concerning Human Understanding* is simply a recasting of the first book of the *Treatise,* and no one will deny the existence of certain philosophical homologues between

---

[6] F. L. Lucas in *The Art of Living,* has a chapter devoted to a discussion of Hume's congeniality, although it contains not a few errors of fact.

the two. But in view of Hume's repudiation of the *Treatise,* now prefixed to most editions of the *Enquiry concerning Human Understanding* or the *Enquiry concerning the Principles of Morals,* we are
obliged to consider the first *Enquiry* as an entity within itself. Professor
Antony Flew, in his fine book *Hume's Philosophy of Belief,* has remarked upon some of the "revisions":

> Certainly there is a marked difference in style and temper. The egotisms
> which so repelled the mature Hume from the former are not to be found in
> the latter. The self-questioning anxieties and the leaping youthful aspira-
> tions have been replaced by a more assured and controlled flow of argument.
> The stylistic deficiencies of the production of "a solitary Scotchman" have
> yielded to the urbane polishings of the rising professional man of letters.[7]

The accuracy of that evaluation of Hume's first *Enquiry* is immediately
impressed upon the reader as he turns to the initial section, which sets
the tone and purpose for the rest of the volume. Hume has discussed
the possibilities of philosophy and science, what man may expect from
them and what they demand of him. The attack on rationalistic metaphysics opens this way:

> But this obscurity in the profound and abstract philosophy, is objected to,
> not only as painful and fatiguing, but as the inevitable source of uncertainty
> and error. Here indeed lies the justest and most plausible objection against a
> considerable part of metaphysics, that they are not properly a science; but
> arise either from the fruitless efforts of human vanity, which would pene-
> trate into subjects utterly inaccessible to the understanding, or from the craft
> of popular superstitions, which, being unable to defend themselves on fair
> ground, raise these intangling brambles to cover and protect their weakness.
> Chaced from the open country, these robbers fly into the forest, and lie in
> wait to break in upon every unguarded avenue of the mind, and overwhelm
> it with religious fears and prejudices. The stoutest antagonist, if he remit
> his watch a moment, is oppressed. And many, through cowardice and folly,
> open the gates to the enemies, and willingly receive them with reverence
> and submission, as their legal sovereigns. (*Works,* IV, 8; *ECHU,* pp.
> 20–21)

Professor Flew again has the correct comment: "Surely this is a statement sufficiently categorical for anyone. It indicates clearly how we

[7] Antony Flew, *Hume's Philosophy of Belief,* pp. 3–4.

are to construe certain more oblique, ironical, or ambiguous passages in later Sections" (p. 11).

That very passage, of course, has an ironic cast to it representative of the irony in both *Enquiries*. Perhaps it will induce the reader to re-examine the tone and conduct of the arguments in the *Enquiries,* be-cause it would otherwise be necessary to quote long sections of Hume's philosophical works to show, bit by bit, the components that make up the irony. As one might guess, the ironic form is most easily discovered in Hume's attitude toward religion, but it is just as apparent, though not as intense, in his attitude toward the rationalistic, a priori phi-losopher. That Hume's unrelentingly logical mind and his exacting empiricism spelled the downfall of several ancient and modern phi-losophers, whose faith was a contempt for experience as a guide to reason, is a legacy of which philosophy can well be proud. Hume's opinion of the philosophy of the rationalists was, at its strongest, contemptuous, and, at its weakest, tolerantly amused. I should say that, in general, I am in sympathy with his antirationalist position, and con-sequently perhaps I am more alert to his ironic treatment of the rational-ists than a rationalist might be, especially when his irony takes the form of blame-by-praise. In his philosophical writings it is frequently the abstract principles that receive his contempt, while the rationalistic philosopher is the recipient of a calm amusement at man's attempt to justify the ways of God to philosophy, as in this example:

When we reason *a priori*, and consider merely any object or cause, as it ap-pears to the mind, independent of all observation, it never could suggest to us the notion of any distinct object, such as its effect; much less, shew us the inseparable and inviolable connection between them. A man must be very sagacious, who could discover by reasoning, that crystal is the effect of heat, and ice of cold, without being previously acquainted with the operation of these qualities. (*Works*, IV, 28; *ECHU*, p. 46)

Hume's ironic tone in that last sentence is classic in its expression. Little that could properly be called sagacious was ever apt to be the product of vacuous theorizing about physical properties that made ab-solutely no reference to experience or experimental procedures. In-deed, Hume is implying, the man is a fool who is sure that he has ascertained the physical results of cold while living entirely (say) in a tropical climate, completely isolated from the rest of the world, having never had any experience of cold and never observing the formation of ice. There were, apparently, those who might just operate in such a strange mental fashion, and Hume was unwilling to accept the validity of their claims. The ironic tone here is a function of the scepticism which accepts reason as its guide, but a scepticism which also accepts experience as its master.

Hume's irony is healthy, because it aims to correct some philosophical notions which were not only anathema to him but which would be distasteful to any man who asked for facts and reasoning—not theories and verbal posturings—in answer to his questions about knowledge and morality. Hume must be credited with perceiving that philosophy had far too often claimed for itself more knowledge, more authority, and more autonomy than could possibly be justified by its contributions to the progress of humanity. It had given man words to live by, illusions to believe; but it had not created the sort of viable intellectual medium that would handle the problems of an individual human nature besieged by a world not of its own making. Philosophy and philosophers in the past had more often than not explained away the mysteries and vagaries of the universe instead of attempting to understand them, or to accept them. If philosophy was to achieve any meaning in the future, Hume felt, it would have to set achievable goals; or, better still, not set any goal at all but that of enlightenment. If philosophers were to have any role in the construction of the intelligence of the future, then they would have to forego certitude and accept mutability, or, in the words of Karl Popper, forego "Utopian engineering" and accept "piece-meal engineering."[8] The difficulty, of course, was that the sort of philosophical attitude Hume wished to inculcate seemed to be a negative approach to the problems of life. After all, if it were meritorious to be ignorant, why should one seek any knowledge about anything? Would it not be better to envision grand designs than more modest pretensions when it was impossible to know the certainty of anything?

Hume did not think so. He felt that it was better to begin without notions of a grand, idealistic system whose "truth" must be proven at

[8] Karl Popper, *The Open Society and Its Enemies,* pp. 154–155.

all costs. Instead, he suggested that we admit our ignorance about some of the "secret springs" of nature and not seek to explain them in some mysterious way. The admission of ignorance was the honest way to begin the search for knowledge; any pose of preconceived certitude had no epistemological value to the philosopher. A philosopher would best proceed by examining sense data and co-ordinating them into a reasonable evaluation of the world. There would be no Utopian engineering for the epistemologist; he would be pragmatic and questioning, always hoping, naturally, that what he learned would give him enough knowledge to develop a coherent and reasonable conception of human nature. The science of human nature, then, would not begin with frozen goals and methods, but should be loose and adaptable enough to meet and understand any sense data, and to abstract from those data an accurate synthesis of human nature.

Much as he may have disliked the rationalism of Plato or Socrates, Hume learned something from them: the use of Socratic irony. The ignorance to which Hume alludes is to him not ignorance but the best kind of knowledge. Pretending to know nothing is a device by which one may become enlightened about the science of human nature. Too, it is better, in Hume's opinion, to remain ignorant about some specific working of the universe or of the mind than it is to invent, to hypostatize, or to imagine some supernatural, metaempirical reason to explain away that mystery. The ignorance in which Hume sees real merit is not that absence of knowledge and thought characteristic of the "vulgar mind" (as Hume called it), but is instead a concomitant of a reasoned, empiric search for truth. It is a search which accepts only the validity of reasoning from fact or number and which is extremely sceptical of the claims of any philosophy which pretends to omniscience. Under these circumstances, it is something less than a divine revelation for us to learn that he sometimes treated the rationalists ironically.

Although Hume's irony is most frequently aimed at rationalists and religionists, it is not uncommon to find a shaft of irony aimed at philosophy and philosophers in general. Hume considered the philosophical habit of mind a worthwhile one, so long as the zeal for philosophy and philosophical inquiry did not flood out one's involvement in the main stream of human affairs. ("Amidst all your philosophy, be still a man.") Philosophy was not what some people took it to be, a substitute for religion, because of the vast differences in procedure and analysis in the two separate disciplines. It is typical of Hume that he is able to remove himself from the intricacies of the argument in the first *Enquiry* and to achieve a certain cultural perspective. At the beginning of Section V, "Skeptical Solution of These Doubts," Hume withdraws, as it were, from the argument and asks the reader to look at the problems from a different point of view:

The passion for philosophy, like that for religion, seems liable to this inconvenience, that, though it aims at the correction of our manners, and extirpation of our vices, it may only serve, by imprudent management, to foster a predominant inclination, and push the mind, with more determined resolution, toward that side, which already *draws* too much, by the biass and propensity of the natural temper. It is certain, that, while we aspire to the magnanimous firmness of the philosophic sage, and endeavor to confine our pleasures altogether within our own minds, we may at last, render our philosophy, like that of EPICTETUS, and other *Stoics*, only a more refined system of selfishness, and reason ourselves out of all virtue, as well as social enjoyment. While we study with attention the vanity of human life, and turn all our thoughts toward the empty and transitory nature of riches and honors, we are, perhaps, all the while, flattering our natural indolence, which, hating the bustle of the world, and drudgery of business, seeks a pretense of reason, to give itself a full and uncontrouled indulgence. (*Works*, IV, 35; *ECHU*, p. 54)

Philosophers, like the rest of us, Hume says, are not incapable of straining at a gnat and swallowing a camel; that is the irony of their profession.

Hume has a reason, as usual, for beginning the section in this way: to prepare the reader for the camels to come, many of which will not go down so easily. In the same paragraph he remarks, a few sentences later, that it is surprising that this sceptical philosophy "which, in almost every instance, must be harmless and innocent, should be the subject of so much groundless reproach and obloquy." To Hume it must certainly have been "harmless and innocent," but to the priest or the metaphysician, it was worse than sin or paganism. This remark is an example of both-and irony, that which is both literally true and ironic. Hume makes the irony clear in the next sentences: "But, perhaps, the very circumstance which renders it [scepticism] so innocent is what chiefly exposes it to the public hatred and resentment. By flattering no irregular passion, it gains few partizans. By opposing so many vices and follies, it raises to itself abundance of enemies who stigmatize it as libertine, profane, and irreligious." Hume is leading the reader, not as gently as some might have wished, from an observance of the ironic disproportion between zeal and true philosophy to the recognition that correct reasoning, which does not pander to one's secret desires, is likely to be the most abominable human activity to reactionaries and dogmatists. In order to make the unsympathetic reader aware of the problem, Hume formulates it ironically; indeed, the unsuspecting rationalist might think that the sceptic was beginning to make a few concessions to his side. To make such an assumption in Hume's writings is to invite certain disillusionment.

In the *Enquiry concerning Human Understanding,* as in other works, scepticism is, in many of its forms, an adjunct to irony. The ironic mode, after all, is one in which the meaning is quantitatively different from a superficial rendering of the words. The writer of a piece of sustained irony, such as Swift's *Modest Proposal,* is, to put it mildly, completely sceptical of the real truth of the superficial level of his words. In Swift's case his scepticism about the economic and moral efficacy of solving the problem of overabundant babies and underabundant food is complete and unrelenting. This scepticism in dealing with moral problems is the sort that, because of the convictions of the author and of the general value structure of civilized man, can never be retracted. Hume's blend of irony and scepticism has much the same purpose as Swift's, though few men were more unlike. In the *Modest Proposal,* for example, Swift prepares the reader for what follows by the utter plausibility of his approach; Hume prepares the reader by what seems to be a plausible objection to philosophy, but notes that scepticism is exempt from this objection. In the paragraph we have just examined the ironic intent is made clear by a variety of devices: historical contrast, a philosophical plausibility engraved onto some curious fact, and the achievement of some cultural or social perspective.

Hume's scepticism is nowhere more famous, or notorious, depending upon one's religious convictions, than in the essay "Of Miracles," which is also one of his best essays.[9] Professor Flew justifiably observes that "everyone . . . who has written at any length on Section X ["Of Miracles"] of this *Inquiry* seems to have misunderstood and misrepresented at least some part of it." In that case, I shall consider myself in fairly respectable company, if what I have to say about the essay proves inaccurate. Section X should not be read alone but in conjunction with Section XI, "Of a Particular Providence and of a Future State." Although Hume is frequently accused of being "naughty" or mischievous in "Of Miracles," his argument is, in fact, genuine and sincere; those who dismiss it as mere cavil have fooled only themselves. As far as I can see, the argument of the essay is unanswerable—if we know what Hume is doing. His contention that *faith,* not reason, is the foundation of "our most holy religion" is so generally accepted by responsible theologians today as to be beyond dispute.

In beginning his discussion of miracles Hume apparently puts substantial emphasis upon human testimony:[10]

To apply these principles to a particular instance; we may observe, that there is no species of reasoning more common, more useful, and even necessary to human life, than that which is derived from the testimony of men, and the reports of eye-witnesses and spectators. This species of reasoning, perhaps, one may deny to be founded on the relation of cause and effect. I shall not dispute about a word. It will be sufficient to observe, that our assurance in any argument of this kind is derived from no other principle than our observation of the veracity of human testimony, and of the usual conformity of facts to the report of witnesses. It being a general maxim, that no

[9] Not everyone shares this view; for example, C. D. Broad in *Five Types of Ethical Theory,* p. 9, writes: "It is unfortunate that the general public should know him mainly as the author of the one thoroughly silly production of his pen, viz., the notorious *Essay on Miracles* [*sic*]." Whether Hume wrote anything that was *thoroughly* silly is at least open to question; I should think better candidates for the epithet "silly" would be the essays Hume described as "frivolous" ("Of Impudence and Modesty," among others), the skit directed against Fraser, and the *Bellmen's Petition,* which will be discussed soon. At least Hume intended those works to be partly silly, in the way that a *Modest Proposal* is "silly." But to call the essay "thoroughly silly" is itself "thoroughly silly."

[10] For a recent discussion of Hume's criteria for accurate testimony regarding miracles, see Ralph S. Pomeroy's article "Hume on the Testimony for Miracles" in *Speech Monographs,* **XXIX** (1962), 1–12.

objects have any discoverable connexion together, and that all the inferences, which we can draw from one to another, are founded merely on our experience of their constant and regular conjunction; it is evident, that we ought not to make an exception to this maxim in favour of human testimony, whose connexion with any event seems, in itself, as little necessary as any other. Were not the memory tenacious to a certain degree; had not men commonly an inclination to truth and a principle of probity; were they not sensible to shame, when detected in a falsehood: Were not these, I say, discovered by *experience* to be qualities, inherent in human nature, we should never repose the least confidence in human testimony. A man delirious, or noted for falsehood and villainy, has no manner of authority with us. (*Works*, IV, 90–91; *ECHU*, pp. 119–120)

Superficially, it would seem that Hume offers the reader testimony as one of the most reliable criteria for the "truth" about a certain event. But does Hume really think that men have a common inclination to truth? When he applies standards for reliability and veracity to testimony, the irony of his former praise of testimony becomes apparent:

It is strange, a judicious reader is apt to say, upon the perusal of these wonderful historians, *that such prodigious events never happen in our days.* But it is nothing strange, I hope, that men should lie in all ages. You must surely have seen instances enow of that frailty. You have yourself heard many such marvellous relations started, which, being treated with scorn by all the wise and judicious, have at last been abandoned even by the vulgar. Be assured, that those renowned lies, which have spread and flourished to such a monstrous height, arose from like beginnings; but being sown in a more proper soil, shot up at last into prodigies almost equal to those which they relate. . . .

Upon the whole, then, it appears, that no testimony for any kind of miracle has ever amounted to a probability, much less to a proof; and that, even supposing it amounted to a proof, it would be opposed by another proof; derived from the very nature of the fact, which it would endeavor to establish. It is experience only, which gives authority to human testimony; and it is the same experience, which assures us of the laws of nature. When, therefore, these two kinds of experience are contrary, we have nothing to do but substract the one from the other, and embrace an opinion, either on one side or the other, with that assurance which arises from the remainder. But according to the principle here explained, this substraction, with regard to all popular religions, amounts to an entire annihilation; and therefore we may establish it as a maxim, that no human testimony can have such force as to prove a miracle, and make it a just foundation for any such system of religion. (*Works*, IV, 97, 105; *ECHU*, pp. 122, 137)

Thus, by a careful definition of the standards for testimony, Hume has made ironic, deliberately, his former statement about testimony.

The discussion of testimony is extended to cover products of the human mind other than religion, in passages whose latent irony becomes transparent when set against the essay as a whole. The inclination to report what the heart wants to see is more likely to strike the pious, as Hume argues:

The wise lend a very academic faith to every report which favours the passion of the reporter; whether it magnifies his country, his family, or himself, or in any other way strikes in with his natural inclinations and propensities. But what greater temptation than to appear a missionary, a prophet, an ambassador from heaven? Who would not encounter many dangers and difficulties, in order to attain so sublime a character? Or if, by the help of vanity and a heated imagination, a man has first made a convert of himself, and entered seriously into the delusion; who ever scruples to make use of pious frauds, in support of so holy and meritorious a cause? (*Works*, IV, 104; *ECHU*, pp. 135–136)

Although he is more caustic in his treatment of religious frauds and their use of illogic to convert sinners, he is not unsympathetic with the nature of the human being who is led to pursue such unreasoned conclusions. He realized that it was contradictory to profess to be a seeker after truth and then to use pat answers as a defense for what one wanted to believe regardless of the facts involved. His counsel was, despite the rhetoric, that "reason is, and ought only to be, the slave of the passions." If one's passions were so strong that he could not dispose of them in the search for truth, Hume did not despise the man or his philosophy. He may have been unsympathetic toward some particular philosophy and the curious reasoning that led to it, but he acknowledged it as one of the curiosities of life. It was, in Aristotelian terms, a *mimēsis* of life, and it followed the pattern of life exactly. Life was a permanent ironic contrast between man's professions of, on the one hand, value and knowledge, and, on the other hand, his contradictory execution of those values and knowledge.

Hume's philosophical conduct of the argument about miracles is typical; although seemingly offhand, it is an ironic inversion of the deductive method in logic. A general position about the esteem and reliability of human testimony is promulgated as the major premise. The minor premise, a more particular form of this generalized major premise, asserts that X, Y, and Z, known to be trustworthy and reliable, have testified that a miracle occurred at such-and-such a place on such-and-such a date. This logic, proceeding so well, suddenly explodes: the conclusion is not logical; the fallout from the blast badly damages the authenticity and certainty of the premises. Deduction, that surest and most reliable branch of logic, will not provide an answer when confronted with possibilities and alternatives that cannot be reduced to its predetermined framework.

Hume's understated irony accomplishes two purposes in the essay on miracles. First, the irony seems to assent to the proposition that human testimony is reliable and useful in epistemology; yet a careful examination of testimony finally reveals that it is, for reasons of psychology and of empirical verification, essentially useless and unreliable. Second, the logic employing miracles as empirical support for the truth of the Christian religion is itself unreliable. In simple terms, Hume was, I think, trying to show that conventional modes of logic, while offering a "reasonable" way of thinking about miracles and the Christian religion, were in error because they failed to distribute all the terms or premises of the attempted syllogism. Hume has accomplished one of the neatest tricks in philosophy: he has used the form of a deductive, syllogistic reasoning to demonstrate the illogic of the terms employed in that form. He has projected the ambiguity inherent in the proposition into two levels of meaning, which he shows to be contradictory. By temporarily assuming the alleged "truth" the reasoning which links testimony, miracles, and the Christian religion, Hume was later able to destroy the logic of that "truth" by carrying the logical implications of the propositions concerned to their ultimate limit. Once the "logic" of those propositions is pushed as far as it will go, the inherent contradictions, Hume believes, will be seen. The irony is apparent: what better way to undermine an opponent than to use his own arguments against him?

The procedure is neither unusual nor should it be unexpected in

Hume. He is, after all, discussing and analyzing the most abstruse and subtle of all philosophical propositions, those of cause and effect. Why he personally imbued the discussion with irony, I cannot say; even the most careful scholar cannot see into a man's mind. But the prevalence of irony in all of its subtle (and not-so-subtle) forms in the eighteenth century must have contributed something. Its effectiveness in overturning the apple carts of rationalism and scholasticism cannot be doubted. Combining irony, the subtlest form in literature, with the subtlest forms of philosophy seems an obvious choice. The wonder is not that it might fail, but that it is all too often unnoticed.

The irony is perhaps more noticeable, or, rather, more in keeping with a superficial understanding of the ironic mode, in the section that immediately follows the essay on miracles, "Of a Particular Providence and of a Future State." In this section Hume exhibits his mastery over the dissipated and illogical supernaturalism of some of the ecclesiastics of his time by professing, in an ironic mode, to treat religious concepts seriously. Section XI opens promisingly:

> I was lately engaged in conversation with a friend who loves sceptical paradoxes; where, though he advanced many principles, of which I can by no means approve, yet as they seem to be curious, and to bear some relation to the chain of reasoning carried on throughout this enquiry, I shall here copy them from my memory as accurately as I can, in order to submit them to the judgment of the reader. (*Works*, IV, 109; *ECHU*, p. 142)

As the essay progresses, however, even the stupidest of ten-year-olds could see how artfully the arguments of the "friend" coincided with the arguments of the author in the rest of the *Enquiry*. It is a classic formulation of the disproportion between what is and what seems to be, in which the perspicacious (or the Eiron) recognizes the disproportion, while the unintelligent (the Dupe or the Scapegoat) is deceived. The coincidence is not so astonishing if we consider that it would be quite improbable that even the most retentive mind would remember the numerous details and fine points that Hume's "friend" introduces into the discussion. This artifice disappears altogether when Hume and his "friend" reach practical agreement on all the propositions advanced in the essay. A man who begins an essay by stating he can "by no means approve" many of the principles he discusses and then openly does so is saying the opposite of what he means. This kind of irony is transparent, since its purpose is to establish the logical plausibility of certain principles of which Hume undoubtedly approved. The organization of the argument gives the would-be rationalist or religionist a false sense of security; and, if he is at all perceptive, he will acknowledge the irony of the introduction when it becomes apparent that Hume is not acquiescing to orthodoxy.

One possible explanation commonly advanced for Hume's irony in discussing religious practices and concepts I have already mentioned: personal safety. He is ironic because he fears what will await him at the hands of an angry mob eager to teach the sceptic a good lesson in Christianity, as did the Christians in Byron's lines:

> Christians have burnt each other, quite persuaded
> That all the Apostles would have done as they did.
> (*Don Juan*, I, 83)

Yet another reason may be advanced: Hume found the ironic mode best suited to his philosophy, his style, and his psychological make-up. It offered him a means of organization and argument that was more effective than the rather dull approach of Locke or, in his late writings, Berkeley. Often, in discussions of religious problems, Hume makes little effort to protect himself, but is openly ironic. He was never persuaded that the distortions of religion, the result of men's attempts to justify their rapacity, greed, chicanery, or a host of other vices, could be justified by broad religious, much less Christian, principles. Sceptics are always quicker to see the disparity between men's deeds and men's actions than someone to whom such anomalous human behavior is neither curious nor contradictory. To Hume it was a form of hypocrisy, but also a fault so eminently human that it could not be despised unless the whole of human nature was also despised. Hume's treatment of this form of human hypocrisy is ironic in its very casualness:

The great source of our mistake [in attributing all goodness and wisdom exclusively to the Deity] in this subject, and of the unbounded licence of conjecture, which we indulge, is, that we tacitly consider ourselves, as in the place of the Supreme Being, and conclude, that he will, on every occasion, observe the same conduct, which we ourselves, in his situation, would have embraced as reasonable and eligible. (*Works*, IV, 119–120; *ECHU*, p. 154)

The irony functions here to delineate the colossal egotism which causes
men to identify the Deity's aims with their own, or to assume that the
desires of the Deity are coextensive with theirs, and that He would
do exactly as they do. Hume, not exactly in sympathy with such ecclesiastics, thought such beliefs presumptuous, and with good reason.
He was not so much irritated by them, however, as he was amused.
This ability to enjoy the foibles of human nature and the doubleness
of men's actions is typical of all his writings.

In the last section of the *Enquiry concerning Human Understanding* Hume arrives at a discussion "Of the Academical or Sceptical
Philosophy." The procedure, organization, and conduct of the argument are in this section similar to those of the preceding sections, in
which the problem is identified (although we discover later that it is
not as much a problem as we suspect). What religionist could resist
the comforting words of the opening?

There is not a greater number of philosophical reasonings, displayed upon
any subject, than those, which prove the existence of a Deity, and refute the
fallacies of *Atheists*; and yet the most religious philosophers still dispute
whether any man can be so blinded as to be a speculative atheist. How shall
we reconcile these contradictions? The knights-errant, who wandered about
to clear the world of dragons and of giants, never entertained the least doubt
with regard to the existence of these monsters.

The *skeptic* is another enemy of religion, who naturally provokes the indignation of all divines and graver philosophers; though it is certain, that
no man ever met with any such absurd creature, or conversed with a man,
who had no opinion or principle concerning any subject, either of action
or speculation. This begets a very natural question: What is meant by a
skeptic? And how far is it possible to push these philosophical principles of
doubt and uncertainty? (*Works*, IV, 122; *ECHU*, p. 158)

These passages might imply that the sceptic is sceptical of scepticism,
but Hume concludes the section by advocating a kind of controlled
scepticism which assumes an ultimate uniformity of nature, an act of
custom that has become a belief. It is not the sceptic who is attacked,
but the dogmatist, a three-dimensional man who insists upon acting as
if he lived in a two-dimensional world. The objection to the volumes
"of divinity or school metaphysics" is the real purpose, as we knew
all along, of Hume's inquiry. Hume is led to advocate a kind of natural-

ism that is an enemy to both atheism and theism alike, and if he handles
them both ironically, they deserve it. In a work that began upon an
ironic note, Hume has ended with an ironic bow to himself, by dis-
covering in some forms of scepticism a kind of dogmatism that is unacceptable. But the rationalist and the religionist receive severe treatment, because their flights from reason and experience are the most
useless ones to Hume.

Despite the serious purpose and inquiries of the first *Enquiry,* Hume
was not to permit himself the luxury of representing the stereotyped
philosopher as brooding thinker. His letters, while mentioning the
Enquiry concerning Human Understanding, also offer a glimpse of the
philosopher at play, an image which, considering Hume's bulk, must
not be taken too literally. Hume reminds us of no one so much as he
does of Bertrand Russell, whose ability to incorporate wit and philosophy is unmatched. Hume's correspondence probably afforded the
philosopher some much-needed relief from the work of composition,
from the tedium of communications with his publishers, and from an
inclination toward a gloomy temperament that his early lack of success
might have engendered. The letters and the occasional writings will
suggest a background for the subtler forms of irony that we find in his
most serious and didactic works.

In writing James Oswald (1715–1769) of Dunniker he recounts
the adventures of one Hugh, Lord Polwarth, later third Earl of
Marchmont (1708–1794). The letter was written in January 1748,
when the first *Enquiry* was finished and awaiting publication. Hume
explained that Lord Marchmont, whose first wife had died in 1747,
was taken with a "fair nymph" of sixteen or seventeen, whom he married 30 January 1748; Hume was a little surprised at the speed of the
infatuation: "They say many small fevers prevent a great one. Heaven
be praised, that I have always liked the persons & company of the fair
sex: For by that means, I hope to escape such ridiculous passions"
(*HL,* I, 110). One of Hume's delights in corresponding with his
friends was to offer an explanation for his (or others') actions that
was antithetical to the one expected. Bernard Shaw was to perfect this
technique. Hume argues, in effect, that by enjoying the company of the
fair sex he will be less susceptible to their charms; only those who find

themselves uncomfortable in their company will marry in great haste or commit similar follies.

By 1751 Hume's good humor was at its peak. His books were enjoying a modicum of popularity, he was spending many pleasant hours with his friends, and he was earning enough from his writing to live on. At this time he was contemplating an extended ironic broadside against religion. The result, the *Bellmen's Petition*,[11] is undoubtedly bad writing, but it was not written to be anything but a skit for the enjoyment of his friends. He confessed his plan to his friend John Clephane in February 1751:

> But since I am in the humour of displaying my wit, I must tell you that lately, at an idle hour, I wrote a sheet called the Bellman's Petition: wherein (if I be not partial, which I certainly am) there was some good pleasantry and satire. The printers in Edinburgh refused to print it, (a good sign, you'll say, of *my* prudence and discretion). Mr Mure, the member [of Parliament], has a copy of it; ask it of him if you meet with him, or bid the Colonel, who sees him every day at the House, ask it, and if you like it read it to the General, and then return it. (*HL*, I, 149)

Later, in a letter to Gilbert Elliot, dated 18 February 1751, he had some observations about the objects of his wit:

> I send you enclos'd a little Endeavour at Drollery against some People who care not much to be jok'd upon. I have frequently had it in my Intentions to write a Supplement to *Gulliver*, containing the Ridicule of Priests. Twas certainly a Pity that Swift was a Parson. Had he been a Lawyer or Physician, we had nevertheless been entertain'd at the Expense of these Professions. But Priests are so jealous, that they cannot bear to be touch'd on that Head; and for a plain Reason: Because they are conscious they are really ridiculous. That Part of the Doctor's Subject is so fertile, that a much inferior Genius, I am confident, might succeed in it. (*HL*, I, 153)

(Part II of *Gulliver's Travels* contains some blistering reflections on bishops, but not perhaps the kind Hume wished to see.) The *Bell-*

---

[11] *Petition of the Grave and Venerable Bellmen, or Sextons, of the Church of Scotland, To the Honourable House of Commons,* anon. No copy of this version is extant. Reprinted in *The Scotch Haggis,* pp. 187–191; quotations are taken from this edition. The *Bellmen's Petition* is reprinted in the Appendix.

men's Petition was occasioned by the decision of the General Assembly of the Church of Scotland to ask Parliament for a higher stipend, a request that was quite within reason and certainly modest. The nobility and landed gentry (among them Hume's elder brother, John Home) opposed the increase, however, probably because the burden of paying it would fall on them. For once, David and John were united in their opinion, but for very different reasons: John, for financial reasons; David, for anticlerical reasons. Hume's sympathies are surely in the wrong here, since the clergymen were entitled to more than the pittance they received. For example, 147 ministers received only the bare legal minimum of £ 45 a year, 41 received only £ 40, and 16 received only £ 35.[12] For many years, the Church of Scotland had hoped to raise the salaries of the more poorly paid ministers, who were having trouble enough storing treasures on earth without having to worry about storing up treasures in heaven. Be that as it may, Hume did not agree that they were entitled to any raise, and the *Bellmen's Petition* is a parody on their demands.

Since Hume was on the side of the landed gentry, the argument advanced by the bellmen to the landed gentry was not one Hume thought worthwhile:

That it seems impossible the landed gentry can oppose the interests of your Petitioners; since by securing so perfectly as they have hitherto done, the persons of their fathers and elder brothers of the foresaid gentry, your Petitioners next, after the physicians, are the persons in the world to whom the present proprietors of land are the most beholden.

That as your Petitioners are but half ecclesiastics, it may be expected they will not be altogether unreasonable nor exorbitant in their demands.

That the present poverty of your Petitioners in this kingdom is a scandal to all religion, it being easy to prove, that a modern Bellman is not more richly endowed than a primitive apostle, and consequently possesseth not the twentieth part of the revenues belonging to a Presbyterian Clergyman.[13]

The irony in this particular excerpt moves in more than one direction. In the first paragraph the sly reference to primogeniture, written at a time when Hume's income was still tenuous, indicates that the bellmen

---

[12] J. Y. T. Greig, *David Hume,* p. 180.
[13] *The Scotch Haggis,* p. 189.

were not the only objects of parody in this particular composition. Hume was not himself financially secure and may possibly have resented the tradition that ruled him out of a fair share of his father's estate. An insecure financial position, however, did not keep him from poking fun at the churchmen. If the petitioners, who were only half ecclesiastics, were not unreasonable in their demands, what would happen if they were complete or full ecclesiastics? The implication is that they would be much more exorbitant and uncompromising in their demands, as a result of their more heavily authenticated piety. The landed gentry should consider themselves fortunate that this petition comes but from "half ecclesiastics" since the more ecclesiastical of their brethren would not be so easy to please, although they are considerably more secure. Apparently, it is easy for a rich man to get into the kingdom of heaven, provided he also happens to be a cleric.

The bellmen (as an earlier part of the tract states) also serve as gravediggers, an occupation which would humble even the most freethinking mind: "That whatever freedom the profane scoffers and freethinkers of the age may use with our Reverend Brethren the Clergy, the boldest of them trembles when he thinks of us; and that a simple reflection on us has reformed more lives than all the sermons in the world."[14] The prospect of the grave is enough to bring even the most sceptical of the sceptics around, and thus the bellmen convert sinners where the more highly paid of the clan do not succeed. Since Hume was frequently thought the boldest and most audacious of the freethinkers, this personal reference is particularly ironic. He was not apt to let the prospect of the grave bring about a death-bed conversion, since he was more impressed by facts than by prospects. And if he trembled when he thought of the function of the bellmen, he probably would not have been writing an ironic petition in their behalf. In this particular instance the purpose of the irony is to point out that the bellmen are not really as influential as they think they are.

The irony in this parody is typical of much of Hume's irony. In a seemingly straightforward piece of prose writing will appear a sentence or two—sometimes only a word or two—whose implications do not at all jibe with the over-all meaning of the passage. When we look

[14] *Ibid.*

at it more closely we discover that the purpose of those short sentences or words is to change the meaning more than any other part of the passage could. The irony in Hume's writings may hinge on just such words or sentences, which the careful reader cannot overlook, although the cursory reader may. It is the sort of irony which may make the reader feel as if he has been unfairly tricked. With Hume, however, that is not true. He expects the reader to be alert for these implications and then to seek out the exact (if possible) meaning of a particular passage. It is especially important in Hume's religious irony, since one or two words, or a single sentence, may very well change the meaning of an entire passage, just as the simple word "not" can reverse the meaning of a proposition. As a sceptic Hume was apt to make the most damning criticism possible of religious arguments, a practice which made the eighteenth-century cleric seethe with rage or indignation. After making one of these damaging critiques, Hume will insert a statement to the effect that the reader must not consider these arguments as destructive to his religion, that they are the cavils of a rampaging imagination. But these confessions of piety are so artfully qualified that only one of Bertrand Russell's "unusually stupid children of ten" (Preface to *Unpopular Essays*) would take them seriously.

From the *Bellmen's Petition* to the *Enquiry concerning the Principles of Morals* is a long step, although the *Bellmen's Petition* was actually written after the second *Enquiry* was at the publishers. (In a letter to Robert Wallace, written about 22 September 1751, Hume says "There has been printed at London, but not yet publish'd an *Enquiry concerning the Principles of Morals* of which I have order'd a Copy to be sent you" *NHL*, p. 29.) Thought by many today to be less impressive than the first *Enquiry*, it was nevertheless Hume's favorite: "In the same Year [1751] was published my *Enquiry concerning the Principles of Morals*, which, in my own opinion (who ought not to judge on that subject) is of all my writings, historical, philosophical, or literary, incomparably the best: It came unnoticed and unobserved into the World" (*My Own Life*). Yet we must give Hume credit for developing one of the first systems of modern ethics to exist outside the boundaries of religion. In his life he exemplified the benevolence he so highly praises in the second *Enquiry* and thus proved that religion was not a necessary counterpart to morality. In view of the religious orientation of most ethical systems, it should not surprise us to see Hume treating them with something less than reverence.

It is easy to be sarcastic about imperfection in human ethics, but it is not easy to be ironic; it is, for example, hard to imagine a modern counterpart to *Gulliver's Travels*. But the kind of irony Hume found useful in writing his second *Enquiry* falls between *Gulliver's Travels* and outright sarcasm, which is never very effective. To demonstrate some of the difficulties involved in a concept of justice Hume writes:

Suppose, that, though the necessities of human race continue the same as at present, yet the mind is so enlarged, and so replete with friendship and generosity, that every man has the utmost tenderness for every man, and feels no more concern for his own interest than for that of his fellows: It seems evident, that the USE of justice would, in this case, be suspended by such an extensive benevolence, nor would the divisions and barriers of property and obligation have ever been thought of. . . . Why raise landmarks between my neighbour's field and mine, when my heart has made no division between our interests; but shares all his joys and sorrows with the same force and vivacity as if originally my own? Every man, upon this supposition, being a second self to another, would trust all his interests to the discretion of every man; without jealousy, without partition, without distinction. And the whole human race would form only one family; where all would lie in common, and be used freely, without regard to property; but cautiously too, with as entire regard to the necessities of each individual, as if our own interests were most intimately concerned.

In the present disposition of the human heart, it would, perhaps, be difficult to find compleat instances of such enlarged affections; but still we may observe, that the case of families approaches towards it; and the stronger the mutual benevolence is among the individuals, the nearer it approaches; till all distinction of property be, in a great measure, lost and confounded among them. (*Works*, IV, 180–181; *ECPM*, pp. 16–17)

Hume begins the first paragraph of the above by an ironic overstatement of the problem of justice, and, as rhetorical contrast, begins the second paragraph by an ironic understatement of the improbability of finding such wide-scaled benevolence in the universe. These sentences are another way, perhaps more openly ironic, of expressing the doubleness or duplicity that is too frequently characteristic of human beings. This passage is particularly enlightening when compared to his final publication, the *Dialogues concerning Natural Religion.* We begin to see now an inclination in Hume's thoughts to argue that much can be done to improve mankind, but won't be. It is a familiar argument for reformers, but Hume is not a reformer in the pejorative sense of that term. To be sure, he hoped to reform the moral behavior (the principles were usually acceptable enough, but were never applied in practice), but against him was working the "natural" inclination of mankind. Not accepting any dogma about the goodness or the badness of man, Hume could sympathize with the difficulties of choice that were the concomitants of any ethical behavior.

When reading the second *Enquiry* we can measure the intent of the irony by giving attention to the examples. Just as the Academy of Lagado in *Gulliver's Travels* provides us with a number of ironic examples, so does Hume point out inanities in various systems of ethics, primarily those with a religious orientation. In the same chapter on justice, in Part ii, Hume argues that it is at best ingenuous of us to imagine that a man "pronouncing a few magical syllables" over a garment has made it fit for service and unlikely to subject the wearer to the severe punishment he might have received if he wore it without the benefit of these pronouncements. In the argument Hume is contrasting patterns of behavior which, in all cases, seem unreasonable; but the reader is soon shown that only some of them are unreasonable. Why, asks Hume, should the "reciting of a liturgy by a priest, in a certain habit and posture . . . dedicate a heap of brick and timber, and render it, thenceforth and for ever, sacred?" In a footnote to that observation, Hume continues the irony:

It is a doctrine of the Church of Rome, that the priest, by a secret direction of his intention, can invalidate any sacrament. This position is derived from a strict and regular prosecution of the obvious truth, that empty words alone, without any meaning or intention in the speaker, can never be attended with any effect. If the same conclusion be not admitted in reasonings concerning civil contracts, where the affair is allowed to be of so much less consequence than the eternal salvation of thousands, it proceeds entirely from men's sense of the danger and inconvenience of the doctrine in the former case: And we may thence observe, that however positive, arrogant, and dogmatical any superstition may appear, it can never convey any thorough persuasion of the reality of its objects, or put them, in any degree, on a balance with the common incidents of life, which we learn from daily observation and experimental reasoning. (*Works*, IV, 193 n–194 n.; *ECPM*, p. 31 n.)

Thus, examples provide Hume with all the evidence he needs to argue that ethics is at best an uncertain science, and that the only sure guides are custom and reasoning in the light of experience. Too, the examples dramatize, ironically, the various shortcomings in man's ethics; Hume hoped that once man was made aware of inequities and unreasonable activities, he would correct them. This hope, unfortunately, was not justified.

The second *Enquiry* represents an attempt to bring empiricism and experimental reasoning into the field of ethics. As one of the first modern philosophers to develop a completely secular system of ethics based on the principle of benevolence, Hume mentions the Deity only perfunctorily in the first part of the *Enquiry concerning the Principles of Morals,* and then passes on to consider some of the practical problems of ethics. Along with the *Enquiry concerning the Principles of Morals* Hume published a lesser-read essay on morals, *A Dialogue.* Mentioned only a few times in Hume's letters, its neglect today is curious, even though it may pose some difficulties for the reader who expects his philosophy spoon-fed. One of the difficulties in reading *A Dialogue* is the result of the form as a dialogue, the participants being an unidentified "I" (presumably Hume) and his friend, Palamedes. For several reasons, one is occasionally hard pressed to determine who is speaking and, consequently, who is responsible for what view. Since Hume is hard enough to read and to understand without additional difficulties, the confusion that can arise in *A Dialogue* is enough to put off all but the persistent reader. The essay does not contain any view or opinions on morals radically different from any of his other essays on morals, at least so far as I can determine. To the student of Hume's thought, however, *A Dialogue* is important, because the approach to the problems of a reasoned ethic is strange and unusual in Hume. Since it was published and probably written within the same general period that the *Enquiry concerning the Principles of Morals* was composed, we should not expect to find different or even diverging studies of the principles of morals. For our purposes, the manner by which Hume handles the problem is instructive, and we may examine his approach for ironic tone.

The work is in fact a dialogue, opened by Palamedes who discusses morality in a country of the world called Fourli. While in Fourli, Palamedes lived with Alcheic, who was universally admired for his fine character. As a youth, Alcheic had been courted by many lovers, but he conferred his favors on the sage Elcouf. We subsequently learn that such pederastic behavior was the expected norm in Fourli, and that the intelligent, graceful youth was encouraged in its practice. Alcheic's wife, who also happened to be his sister, was not at all dismayed by this infidelity. Other characteristics of moral behavior for which Alcheic is admired include murder, parricide, and masochism.

In the society in which Palamedes was a visitor nothing was more admired than the ill treatment of one's guests; to offer a guest the best portions of the food at a party was not only simple-minded but boorish. In this society, conversation among the inhabitants consisted primarily of sneer, banter, and raillery; and Palamedes had difficulty in separating the jest from the earnest. The upshot of all this now becomes clear:

> You are too good a scholar not to discover the ironical SOCRATES and his ATHENIAN club in my last story; and you will certainly observe, that it is exactly copied from XENOPHON, with a variation only of the names. And I think I have fairly made it appear, that an ATHENIAN man of merit might be such a one as with us would pass for incestuous, a parricide, an assassin, an ungrateful, perjured traitor, and something else too abominable to be named; not to mention his rusticity and ill-manners. (*Works*, IV, 293; *ECPM*, p. 146)

Palamedes has, by means of an allegory, been describing the ethic of a certain fictitious nation for the purpose of illustrating, in his words, that "There are no manners so innocent or reasonable, but may be rendered odious or ridiculous, if measured by a standard, unknown to the persons."

Plainly, then, what Hume is driving at in this essay is the principle of ethical relativism. It is not my purpose here to discuss the merits and defects of the principles of ethical relativism, but to show Hume's use and delineation of them. The discussion in the concrete terms of Palemedes is dramatically superior to any abstractions that might be offered in support of ethical relativism. The analogy between the country of Fourli, where certain activities are far removed from what in the modern world is ordinarily considered moral, and Socrates' Athenian club is sufficient to let the reader grasp the point. Thereafter the discussion is more straightforward, with other examples of behavior thought to be heinous by Hume's contemporaries, but considered highly moral or at least amoral by other people in other times. As the protagonist says, "the principles upon which men reason in morals are always the same; though the conclusions which they draw are often very different." The proper interpretation of this passage is, I think, that men have historically reasoned on the same principles in morals. The principles are not immutable, but they simply happen to be the ones men have always reasoned on (which may indeed be the source of their errors). That is a general summary of his argument, while Palamedes argues that all moral distinctions are the result of law, custom, and fashion, that human nature is not intrinsically moral or immoral.

Which of the two moralists in *A Dialogue* more accurately represents Hume's view is a decision we need not linger on, although I have suggested that he would probably incline to the view of the "I" in the essay; but he would not reject in toto the arguments of Palamedes. To us the importance lies in the manner in which his subject is treated. Assuredly, the practices Palamedes describes in the first part of the dialogue are not ones to which Hume's era would give moral sanction. But Hume was interested in showing that even those whom we esteemed the most civilized were, from the same set of principles, capable of drawing conclusions different from ours about morality. His point was that the custom of the time would find nothing objectionable in certain circumstances or practices that his own time would abominate. For that reason he would not reject Palamedes' arguments, for he was aware that intelligent men, reasoning from the same set of circumstances or general principles, could arrive at greatly varying conclusions.

The irony of the *Dialogue* is that in Hume's time the intelligent, as well as the not-so-intelligent, men admired the ancients, but were al-

ways able to ignore practices which they would have considered immoral. Hume was eager for them to recognize that they could still admire the ancients without feeling squeamish about it. Morality to them
was the very opposite of that of the Fourlians. In order to demonstrate
that intelligent men could come to different conclusions reasoning
from the same set of principles, Hume employs a literary form capable
of drawing that contrast with the utmost subtlety. He does it through
the character of Palamedes. Palamedes' device is irony, for he wants his
friend to see that no inconsistencies were at stake in the Fourlis' moral
principles; they were simply other human beings, who were different,
no more, no less. It would have been an ironic twist of fate if men's
minds were so narrow as to ostracize truly admirable people for differences in moral attitude. (Obviously, friends and acquaintances are
chosen with some regard to their system of morality, but moral attitudes
and moral systems are not identical.)

The two *Enquiries*, the *Political Discourses*, and *A Dialogue* were
the substantial works of this middle period and went through several
editions. The *History of England* began to appear in 1754, but that is
the subject of another chapter. So Hume was busy and he was successful. If we recall his early apprehension about the success of his writings, we can easily conclude that he was a happier man at this time of
life than he had been in the 1740's. That conclusion, while accurate, is
a little facile. Hume's letters reveal that he was never entirely de-
pressed about the reception of his works. By this time Hume has
learned to joke about himself; if not learned, then encouraged his inclination to see himself in an irreverent or a joking light. One example
from his letters will perhaps serve as sufficient background for Hume's
state of mind. The following excerpts were written in April 1751 to
Mrs. Matthew Dysart of Eccles:

Our friend [David's brother, John, who had just married], at last,
pluckt up a resolution, & has ventur'd on that dangerous encounter. He
went off on Monday morning; and this is the first action of his life, wherein
he has engag'd himself without being able to compute exactly the consequences. But what Arithmetic will serve to fix the proportion betwixt good
& bad Wives, & rate the different classes of each? Sir Isaac Newton himself,
who cou'd measure the courses of the Planets, and weigh the Earth as in a
pair of scales, even he had not Algebra enough to reduce that amiable Part

of our species to a just equation: and they are the only heavenly bodies, whose orbits are as yet uncertain. . . .

My Compliments to his Sollicitorship [Alexander Home, Solicitor-General for Scotland]. Unfortunately, I have not a horse at present to carry my fat carcass to pay its respects to his superior Obesity. But if he finds travelling requisite either for his health or [the] Captains, we shall be glad to entertain him here, as long as we can do it at anothers expence: In hopes we shall soon be able to do it at our own.

Pray tell the Sollicitor, that I have been reading lately in an old Author called *Strabo*, that in some cities of ancient Gaul, there was a fixt legal standard establish'd for corpulency, & that the Senate kept a measure, beyond which, if any Belly presum'd to encrease, the Proprietor of that Belly was oblig'd to pay a fine to the Public, proportionable to its rotundity. Ill wou'd it fare with his Worship & I, if such a law shou'd pass our Parliament. For I am afraid we are already got beyond the statute.

I wonder, indeed, no Harpy of the Treasury has ever thought of this method of raising money. Taxes on Luxury are always most approv'd of: and no one will say, that the carrying about a portly Belly is of any use or Necessity. Tis a mere superfluous ornament and is a proof too, that its Proprietor enjoys greater plenty than he puts to a good use: and therefore, 'tis fit to reduce him to a level with his fellow-subjects by Taxes & impositions.

As the lean people are the most active, unquiet, & ambitious, they everywhere govern the world, & may certainly oppress their antagonists whenever they please. Heaven forbid that Whig & Tory shou'd ever be abolish'd: For then the Nation might be split into Fat and Lean & our Faction, I am afraid, wou'd be in piteous taking. The only comfort is, if they opprest us very much, we shou'd at last change sides with them.

Besides, who knows, if a tax were impos'd on Fatness, but some jealous Divine might pretend, that the Church was in danger.

I cannot but bless the memory of Julius Caesar, for the great esteem he exprest for Fat men, and his aversion to lean ones. All the World allows, That that Emperor was the greatest Genius that ever was; and the greatest Judge of mankind. (*HL*, I, 158–160)

It is perhaps sufficient to say that Hume's life and writings were infused with irony at this time of his life, but it would be incorrect to say that Hume did not practice the ironic mode well. Much of the incorrectness of discussions about Hume lies in the failure to perceive the arrangement of the argument. Confronted with what seem to be inconsistencies, ambiguities, and trivia, the Hume critic has all too often dismissed the passages as bad writing or bad philosophy. This is particularly true of the *Enquiries*, which so puzzled Selby-Bigge that in his edition of them he remarked that Hume's "pages, especially those of the Treatise, are so full of matter, he says so many different things in so many different ways and different connexions, and with so much indifference to what he has said before, that it is very hard to say positively that he taught, or did not teach, this or that particular doctrine." The idea of doctrine, of course, was repugnant to Hume, whether it be philosophical, religious, or political doctrine. His letters frequently raise questions about ideas advanced as certain, when their only validity is intuitional. The long essay "Of the Populousness of Antient Nations" begins with a series of empirical objections lodged against the doctrine of the superior populousness of antiquity. The verbal weaknesses in Hume's writings are, more often than not, subtleties of language that become apparent when seen against the pattern of his life and his thought at the time of their composition. To think that a man's thought can always be correctly inferred without reference either to his life or to his intellectual milieu is a mistake, and, curiously, it is these emphatic forces in Hume's life that many scholars or commentators ignore. Of his intellectual milieu little need be said, since it and his life are thoroughly covered in Mossner's biography. But one must also see the effect of his life and his intellectual milieu on his writings.

This effect is apparent in the literature of this period in Hume's life, more so than it was in the early 1740's, when his abilities as a writer were just being formed. Hume still has the young man's optimism that human nature can be reduced to experimental reasoning, although he does not think man will become a slave to blind reason. Nor does he wish to see him any more a slave to reason than to the passions. But his life, to judge from the way he corresponds with his friends and from his lighthearted attitude toward philosophies in conflict with his, was full of good humor and pleasantry. In such circumstances, it is impossible not to imagine that irony would offer itself as both a method and a mode of writing. When the reader suspects that Hume is diverting or confusing the issue, he would do well to reconsult the text, while remembering Hume's attitude in other writings and activities of the period.[15] It is futile, if not foolish, to separate an author's thought from his life and the intellectual milieu in which he lived. Irony does not exist alone as an abstract concept, but it is related to the concrete human being we may call an ironist. One cannot understand or always perceive the ironic mode in Hume's writings without an awareness of his life. No man is capable of entirely separating the way he lives from the way he thinks, and we seldom react to even the possibility of irony without some curiosity about the author, his personal convictions, his way of life, or his attitude toward other human beings and human institutions. Perhaps we could assume that knowledge of a man's life and his intellectual milieu was unnecessary for an understanding of his writings, if he lived in a cultural vacuum and was never influenced by his environment. Of a man who was engaged in religious, literary, and political discussions and altercations, and who wrote the first comprehensive history of England, that cannot be said.

[15] A recent example of this failure to perceive Hume's intentions is John H. Randall, Jr., "David Hume: Radical Empiricist Pragmatist," in *Freedom and Experience: Essays Presented to Horace M. Kallen,* ed. by Sidney Hook and Milton R. Konvitz, pp. 289–312.

3. The Expansion of a Literary Mode

*"But notwithstanding this Variety of Winds and
Seasons, to which my Writings had been exposed, they had still been making such Advances, that the Copy Money, given me by the
Booksellers, much exceeded any thing formerly
known in England: I was become not only independent, but opulent."*

The period in Hume's life on which we now
focus our attention, approximately 1754 to
1762, was in many ways the most satisfying of his life, as the excerpt
from his autobiography that forms the epigraph for this chapter might
indicate. He published his *History of England* and the *Four Dissertations,* exchanged "love-letters" and other intimacies with the Comtesse
de Boufflers, and was involved in several religious skirmishes of the
time. Superficially nationalistic, Hume was "pointing with pride" at
the literary achievements of Scotland and doing what he could to aug-
ment them. Unlike many of his contemporaries, he devoted himself to
the writing of standard English, encouraging his countrymen to do the
same. I have mentioned his list of Scotticisms, prefixed to some copies
of the *Political Discourses* (1752) and reprinted in the *Scots Magazine*
(XXII [1760], 686–687); also, Hume was otherwise attempting to
unite Scotland with the English literary tradition. He had remarked,
in writing to Gilbert Elliot of Minto in 1757, "Is it not strange that, at
a time when we have lost our Princes, our Parliaments, our independent Government, even the Presence of our chief Nobility, are unhappy,
in our Accent & Pronunciation, speak a very corrupt Dialect of the
Tongue which we make use of; is it not strange, I say, that, in these
Circumstances, we shou'd really be the People most distinguish'd for

Literature in Europe?" (*HL*, I, 255). Unfortunately, not all the Scots-men improving Scotland's position in literary history were as well equipped as Hume; the result was a series of interesting failures in which the established literary figures of Scotland sponsored young writers who today are almost totally forgotten. Hume's sponsorship of the poet Thomas Blacklock is a case in point.[1] But it is worthwhile to note the energy Hume applied to helping others in their literary en-deavors, for it belies the notion that he was so avid for self-fame that he was indifferent to the talents of others.[2] It is also a measure of the energy he could pour into scholarship when interested in a project; and most of Hume's writings reflect a serious, pervasive absorption with his subject. This is particularly true of the oft maligned *History of England*. Hume's letters to friends and booksellers, for example, are full of requests for books that he would need in writing the *History*. Although he was not a scientific or pedantically conscientious scholar, Hume applied to the writing of history those qualities that many his-torians lack—"style, judgment, impartiality, care."[3]

As early as 1745 Hume had been preparing to write a history of England, and by 1749, after he had returned from Turin, he began work in earnest. Three extant memoranda[4] from that year cover the entire course of British history up to 1739. Only in 1752, when Hume was made librarian of the Advocates' Library, now the National Li-

[1] See Ernest Campbell Mossner, *The Forgotten Hume*, Chapter Two. Their relationship ended unhappily with the praise Blacklock had for Beattie's *Essay on Truth*.

[2] Even so sympathetic a writer as Thomas H. Huxley could say of Hume: "It must be confessed that, on this occasion, no less than on that of his other publications, Hume exhibits no small share of the craving after mere notoriety and vulgar success, as distinct from the pardonable, if not honourable, ambition for solid and enduring fame, which would have harmonized better with his philosophy" (*Hume*, p. 14).

[3] See David B. Horn on Hume's *History of England* in the Hume memorial volume published by the University of Edinburgh celebrating the 250th anni-versary of Hume's birth in 1961, *A Record of the Commemoration Published as a Supplement to the University Gazette*, pp. 25–28. For the four qualities Hume found wanting in English historians, see *HL*, I, 170.

[4] National Library of Scotland, MSS 733, 734; Henry E. Huntington Library, MS HM 12263. Professor Ernest Campbell Mossner has a useful discussion of Hume's historical technique in "An Apology for David Hume, Historian," *PMLA*, LVI (1941), 657–690.

brary of Scotland, did he have the time, opportunity, and resources to devote himself entirely to the writing of history. The six volumes of the *History of England* appeared between 1754 and 1762 and became a popular classic within Hume's lifetime, remaining the standard history of England until the late nineteenth and early twentieth centuries. How many times it was reprinted is anyone's guess; I have counted thirty-seven separate editions, and it is hardly to be doubted that more, probably over a hundred, exist or were printed.[5] So the work that occupied him throughout the 1750's did more for his immediate reputation and financial success than any other work.

Hume's contemporaries knew him primarily as a historian, as indeed did our own great-grandfathers. Even as late as 1922 one of those ephemeral popular encyclopedias could say of Hume:

He wrote a number of works on philosophy, morals, and religion that have brought him little fame, but his *History of England* is a masterpiece. It is written in a clear, attractive style, hardly second to that of Macaulay. Hume was the first English historian to make place for chapters on literature and the condition of the common people. His history contains a few sentences that have warranted a charge of hostility to orthodoxy, but the high merit and originality of his work made it an undisputed standard until Green's history appeared.[6]

That mild passage gives no evidence of the controversies Hume's *History* created; but it should come as no surprise that almost anything Hume wrote was likely to bring cries of dismay from diverse quarters.

A *History of England* written by a sceptical Scottish philosopher might be expected to stir up the illiterates accustomed to blatantly one-sided "discussions" of things historical and political. Any intrusion into religion and politics which eschews blanket praise and seeks to determine real values and real defects is bound to irritate at least one

---

[5] T. E. Jessop in his *Bibliography of David Hume and of Scottish Philosophy from Francis Hutcheson to Lord Balfour*, pp. 30–32, lists fifty-four editions published after Hume's death. Since several of the editions I have seen differ from Jessop's listing (and I have not made a systematic search), it would seem probable that editions and adaptations of the *History of England* would approach at least a hundred.

[6] Unsigned article in *The Standard Reference Work for the Home, School, and Library*, IV, no page numbers, "Hume."

person and probably more. Thus, the charges of "atheism" and "Tory-ism" were the ones most consistently leveled at Hume by his contem-poraries.[7] What would seem to be a spirit of irreligion does pervade the *History*, but it must be remembered that Hume was trying to assess the real value of the church in historical perspective; and that he had to be more a "friend to truth" than to bias or partiality. No writer ex-pects to complete any work for which he can claim lack of bias, but Hume's historical method was not used expressly to "prove" a certain conception of history. The kind of consideration I want to give to the *History of England* will touch upon its politics and religion as the cen-tral interests in an analysis of the ironic mode. Naturally, the ironic mode touches upon more than religion and politics, but it would be somewhat unwieldy at the present time to discuss definitively the scope and accuracy of Hume's history. It is not a case of deciding whether Hume is "right" in a certain representation of English history, but to what extent he is ironic. Thus, what we are trying to pinpoint is Hume's actual feeling about the periods he summarizes. For the present we must discount the statement in his autobiography, a state-ment probably ironic, that the alterations in the *History* were all made "invariably to the Tory Side." A more accurate expression of any Toryism or Whiggism that may appear in the *History* was clarified by Hume in a letter to John Clephane in 1756: "With regard to politics and the character of princes and great men, I think I am very mod-erate. My views of *things* are more conformable to Whig principles; my representations of *persons* to Tory prejudices. Nothing can so much prove that men commonly regard more persons than things, as to find that I am commonly numbered among the Tories" (*HL*, I, 237). This recognized dichotomy is observed in many places throughout the *History*, as Hume makes a distinction between the way he analyzes men and the way he analyzes things and events.

Hume began his history *in medias res*, with a discussion of the reigns of James I and Charles I; this volume was published in 1754 by Gavin Hamilton, not without some difficulties and misunderstand-

---

[7] Ernest Campbell Mossner in "Was Hume a Tory Historian? Facts and Re-considerations," *The Journal of the History of Ideas*, II, (1941), 225–236, makes a detailed analysis of Hume's Toryism and finds it wanting.

ings.[8] Initially, the *History* was a failure, and in his autobiography Hume writes of it at some length:

> I was, I own, sanguine in my Expectations of the Success of this work. I thought, that, I was the only Historian, that had at once neglected present Power, Interest, and Authority, and the Cry of popular Prejudices; and as the Subject was suited to every Capacity, I expected proportional Applause: But miserable was my Disappointment: I was assailed by one Cry of Reproach, Disapprobation, and even Detestation: English, Scotch, and Irish; Whig and Tory; Churchman and Sectary, Free-thinker and Religionist; Patriot and Courtier united in their Rage against the Man, who had presumed to shed a generous Tear for the Fate of Charles I, and the Earl of Strafford: And after the first Ebullitions of this Fury were over, what was still more mortifying, the Book seemed to sink into Oblivion. Mr Millar told me, that in a twelvemonth he sold only forty five Copies of it. I scarcely indeed heard of one Man in the three Kingdoms, considerable for Rank or Letters, that cou'd endure the Book. I must only except the Primate of England, Dr Herring, and the Primate of Ireland, Dr Stone; which seem two odd Exceptions. These dignifyed Prelates separately sent me Messages not to be discouraged.

Perhaps without knowing it, Hume has revealed one of the reasons for this initial failure. If the book did not sell, then those who had read it must necessarily be few; no matter how thumb-worn an owner's copy might become, it would still have limited circulation. Among those objecting to the book, then, must have been a considerable number who never read it, but knew only its reputation—and the author's. Hume, accused all of his life as a subverter of true religion, could not expect, even under favorable circumstances, a kind reception from all of the public. Much of the tirade against the book probably reflected current sentiment against the man, David Hume. None of the eighteenth-century fundamentalists was likely to approach the book with an open mind, and its publication simply afforded them an opportunity to get in a few licks at Hume. I should suspect that most of the early objections raised to the first volumes of the *History of Eng-*

[8] For a complete summary of the difficulties Hume encountered in getting his *History of England* published, consult the following article: Ernest Campbell Mossner and Harry Ransom, "Hume and the 'Conspiracy of the Booksellers': The Publication and Early Fortunes of the *History of England*," *University of Texas Studies in English*, XXIX (1950), 162–182.

land were, in reality, raised about its author, who was one of the most vilified men of the eightenth century.[9]

After this unfortunate, and perhaps underestimated, reception, and the "Conspiracy of the Booksellers," sales of the *History* picked up, and the completed volumes were eminently successful, much more so than Hume had expected. When he began he had some uncertainties about writing a complete history of England.[10] Although he ultimately decided to complete his work, he was hesitant for these reasons: (1) no public libraries were available in London until the British Museum opened in 1759; (2) he needed to gain admission to the libraries of

[9] Dr. Johnson's innumerable unkind comments about Hume are the most obvious proof of the kind of vilification Hume received from some of his contemporaries. As late as 1773, Dr. Johnson had not read the *History of England*: "I [Johnson] have not read Hume; but, doubtless Goldsmith's *History* is better than the *verbiage* of Robertson, or the foppery of Dalrymple." (Boswell, *Life of Johnson,* ed. by G. B. Hill, rev. by L. F. Powell, II, 236–237.) Apparently Dr. Johnson did manage to read it before his death, to judge from the following anecdote, entitled *Singular and laughable Instance of* IGNORANCE: "Doctor Johnson, whilst he was a teacher of youth, had two very good classick scholars, yet it was thought necessary that something more familiar should be known, and he bid them read the History of England [i.e., Hume's]. After a few months had elapsed, he asked them, 'if they could recollect who first destroyed the monasteries in our island? One modestly replied, that he did not know; the other said, Jesus Christ [*sic.*]." (Cited in "Mr. Addison's *Interesting Anecdotes, Memoirs, Allegories, Essays, and Poetical Fragments; tending to Amuse the Fancy, and Inculcate Morality* [London, 1794], p. 76. Several of these collections with almost identical title pages were printed in 1794; sometimes they were bound together, sometimes separately. If the reader wishes to check this anecdote, I can only wish him luck in locating the same 1794 edition I quote from; it contains two collections, both printed in 1794 with identical wording in the title pages, and has "I" stamped on the spine.)

[10] See Ernest Campbell Mossner, ed.: "New Hume Letters to Lord Elibank," *Texas Studies in Literature and Language,* IV (1962), 440, 448, and 448 n. Hume says: "The History of the House of Tudor is recommended to me; and indeed I am fully convinc'd, that I shou'd have done much better had I wrote these Reigns previously to the History of the House of Stuart. For after having shown by a long Series of Facts the Nature of the English Government during that Period, it wou'd have been easy to correct the Prejudices of those, who think that James the I & Charles the I ought to [be] judg'd by the Same Standard which we would apply to George the I & 2d. However, it has been remarked to me, that Tacitus went backwards, and wrote his Annals after his History; and that there is nothing absurd in a man's enlarging his Plan after this manner. I may hereafter think of this Scheme, if it happen, as is probable, that Idleness becomes a Burthen to me."

important English families, a procedure that could not be hurried; and
(3) he was mildly apprehensive about the treatment the volumes
would receive from Whig ministers.[11] In this discussion I shall follow
Hume's chronology to see if there is any noticeable new development
of the ironic mode and to see if Hume really did tone down the objectionable passages on religion to make them acceptable to theists, or
if he simply disguised them.

As a historian Hume perhaps felt that the ironic mode was not
always suited to the purposes of historiography, as he suggests in a
footnote to the essay "Of the Populousness of Antient Nations": "The
authorities cited above, are all historians, orators, and philosophers,
whose testimony is unquestioned. 'Tis dangerous to rely upon writers
who deal in ridicule and satyr" (*Works*, III, 408 n.). This is straight
argument: Hume warns against the reliability of writers whose *constant* tool is ridicule and satire. Asking what posterity would make of
a passage from "Dr. Swift," he quotes from *Gulliver's Travels* a description of Englishmen as the scum of the earth—assassins, inform-
ers, bribers, and so forth, the worst sort of human kind. But Hume
adds a qualification: "Such a representation might suit the government of ATHENS; but not that of ENGLAND, which is a prodigy even
in modern times, for humanity, justice, and liberty." Here the irony is
plain enough, for Hume did not think England anywhere near perfect
at that time, and a reading of the *History* indicates that England was
distinguished only sporadically for "humanity, justice, and liberty."
(He did, however, think that the revolutions of the late 1660's gave
birth to a theoretically fine system of justice, which was not observed
as it should be.) Regardless of the reader's knowledge, Hume would
expect him to see his irony. Seeing irony, however, is one thing; rely-
ing on writers who deal in irony and satire while writing history is
another. Hume's conception of history would certainly leave room for
an irony that would juxtapose events to dramatize their foolishness. A
glance at his conception of history, expressed in their essay "Of the
Study of History," will clarify his approach to historical scholarship:

In reality, what more agreeable entertainment to the mind, than to be
transported into the remotest ages of the world, and to observe human so-

[11] Mossner, "New Hume Letters to Lord Elibank," p. 448 n.

ciety, in its infancy, making the first faint essays towards the arts and sciences: To see the policy of government, and the civility of conversation refining by degrees, and every thing which is ornamental to human life advancing towards its perfection. To remark the rise, progress, declension, and final extinction of the most flourishing empires: The virtues, which contributed to the greatness, and the vices, which drew on their ruin. In short, to see all human race, from the beginning of time, pass, as it were, in review before us; appearing in their true colours, without any of those disguises, which, during their life-time, so much perplexed the judgment of the beholders. What spectacle can be imagined, so magnificent, so various, so interesting? What amusement, either of the senses or imagination, can be compared with it? Shall those trifling pastimes, which engross so much of our time, be preferred as more satisfactory, and more fit to engage our attention? How perverse must that taste be, which is capable of so wrong a choice of pleasures? (*Works*, IV, 389–390)

The above description of history and the study of it might more properly be called a panegyric to history, but it gives us a clue to the writing of history. The deliberate understatement at the end is a kind of irony, since Hume engaged in a number of "trifling pastimes" (such as the writing of his philosophical works) whose pleasure was not overshadowed by the reading of history. History is a synthesis of important events of the past, analyzed for their function in the shaping of the drama of human life, and organized in a manner that gives the reader a historical perspective, that is, a point of view that enables him to see that Galileo's discoveries were more important than the Thirty Years' War. It is not likely that a historian, to judge by Hume's description of history, will be perpetually ironic in his synthesis of the important events of an age. Hume can apply his irony to both things and people, especially those for which he does not have the highest regard.

In theory, Hume would seem to be on the side of the Commonwealthmen, and his Parliament is Cromwellian.[12] But Hume abominated Cromwell, and when writing about him and his role in English history Hume makes sure that the reader does not mistake his irony. Writing of the man whom Cromwell succeeded as commander of all the armed forces in Great Britain, Sir Thomas Fairfax, Hume says,

---

[12] See Caroline Robbins, *The Eighteenth-Century Commonwealthman*, p. 216.

"This artful and audacious conspirator had conducted himself in the parliament with such profound dissimulation, with such refined hypocrisy, that he had long deceived those, who, being themselves very dextrous practitioners in the same arts, naturally entertained the more suspicion against others" (*History*, VII, Chap. LIX, 91). In that example Hume is appealing to what must be a basic belief in human beings: that politicians, by their very nature, cannot eschew deception and chicanery. More specifically, it makes an ironic comment about the extent of corruption in Parliament during Cromwell's time, especially prior to the establishment of the Protectorate. But let us notice that the irony is by no means subtle; without knowing a single event or person in British history, even Russell's rather dense ten-year-old could understand Hume's point.

When Cromwell's army marched into Parliament the popular support of the step was widespread, although a change in the status quo is not always a guarantee of popularity. As we know, however, nothing but more corruption ensued, and the Parliament under Cromwell's iron fist was not better than its predecessor. In order to allocate some of the new tax money to their own pockets, the members of Parliament came up with an ingenious solution complementing their cupidity: "The method of keeping accounts, practised in the exchequer, was confessedly the exactest, the most antient, the best known, and the least liable to fraud. The exchequer was, for that reason, abolished, and the revenue put under the management of a committee, who were subject to no controul" (*History*, VII, Chap. LIX, 94–95). That statement has the virtue of being true and ironic at the same time. Although today we may not think the method of the exchequer before Cromwell was very efficient, Hume and his time apparently did. Consequently, when Hume says it was changed because it was so efficient, we know exactly what he means: that its efficiency was such that it would reveal any frauds perpetrated against the treasury. In order to line their own pockets Cromwell and his conspirators had to devise a method which was not so easily accountable.

Finally, in describing Cromwell's character, Hume begins on an ironic note:

The writers, attached to the memory of this wonderful person, make his

character, with regard to abilities, bear the air of the most extravagant panegyric: His enemies form such a representation of his moral qualities as re-
sembles the most virulent invective. Both of them, it must be confessed, are
supported by such striking circumstances in his conduct and fortune as bestow on their representation a great air of probability. [Here follows a long
description from Cowley's *Discourses,* a passage denigrating Cromwell.
Hume then comments as follows.] My intention is not to disfigure this picture, drawn by so masterly a hand: I shall only endeavour to remove from
it somewhat of the marvellous; a circumstance which, on all occasions, gives
much ground for doubt and suspicion. (*History,* VII, Chap. LXI, 295–296)

That is the sort of irony of which Hume is particularly fond: a recognition of the crosscurrents which compose personalities. Friends see
only a person's good qualities; enemies, the bad; Hume is ironically
impartial and says that both are right. The word "wonderful," however, gives the reader an insight to Hume's own feelings about Cromwell. While Hume was mostly in favor of the ideas of liberty proposed
by the Commonwealth, he was flatly opposed to men like Cromwell,
who were so very different from himself. This representation of Cromwell is perhaps a "Tory prejudice"; but it is a prejudice which a great
many civil men of the eighteenth century and, indeed, of our own,
share. Hume's philosophical emphasis was, we must remember, on
human beings, their good points and their bad points; and if he discusses people more than events in the *History,* the imbalance is not unexpected. Men are frail creatures and capable of mistakes in judgment,
which, paradoxically, is one of their distinguishing traits. While Hume
has no wish to eradicate those failings which make human beings human, he does want to leave room for their improvement. They are not
above the judgment of the historian, and Hume arranges his facts to
speak for themselves, knowing that adroitly arranged facts could be
far more impressive than slander or abuse. The unfavorable opinion of
Cromwell may not support Hume's claim to impartiality, but he tries
to give the reader a balanced view of the Commonwealth. It is not
Cromwell's Whiggery he disliked so much, but the man himself, for
the remainder of the discussion of the Commonwealth transparently
favors the increasing liberty in English life.

The charges of atheism, impiety, or heathenism were so often leveled against Hume that they ceased to have any meaning because of

the incessant repetition. Hume had opponents who were stauncher in their arguments than mere namecalling, and those were the ones he was interested in hearing and answering. He wanted to meet them on an equal footing, that of enlightened men seeking the truth about religion, probing into each other's minds for a solution, if any, to some of the questions that were perennially raised by human beings. All too often his opponents had neither his gracefulness nor his charity and thought of Hume only as someone dogmatically inimical to religion. If religion comes off badly in the *History*, it is not malice, but justice, that prevails. Over and over, in discussing the reigns of James I, Charles I, and Cromwell, Hume calls attention to the acts of religious fanatics, letting their actions speak for their own stupidity. For this practice he was frequently accused of a superogatory bias against religion, although the same absurdities pointed out in any other field of study would have brought clamors of approval. The practice in Cromwell's reign of instituting commissioners, called "tryers," as clergymen is objectionable, because it emphasizes ignorance and narrow-mindedness as qualities for propagating "true religion." These men usually had as much preparation for the cloth as they had for government:

Instead of supporting that union between learning and theology, which has so long been maintained in Europe, these tryers embraced the latter principle in its full purity, and made it the sole object of their examinations. The candidates were no more perplexed with questions concerning their progress in Greek and Roman erudition; concerning their talent for profane arts and sciences: The chief object of scrutiny regarded their advances in grace, and fixing the critical moment of their conversion. (*History*, VII, Chap. LXI, 269)

It is not religion as an entity that Hume objects to, but its abuses, its fanaticisms, its bigotries, its intolerances, its hypocrisies; Hume accepts and even desires a religious tradition which explores the connections between knowledge and theology. An unlearned man was not qualified to judge the accuracy of theological sentiments divorced from the background and tradition of scholarship and study with which theology was so long associated. Although Hume found much in theology, especially medieval theology, that was useless or ridiculous, he reprobated just as much a fundamentalist theology born of ignorance or enthusiasm. Thus, it is easy to see why statements like the above (and it is one of many) conferred upon Hume the reputation of an irreverent scoffer, to choose one of the milder epithets. But the religious Neanderthals will, in any century, object to a philosophy that is just the slightest heterodox. Hume is not opposed to religion per se; but what passed for religion in his and earlier times was, in his opinion, often cultural and social regimentation. Other examples of religious folly abound in the *History*, such as the practice of the "pretended saints" to change their names to Old Testament names, even adopting an entire "godly" sentence as a name: "Accepted, Trevor of Norsham," or "Kill Sin, Pimple of Witham," or "If Christ had not died for you, you had been damned, Barebone." Hume reports that the people tired of this long name and gave Barebone the appellation "Damned Barebone."[13] I mention this as evidence that while the image of religion Hume presents is not favorable, neither is it fanciful.

It is useful to keep in mind these examples of fanaticism for a reason that should be common enough: they provide a context in which we must consider the other, seemingly favorable mentions of religion in the *History*. It should be seen that it is not religion that Hume is so much concerned with, but factionalism, partisanship, and shortsightedness; all of the examples are justifiably extreme. Appearing as disinterested observer, Hume chronicles instances of human eccentricity carried to a foolish, dangerous extreme. So the examples of religious idiocy belong to a category: unreasonable acts. Introduce a little calm reason, and perhaps some of Bishop Butler's "Cool Self-Love," into these acts, and their unseemliness will become apparent. If Hume is then reckoned hostile to religion because of these examples, he must also be reckoned hostile to politics, to history, and to economics. His hostility is not to one of these "disciplines," but to the ignorance they display. It so happened that religion and religious zealots provided more abuses of reason than economists, historians, and politicians. Strictures against abuses in these fields of human endeavor are just as

---

[13] Some of these interesting names do not appear in the 1773 edition from which I usually quote; they can, however, be found in editions cited as "A New Edition, with the author's last corrections and improvements." See *History of England*, V, 442 n.

firm as those against religious abuses. To undermine religion seemed
to Hume a questionable goal, but he had no hesitation in attacking
what was in fact irreligion disguised as fervor. Indeed, he remarks
upon several occasions that Cromwell frequently used religion hypo-
critically in order to gain more political power or to keep the populace
under his control. That religion should be used as a tool for subjuga-
tion and oppression was immoral if not unthinkable to Hume. The
antipathy for religion which had been extended way beyond the
bounds of reason and good taste complements his dislike for "enthusiasm," one of the recurring objects of his scepticism.

The proper office of religion in a zealous age is suggested by Hume
in discussing the reign of Charles I:

> Whatever ridicule, to a philosophical mind, may be thrown on pious cere-
> monies, it must be confess'd, that, during a very religious age, no institution
> can be more advantageous to the rude multitude, and tend more to mollify
> that fierce and gloomy spirit of devotion, to which they are subject. Even the
> English church, tho' it had retained a share of popish ceremonies, may justly
> be thought too naked and unadorned, and still to approach too near the ab-
> stract and spiritual religion of the puritans. [Bishop] Laud and his associ-
> ates, by reviving a few primitive institutions of this nature, corrected the
> error of the first reformers, and presented, to the affrighted and astonished
> mind, some sensible, exterior observances, which might occupy it during
> its religious exercises, and abate the violence of its disappointed efforts.
> The thought, no longer bent on that divine and mysterious Essence, so
> superior to the narrow capacities of mankind, was able, by means of the
> new model of devotion, to relax itself in the contemplation of pictures,
> postures, vestments, buildings; and all the fine arts, which ministred to
> religion, thereby received additional encouragement. The primate, 'tis
> true, conducted this scheme, not with the enlarged sentiments and cool
> disposition of a legislator, but with the intemperate zeal of a sectary; and
> by over-looking the circumstances of the times, served rather to inflame
> that religious fury, which he meant to repress. But this blemish is more
> to be regarded as a general imputation on the whole age, than any par-
> ticular failing of Laud; and 'tis sufficient for his vindication to observe,
> that his errors were the most excusable of all those which prevailed during
> that zealous period. (*History,* VII, Chap. LVII, 41–42)

This passage is typical of Hume in the two or three qualifying words that leave no doubt about his position. The qualified praise has an ironic ring to it when the reader learns that Laud's actions had a result opposite to the intended one. Laud, who was unjustly put to death for siding with the King in the rebellion that led to the Commonwealth, receives another kind of ironic praise for turning, or attempting to turn, men's thoughts away from "that divine and mysterious Essence so superior to the narrow capacities of mankind" to more praiseworthy pursuits: the fine arts. If religion could be supplanted by devotion to the fine arts, then its "truth-value" could not be very great. In praising religious activity Hume is really criticizing the truth-value of religion, implying that devotion could be easily shifted from contemplation of the spiritual to contemplation of the outward manifestations of the spiritual. As such, it became a worship of religion, not a worship of a "divine and mysterious Essence." Two kinds of irony are present in this passage. One, the creation of tension between what was aimed for and what was achieved, implies that devotion and zeal unchaperoned by good sense inevitably lead to greater chaos. The other, the result of a shift in emphasis, suggests that what is often interpreted as genuine religious devotion is in fact a psychological attachment to something that seems pervasive and enduring; and that this attachment can be redirected to other goals. This particular passage occurs at the end of Chapter LVII and provides a fitting commentary on many of the excesses discussed in it.

Hume was not one to deny that religion could assuage mental anguish, but he accepted only examples of devotion born of an act of faith and temperate in its worship. In the process of shedding "a generous Tear for the Fate of Charles I" (as, Hume notes in his autobiography, his adversaries accused him of doing) Hume describes the circumstances preceding Charles I's execution:

The great source, whence the King derived consolation amidst all his calamities, was undoubtedly religion; a principle, which, in him seems to have contained nothing fierce nor gloomy, nothing which enraged him against his adversaries, or terrified him with the dismal prospect of futurity. While everything around him bore a hostile aspect; while friends, family, relations, whom he passionately loved, were placed at a distance, and unable to serve him; *he reposed himself with confidence in the arms of that Being, who penetrates and sustains all nature, and whose severities, if received with piety*

and resignation, he regarded as the surest pledge of unexhausted favour.
(*History*, VII, Chap. LIX, 118. Italics added)

Again, the irony is dependent on the arrangement of the words: the
pious are pleased to learn of the "Being who penetrates and sustains
all nature," and they probably fail to see the irony in the remark that
His severities are considered as the best signs of favor; the more unfortunate one's condition, the more he is favored by God. Hume's disagreement is evident. Self-deception had caused as much harm in the
world as deception by politicians and confidence men, and it had to be
rigorously opposed. The devout, both Catholic and Protestant, were
fond of regarding hardship and personal sacrifice, if not actual pain, as
proof of God's plenty and wisdom. That Hume found this view curious is unsurprising in a man who wanted to introduce "experimental
reasoning" into the "science of human nature." To react against misfortune as if it was not of God's choosing was often regarded by
Hume's contemporaries as impious, while Hume thought it subversive
to whatever was good in religion to regard "severities" as proof of
God's favor. To do that would entail, as a matter of logic, regarding
good fortune as the work of the devil. Hume, if he conceived of an
anthropomorphic deity at all, certainly did not regard him as a creature
needing continual applause and obeisance, while making known his
favorites by inflicting them with hardships. Part of the whole argument of "natural religion" (to be discussed later) was Hume's attempt to correct this unfortunate notion, although he did it from the
secular side of the fence. The criticism of religion offered in this passage is subtle, but it recognizes a danger (that of assuming hardship
to be evidence of God's favor) in religious fervor that the zealots
themselves did not see. In fact, Hume is not so much their worst enemy
as he is their friend. Someone maliciously hostile to religion could be
caustic and abrasive in pointing out the anomaly of the God-blessed
Christian overwhelmed by God-given misfortunes. But it is not likely
that any ecclesiastic reading this passage and perceiving the irony
would think of Hume's criticisms as a contribution to the improvement
of theology.

It will be seen, even from this brief discussion of part of the
History, that it embodied an esthetic principle dear to the hearts of the

Renaissance, Restoration, and eightenth-century critics: instruction. While it would be beyond the scope of this book to quote all of the obvious passages, Hume's approach to the process of historical narration is frequently intentionally instructive. The discussion which closes the reign of Charles I is an often quoted example of the lessons, Hume argues, that are to be learned from history. In his straightforward discussions of historical events, Hume is careful to make sure that his irony is transparent. He was aware of the danger of having his irony interpreted literally, although he occasionally wished to have some of his religious irony go unobserved by the fundamentalists. One of his devices we have already seen in specific form; it involves using a word in both its usual sense and its etymological sense. When Titus Oates spread the story of a Catholic plot to kill the King and seize the government, Hume points up the folly of his efforts with a one-sentence introduction to what is otherwise an uncluttered summary of Oates's narrative: "The wonderful intelligence, which Oates conveyed both to Godfrey and the council, and afterwards to the Parliament, was to this purpose" (*History*, VIII, Chap. LXVII, 64). The discussion then is sober and literal, although Hume is not impartial; but the opening sentence had prepared us for this judgment against Oates. Hume continues to ridicule the "Popish Plot" remarking that

... the whole texture of the plot contains such low absurdity, that it is impossible to have been the invention of any man of sense or education. It is true, the more monstrous and horrible the conspiracy, the better was it fitted to terrify, and thence to convince the populace: But this effect, we may safely say, no one could beforehand have promised upon; and a fool was in this case more likely to succeed than a wise man. Had Shaftesbury laid the plan of a popish conspiracy, he had probably rendered it moderate, consistent, credible; and on that very account had never met with the prodigious success, with which Oates's tremendous fictions were attended. (*History*, VIII, Chap. LVII, 75)

In seeking to find the truth, the crown and Parliament both involved themselves in much nonsense. Anyone turning "state's evidence" was promised anonymity (and five hundred pounds, a prior inducement) and absolute protection. In short, the power structure was looking for a scapegoat: "Thus were indemnity, money, and security offered to the fairest bidder: And no one needed to fear, during the present fury of the people, that his evidence would undergo too severe a scrutiny" (*History,* VIII, Chap. LXVII, 76).

Hume has learned to be ironic about matters where some general public agreement exists, and the irony becomes less subtle, more available to the "general" reader than was his religious irony. This is not to say that Hume's attitude toward human failings and foolish institutions has softened. He was seldom intolerant of fancies and fatuousness in other human beings; human reason was not perfect, and one could not expect human action to be. But he judged human beings sternly nevertheless. The irony in the early works, primarily in the *Treatise,* is uncertain and diffuse, sometimes abstract. Hume is now directing his irony toward human beings and institutions. In *A Dialogue* he treats an idea ironically, as he does in "Of Miracles." Ironic treatment of people and institutions is not new in Hume's writings, but he handles it with a sureness—and an insistence—that had not appeared previously. I would not pretend that this is a remarkable development. What would be more natural than a man's improving his rhetoric as he grows older and writes more? It is only the shift in emphasis that should be noted. Though still not a "successful" writer, Hume has avoided some of the deference to other people that led him to palliate his scepticism in early writings.

The seeming logic of this rhetorical development does not, however, gather more and more speed: we should not assume that the irony will be better in the volumes of the *History* written after the discussion of the Stuarts. Of the chapters devoted to the Tudors, Hume notes in his autobiography that the "Reign of Elizabeth was particularly obnoxious" to his audience, but that he was "callous against the impressions of public Folly." It is easy to see why the public would object. The ties between church and state were reprehensibly strong, and the bloody religious wars were examples of human folly and stupidity that Hume rightly condemned. The moralist, Hume felt, cannot abdicate his position, especially where public sentiment is willfully blind to actualities. In discussing the Puritans, Hume is less than kind about their extravagances and their claims to an inside track to the Deity. Since the Puritans are easy objects of criticism, Hume is careful to seek out any possible virtues, sometimes simply to contrast to their vices. He admits that the inauguration of Elizabeth carried with it at least one portent: a moderate degree of enlightenment in religious matters, and he notes with approval her efforts to see that Catholics were not persecuted the way they had persecuted the Protestants.

What probably enraged the partisans of various religious factions more than anything else is Hume's ironic conduct of the discussion, a technique seen in the essay "Of Miracles." The opening of the third chapter on Elizabeth is seemingly full of praise for the Church of England, which is cited as proceeding with "reason and moderation" in shaking off the yoke of papal authority; revenge for the atrocities of Bloody Mary was discouraged; and nothing new in the church's liturgy was added just for revenge. He observes, in the conclusion of the opening paragraph, that "the new religion, by mitigating the genius of the antient superstition, and rendering it more compatible with the peace and interests of society, had preserved itself in that happy medium, which wise men have always sought, and which the people have so seldom been able to maintain" (*History*, V, Chap. XL, 156–157). One is not surprised, after the last part of that sentence, to see that the next paragraph begins "But . . ." A few pages later we learn that the church and the state had not achieved perfect amity, because Elizabeth attempted to bring public worship "still nearer to the Romish ritual," thinking that the Reformation had gone far enough. Empowered by Parliament to enact any new ceremonies she considered proper, she exacted rigid devotion to established laws of the "church-state" and punished all nonconformity. Consequently, those to whom any relics of Catholicism were anathema had to keep quiet about their objections. Hume's comment on the entire proceeding reveals the ironic conduct of the argument:

So fruitless is it for sovereigns to watch with a rigid care over orthodoxy, and to employ the sword in religious controversy, that the work, perpetually renewed, is perpetually to begin; and a garb, a gesture, nay, a metaphysical or grammatical distinction, when rendered important by the disputes of theologians and the zeal of the magistrate, is sufficient to destroy the unity of the church, and even the peace of society. These controversies had already excited such ferment among the people, that in some places they refused to frequent the churches where the habits and ceremonies were used, would not salute the conforming clergy, and proceeded so far as to revile them in the streets, to spit in their faces, and to use them with all manner of contumely. And while the sovereign authority checked these excesses, the flame was confined, not extinguished; and burning fiercer from confinement, it burst out in the succeeding reigns to the destruction of the church and monarchy. (*History*, V, Chap. XL, 160–161)

The Biblical rhetoric in relating the habits of the nonconformists is unlike Hume, and he seldom employs it without ironic intent. The metaphor in the last sentence makes an ironic contrast between the aims and the results of the sovereign authority's attempts to enforce religious conformity.

Hume continues to make light of the trivial points raised by first one group of religionists and then by their opposed group. The guiding thesis, that politics and religion make strange bedfellows, was not one to which his age was unaccustomed; indeed, across the Atlantic, James Madison, in the years to follow, was to articulate as forcefully as possible the objections to a union of church and state. Hume develops this thesis, by implication, to the same position that Madison does, and it is small wonder that in 1758 it created some excitement. The abuses which Hume chronicles speak more strongly, however, than the objections to his *History* on grounds of religious hostility. It was not hostility, but a desire to enforce the following considerations: (1) that history showed a preponderance of bloody warfare and civil strife when religion and politics were linked; (2) that the strictures, intolerances, and fanaticism of religious groups damaged "true religion" far more than anything else; and (3) that religious controversy was best left to the scholars and theologians. In making these points, Hume has recourse to several kinds of irony, although he seems to have no particular plan for employment of the ironic mode. Often, the conduct of the argument is ironic, while in the next paragraph the irony may hinge upon a contrast between two kinds of action. In still other passages, the reader adds the ironic tone himself. Inevitably, the irony is created by a degree of over-all scepticism that is reluctant to confer absolute sanctity upon the persons or events under discussion.

Elizabeth's intrusion into religious matters and the laws governing them was not one she was qualified to make, being "more jealous" of religious points than matters of state. Hume does not even grant her sincerity: "She pretended, that, in quality of supreme head or governor of the church, she was fully empowered, by her prerogative alone, to decide all questions which might arise with regard to doctrine, discipline, or worship; and she never would allow her Parliaments so much as to take these points into consideration" (*History*, V, Chap. XL, 180). She was supported in this pretense by the "treasurer of the household" and the comptroller. Not everyone agreed with her contention, and Hume, in one example, exposed the triviality of the argument on both sides. One Pistor opposed the other courtiers:

He was scandilized, he said, that affairs of such infinite consequence (viz. kneeling and making the sign of the cross) should be passed over so lightly. These questions, he added, concern the salvation of our souls, and interest every one of us more deeply than the monarchy of the whole world. This cause he shewed to be God's; the rest were all but terrene, yea trifles in comparison, call you them ever so great: Subsidies, crowns, kingdoms, he knew not what weight they had, when laid in the ballance with subjects of such unspeakable importance. (*History*, V, Chap. XL, 180–181)

Pistor's zeal was in vain, since the House refused to amend the liturgy. Immediately following this episode Hume praises the attempts of various members to remove Parliament from the control of the crown, although he notes that the newness of the principles involved did not palliate the controversy.

Hume's feelings are, I think, clearly implied. Much could be lauded in the continuation of the Reformation, but England had a long way to go before achieving any semblance of moderation and reason in religious matters. The approval Hume gives to such moderation is ironic, for he approves of something that doesn't really exist and that is infrequently sought. As another example of over-all irony in the arrangement of the argument, the discussion of Elizabeth's reign is not overtly complimentary or uncomplimentary. Hume's language is appropriately amazed or understated, and to our eyes his judgments of the folly arising from religious zeal are correct. The concern, though, is not with religion per se, but with religion as an instrument of polity. It is not something I would label "religious irony" for its boundaries are wider than that. It involves all of the cultural phenomena capable of "exciting the passions" and it demonstrates the futility, if not the inanity, of passions unguided by reason. Hume has tried to give the reader some intellectual perspective from which to judge the events which, at the time, seemed monumental. Instead, Hume suggests, no event in itself is likely to be worth the expense of time and energy it requires, if it is predicated upon unreasonable tenets. Hume may be atomistic in his epistemology, but he is not in historiography; events are important only when linked to cultures and learning (a similar position is implied in *A Dialogue*). The attachment of ultimate importance to any one event or fact is a folly unbecoming human nature, however "natural" it may be for us to assent to the attachment.

In the passages about Elizabeth's role in the religion of the state Hume has directed his irony against ideas, but ideas as they are embodied by some particular person. So the emphasis for the ironic mode at this period in his life is expressed in terms of human beings living on the borders of irrationality and intemperance. A history of England naturally provides Hume with an opportunity to poke fun at people rather than pure ideas. It is not so much the ideas that Hume objects to, but the fatuousness of the human creature who dignifies them by acting as if they were worthwhile beliefs. I say this because the *History* is replete with instances of human folly, while ideological follies receive lesser attention. He is appropriately putting the blame where it belongs: on people, not on ideas. Yet it is worthwhile to look at Hume's ironic citations of irrational ideas. There, more than anywhere else, he expects the reader to join him as the Eiron looking for the Dupe.

The reign of Henry VII provided numerous examples of political foolishness in the form of various laws enacted during that period. To a large extent, these laws alone provide sufficient comment upon themselves, but Hume sets up the reader with a series of antithetical sentences:

Laws were made against the exportation of money, plate, or bullion: A precaution, which serves to no other purpose than to make more be exported. . . . Horses were forbid to be exported; as if that exportation did not encourage the breed, and render them more plentiful in the kingdom. To promote archery, no bows were to be sold at a higher price than six shillings and four-pence, reducing money to the denomination of our time. The only effect of this regulation must be either that the people would be supplied with bad bows or none at all. (*History, III, Chap.* XXVI, 422–423)

Highly regarded as an economist by Adam Smith, Hume perceived that economic problems met with no easy solution.[14] For that matter, Hume never proposed simple solutions to complex problems, as did many of his detractors in "answering" his works. Wit and ironic deference were constant weapons to be used against oversimplification or illogic. Along with the discussion of shortcomings in laws in Henry VII's reign occurs this solitary sentence: "The profession which then abounded most, and was embraced by persons of the lowest rank, was the church: By a clause of a statute, all clerks or students of the university were forbid to beg, without a permission from the vice-chancellor" (*History*, III, Chap. XXVI, 424).[15] Even religion was the object of unwise laws; but it always has had its share of unwise laws, decrees, practices, or edicts. These examples provide Hume with impressive evidence about the curiosities of not only Henry VII's reign, but the reigns of other monarchs. Examples such as the one above are ironically incorporated into the text to give the reader what Hume thinks is an appropriate outlook on the affairs of an epoch.

As each new chapter of the *History* opens, a reader often feels that England was about to embark on one of its most promising epochs, only to discover, later, that the state of affairs was at best muddy. The opening chapter on Henry VIII catches the spirit of the times: "The death of Henry the Seventh had been attended with as open and visible a joy among the people as decency would permit; and the ac-

[14] For an excellent analysis and discussion of Hume as economist, see Eugene Rotwein's introduction to his volume *David Hume: Writings on Economics.* Smith's high opinion of Hume is too well known to require much mention, but this excerpt from a letter to Smith in 1759 about Smith's just-published *Theory of Moral Sentiments* is evidence of their friendship and of the irony Hume uses in relations with friends: "Supposing, therefore, that you have duely prepared yourself for the worst by all these Reflections; I proceed to tell you the melancholy News, that your Book has been very unfortunate: For the Public seem disposd to applaud it extremely. It was lookd for by the foolish People with some Impatience; and the Mob of Literati are beginning already to be very loud in its Praises" (*NHL,* p. 53).

[15] In other editions of the *History* the word "sometimes" prudently precedes "embraced." A clerk was, of course, a cleric or a theology student.

cession and coronation of his son, Henry the Eighth, spread universally
a declared and unfeigned satisfaction" (*History*, III, Chap. XXVII,
429). Promises and hopes for the new reign were high, but they were
to be thwarted. In the succeeding chapters, by concentrating on the
crucial events rather than the trivia, Hume, as he commonly does, presents a picture of a confused, strife-weary nation. Many of the national
ills can be blamed on poor judgment and poorer administrators, whose
abilities, however excellent, are almost always misdirected. Henry
VIII's choice of Thomas Wolsey as member of council was a case of
especially bad judgment. Hume's recognition of Wolsey's abilities is
ironic:

By this rapid advancement and uncontrouled authority, the character and
genius of Wolsey had full opportunity to display itself. Insatiable in his
acquisitions, but still more magnificent in his expence: Of extensive capacity, but still more unbounded enterprize: Ambitious of power, but still
more desirous of glory: Insinuating, engaging, persuasive; and, by turns,
lofty, elevated, commanding: Haughty to his equals, but affable to his de-
pendants; oppresssive to the people, but liberal to his friends; more generous than grateful; less moved by injuries than by contempt; he seemed
framed to take the ascendant in every intercourse with others, but exerted
this superiority of *nature* with such ostentation as exposed him to envy, and
made every one willing to recal the original inferiority or rather meanness of
his *fortune*. (*History*, III, Chap. XVII, 455–456)

Hume has focused his irony, in this passage as well as in others,
that must go unquoted, on seemingly intelligent people who, overwhelmed by the sense of power, abrogate any association with dignity
or decorum. The irony here calls attention to qualities which if rightly
directed would earn a man the highest praise, the favor of history, and
the acclaim of popularity; if these qualities are misused, their possessor
becomes an object of loathing and distaste. (Or so Hume judges, although he has some kind words for Wolsey in summing up his character. But Hume is also trying to make clear the extent to which
Wolsey was disliked by his contemporaries.) History provides a
unique opportunity to determine whether the vices and irregularities
of men are innate or are forced on them by advantageous positions.
Hume seems generally to think that power is a perpetual struggle;

those in power do everything they can to stay and are, as a consequence, often led to acts of violence and tyranny. When this putative power is combined with religious strife, then little in the way of sanity is to be hoped for. The organization of the material suggests that even the best of intentions will be subverted if events force men to choose between wise policy and expedient politics. They are further weakened, as is the state, by the intrusion of dogma, especially religious dogma demanding absolute particularity in observance by its devotees. By such complicated, and seemingly hopeless events, then, are men led to irrationality and folly. Hume recognizes that it is not an easy matter to abdicate power; he simply questions if political power, at best temporal (regardless of what a Pope might say), is worth such a vitriolic struggle. It is not often the function of the historian to ask questions that he does not answer, but Hume raises questions that are intrinsically valuable, simply because that is his duty as philosopher-historian.

The final volumes of the *History of England*, devoted to the Celtic and Saxon periods as well as to the Middle Ages, were finished in 1761 and met "with tolerable, and but tolerable Success." These volumes were undoubtedly the least interesting to his contemporaries, as the period concerned is to most of us. Hume admitted one of the difficulties of writing a history of this period: "We shall hasten thro' the obscure and uninteresting period of Saxon annals: And shall reserve a more full narration for those times, when the truth is both so well ascertained and so complete as to promise some entertainment and instruction to the reader" (*History*, I, Chap. I, 2). Those words, written after a substantial part of the *History* had been completed, perhaps justify Hume's concentration on major events while omitting minutiae. By now the public was as inured as it could become to Hume's historical narrative, just as Hume told us he was "callous" to the outcries raised against the publication of the Tudor volumes. Either that, or the public had accepted some of Hume's enlightenment and was willing to see history as a series of events, more or less connected, not as a series of "right" and "wrong" attitudes. If Hume managed to discourage attitudinizing in the writing of history, he made a contribution well worth admiring.

Since attitudes about the Druid religion were not assiduously defended during the eighteenth century, Hume can be a little more openly ironic about the life-death power of the "church-state." One of his favorite methods, seen in previous examples, consists in itemizing the various policies of a given group and adding or implying some commentary. The first paragraph on the Druids is a creditable example:

The religion of the Britains was one of the most considerable parts of their government; and the Druids, who were their priests, possessed great authority among them. Besides ministring at the altar, and directing all religious duties, they presided over the education of youth; they were endowed with an immunity from wars and taxes; they enjoyed both the civil and criminal jurisdiction; they decided all controversies among states as well as private persons, and whoever refused to submit to their decree was exposed to the most severe penalties. The sentence of excommunication was denounced against him: He was forbid access to the sacrifices or public worship: He was debarred all intercourse with his fellow-citizens, even in the common affairs of life: His company was universally shunned, as profane and dangerous: He was refused the protection of law: And death itself became to him an acceptable relief from the misery and infamy to which he was exposed. Thus, the bands of government, which were naturally loose among that rude and turbulent people, were happily corroborated by the terrors of their superstition. (*History*, I, Chap. I, 4)

In case the reader misses the point, the opening sentence of the next paragraph corrects him: "No species of superstition was ever more terrible than that of the Druids." But the irony has been directed against both religion and politics, both apparently having an equally bad effect on each other. Otherwise, Hume is less kind in his treatment of the Druids than he ever is in discussing any of the various brands of Christianity in later periods. As a matter of logic, then, his readers should have assumed that he was not malevolent toward Christianity, but was applying a moralist's interpretation to history. Hume knew, however, that he couldn't expect an open mind from every member of his eighteenth-century audience, and he is perhaps freer with non-Christian religions on that account. The zealots are always happy when one of their antagonists is attacked, no matter who the attacker may be.

Hume is not content to embody that great autonomy, "accepted opinion," in his *History*; he feels free to disagree with established opinion whenever he feels the facts and events so warrant. The "new judgment" that he then forms about men and events is important in at least two ways. First, we might expect a sceptical philosopher to disregard common opinion and hearsay when forming a mental image of certain men or events. A concept, however strongly one may be attached to it, is a dangerous guide in attempting to form impartial judgments. The second way in which this "new judgment" is important is an outgrowth of the first. Since Hume could not accept the evidence (if it may be so called) of "accepted opinion" without first subjecting it to empirical examination, he had to mind his scholarship. He was not careless, and he did attend to the research necessary for such a project; as I mentioned earlier, his letters give instances of his writing to friends and booksellers in an effort to gain some of the books and papers necessary for the research. (See *HL*, I, 188, 210, 212, 226, 227, 262, 322–325). While he may not be the most diligent scholar, if we judge by the standards of our age, he was eminently competent for his age; and he at least went to the trouble to quote from texts, not from memory, as other writers of the age were wont to do. The irony that comes to light in the *History* is a product of research and thought, not of petulance or ill humor. That source could be left to other, lesser writers.

Failure to accept an established opinion does not necessarily imply that the writer is hesitant or indecisive about his viewpoint. Hume is conventionally ironic in recognizing his differences with other writers, as he does when discussing William the Conqueror:

Some writers have been desirous of refusing to this prince the title of Conqueror, in the sense in which it is commonly understood; and on pretence, that the word is sometimes in old books applied to such as make acquisition of territory by any means, they are willing to reject William's title, by right of war, to the crown of England. It is needless to enter into a controversy, which, by the terms of it, must necessarily degenerate into a dispute of words. It suffices to say, that the duke of Normandy's first invasion of the island was hostile; that his subsequent administration was entirely supported by arms; that in the very frame of his laws he made a distinction between the Normans and English, to the advantage of the former; that he acted in every thing as absolute master over the natives, whose interests and affections he totally disregarded; and that if there was an interval when he assumed the appearance of a legal magistrate, the period was very short, and was nothing but a temporary sacrifice, which he, as has been the case with most conquerors, was obliged to make of his inclination to his present policy. Scarce any of those revolutions, which, both in history and in common language, have always been denominated conquests, appear equally violent, or have been attended with so sudden an alteration both of power and property. (*History*, I, Chap. IV, 301–302)

Hume goes along with one established opinion and calls William, Duke of Normandy, by his royal title and not his popular one, ironically avoiding the pointless dispute over William's right to the name "Conqueror." Since he has referred to the Duke of Normandy as "William" throughout the preceding pages, his acceptance of the term "Conqueror" is obvious. Hume is judging history by the facts and not by accepted opinion or chauvinism, although he knows how to position his facts to present a certain view. The name is really unimportant so long as the reader knows what man is being talked about and what were his actual accomplishments, as distinct from attitudes toward him. National pride might demand that a conqueror of Britain be called by some euphemistic title, but Hume's accession to this demand is ironic. He says in effect that you know and I know but we will pretend that no one else knows the horrible truth.

In discussing the accomplishments both of men and of the age in which they lived, Hume occasionally displays impatience with their ignorance. Not an impatient or intolerant man himself, Hume did, as we have seen, find impatience and intolerance in others to be reprehensible; and many of the unfavorable judgments made in the *History* stem from his dislike of pretense, self-aggrandizement, and condescension. When an example of the ignorance of an age presents itself, however, Hume can be a little impatient in his ironic presentation of the shortcoming:

We may judge of the ignorance of this age in geography, from a story told by Robert of Aylesbury. Pope Clement VI having, in 1344, created Lewis of Spain prince of *the fortunate islands*, meaning the Canaries, then newly discovered; the English ambassador at Rome, and his retinue, were seized with an alarm, that Lewis had been created King of England; and they immediately hurried home, in order to convey this important intelligence. Yet such was the ardour for study at this time, that Speed in his Chronicle, informs us there were then thirty thousand students in the university of Oxford alone. What was the occupation of all these young men? To learn very bad Latin, and still worse logic.[16]

The irony of the whole paragraph is emphasized by the last sentence. It was surely not the occupation of all those young men to *learn* bad Latin and worse logic; the fact that they did does not speak well for the learning process at Oxford. However great the ardor for learning may have been, the actual learning was not great.

From the necessarily brief consideration that we must give to Hume's *History of England* in this book, it is possible, I think, to ascertain several purposes of the irony. To begin, its over-all, general purpose is to supplement the historical method, to add something to the arrangement and presentation of facts that will guard against dullness. Irony sharpens the wits of both the writer and the reader by commanding a higher level of awareness and perceptiveness than ordinary discourse requires. It would be fatuous to maintain that irony is the method by which the *History* is given shape, but its support of Hume's method can hardly be doubted. In more instances than it would be profitable to enumerate, the reader encounters situations where he can—and often must—add the ironic tone himself. Hume's method may be to let the facts and events speak for themselves, but their arrangement often impels the reader toward a sceptical or an ironic conclusion.[17] By organizing the events of history and the reactions of human nature to these events, Hume suggests a cosmic irony that falls alike on men everywhere. It is the kind of irony Burns creates when writing "The best laid schemes o' mice an' men/ Gang aft a-

---

[16] This particular paragraph does not occur in the 1773 edition; cf. the Aldine Book Publishing Company of Boston's edition (II, Chap. XVI, 277). That it was added in later revisions is evidence of Hume's continuing reluctance to be badgered into softening the criticisms of the Christian religion in the *History*. Also, the passage does not appear in the first edition.

[17] It is an oversimplification to suggest that Hume's method was simply "letting the facts speak for themselves," but that is a guiding principle. Hume's method is most carefully discussed in Mossner's article, "An Apology for David Hume, Historian."

gley." Hume is continually chronicling events where men's plans have been thwarted by the unexpected or by their own ignorance or cupidity. Writing of Richard II's great promise as a leader (*History*, III, Chap. XVII, 12), Hume counters with examples of his want of "solid judgment" which demonstrate the King's immense failures. Hume is actually suggesting that history is more filled with irony and failure than it is with glory, honor, and victory; the higher men's expectations, the greater their disappointments. To see men and events from a temporal perspective changes the complexion of affairs which, at one time, had seemed momentous and earth-shattering, while the truly important events were ignored or forgotten for decades or generations. By juxtaposing promises and actuality, aspirations and defeats, Hume, throughout the entire *History*, creates a cosmic irony that not only tries to restore events to their proper size but even wishes that contemporaries had been able to measure the truly important events. It is, to some extent, history seen through the eyes of the eighteenth-century rationalism,[18] but it is just as much history seen through the eyes of eighteenth-century irony. Hume projects the two or more levels on which an event or a person may be conceptualized and offers the ambiguity of these conceptualizations as an example of cosmic irony.

More openly, this cosmic irony, and the ironic method, lead Hume to one of the re-enforcing purposes of the *History*, that of instructing his readers. Here and there, in the course of the historical process, Hume will pause and discuss the lessons to be learned from certain events. Not a moralist in the sense that Dr. Johnson was, Hume merely gives the reader a gentle push toward the "right" interpretation of events, particularly ones in which turmoil and bloodshed were more common than not. So the juxtaposition of plans and events, with an implied cosmic irony, is designed to dramatize a moral. Like most eighteenth-century writers, Hume preferred to lead the reader to the proper conclusion, rather than to assume that he would reason logically to the proper conclusion. The cosmic irony involves what we may call the irony of history, which is what Hume calls to our attention. Once

[18] This penchant of Hume's is touched upon by Godfrey Davies in "Hume's History of the Reign of James I" in *Elizabethan and Jacobean Studies Presented to F. P. Wilson*, pp. 231–249.

the irony of certain historical events and the characters who partici-
pated in them is seen, then we can, Hume hopes, learn how to deal
with our own problems in a satisfactory way. The goal of enlightenment, which became clearly identified in Hume's age, was incorporated
as the theoretical background of the *History of England*.

The principle of instruction was as highly regarded in the seven-
teenth and eighteenth centuries as it is in our own, although this century has given it a different formulation as an esthetic principle. Hume
had tried, almost desperately, in his earlier works to see that his readers
made some sort of reassessment of their habits of mind. He had tried
to introduce the "experimental Method of Reasoning into Moral Subjects"; when he had little readership among the masses, it is not surprising that he sought to cultivate more readers by means of a work
(the *History of England*) which probably would, and in fact did, have
a much wider audience than the *Treatise* and the various editions of
his essays. The principles of philosophical inquiry, now applied to the
study of history, produced a work designed to breed a sceptical attitude about the absolute importance of men or events in the historical
process. In writing of Edward I's reign Hume argues that "Each age
has its peculiar mode in conducting business; and men, *guided more
by custom than by reason*, follow, without enquiry, the manners, which
are prevalent in their own time" (*History*, II, Chap. XIII, 253. Italics
added). If it were not possible to make his points known in philosophical writings, then in a study of history Hume could dramatize the
faults and achievements of human beings who attempted to reason
about moral subjects. Thus, when Hume juxtaposes certain events so
that the reader will infer their historical irony, his main purpose is enlightenment or instruction—to get mankind to improve itself. Acting
as a buffer against this optimism is the pervasive belief that mankind
isn't likely to improve itself. But Hume never completely divorced
himself from the "official optimism" of the eighteenth century, although he felt more keenly in tune with the second line of Pope's
couplet, "Hope springs eternal in the human breast:/ Man never Is,
but always To be blest."

In the first few lines of the first volume of the *History of England*
we noticed Hume's statement that the *History* was also written to en-

tertain, and much of the irony is directed to that point. Some of the religious irony undoubtedly did not amuse Hume's clerical contemporaries, but it certainly amused him. And the more enlightened clergy joined Hume, perhaps dragging their feet, in perceiving the outrageousness of church abuses in the past and realizing that the irony was apposite. The religious irony would probably amuse the religionists as well, so long as their sect was not the one under Hume's microscope. In addition to the entertainment offered by the treatment of religion and politics, Hume could catalogue some of the more obvious manifestations of ignorance, as in the example about the Oxford students. An erudite entertainment to be sure, but one which Hume's readers would recognize and enjoy. Hume, despite his claims to impartiality, could not be impartial at all times, and no one pretends that he is. Knowing human nature well, he could, however, recognize the entertainment value in making the reader feel slightly superior to his predecessors, although parts of the *History* pointed out, with equal cogency, that the superiority of human nature in Hume's age was a fiction. Though Hume had no doubt about the general improvement in affairs of state, he was not blind to the defects of the eighteenth century. In providing his age with a criterion by which to measure its accomplishments, its aspirations, he was providing a considerable degree of entertainment. Irony is used to heighten that entertainment, although it probably offended a number of the rigidly righteous, as well as the politicians. In an age lacking, perhaps fortunately for them, the beneficence of the television industry to provide them with items of entertainment, histories were almost as popular as novels. Whatever possible involvement the word "entertainment" suggests today, it required active participation in the eighteenth century, except for the drama. And to judge by contemporary accounts of performances at local theatres, even that participation could be considerably less passive than a modern audience's.

Finally, the irony has a purpose that extends beyond instruction and entertainment. Like much irony, especially Swift's, it aims at the correction of human evils. Once man is made aware of shortcomings in human nature, he must then be convinced that human nature is capable of improvement and that human beings have a moral duty to improve it. For Hume, it is not enough just to make man aware of his problems;

Hume must convince him that they should be rectified. Consequently, his irony is prescriptive, as indeed irony almost must be by definition. The prescription for amelioration is invariably implied in the description of the various follies that have all too often been the hallmark of the human race. Hume still believes that human nature can be improved, and, like his age, he could be optimistic about the possibilities. In exposing human folly, he ironically praises the odious. The irony is a corrective, a device for exposing vice and encouraging virtue, although that polarization oversimplifies Hume's intentions. If the *History of England* failed to reform human nature, which its author did not fully expect it to do, it had at least the excellence of forcing men to reconsider, in the light of reason, their goals and their values. For all practical purposes, it was Hume's last attempt[19] to embody his sceptical philosophy in another form. The controlled irony was simply one means by which this philosophy was expressed in the framework of history. While it is not of major importance today as a history of England, to the Hume scholar looking for manifestations of his thoughts in unphilosophical milieus it is useful if not indispensable. To the philosopher, it can act as a supplement, even a clarification, of some of Hume's most provocative innovations.[20] It may be of interest only to the specialist, but an understanding of Hume—his thought and his life—cannot be had unless one reads his *History of England*.

During the time that the *History* was being written, Hume also had time to publish in 1757 the volume entitled *Four dissertations. I. The natural history of religion. II. Of the passions. III. Of tragedy. IV. Of the standard of taste.* Hume first mentioned the book in a letter to his London publisher, Andrew Millar, dated 12 June 1755: "There are four short Dissertations, which I have kept some Years by me, in order to polish them as much as possible" (*HL*, I, 223). While it would be pointless to go into the publishing history of this work, it is sufficient to remark that the "Natural History of Religion" was not the only in-

[19] The *Dialogues concerning Natural Religion,* written about 1752 and published posthumously in 1779, is the major exception; it will be discussed in Chapter Four.

[20] While this is not the place to go into it, I have often wondered if Hume's epistemology is as atomistic as it is generally thought to be. The *History* gives evidence that it is not.

cendiary title.[21] It is, however, the work which shall engage our attention for the present. Having read it, we may see why mid–eighteenth-century readers were on the lookout for any hint of heterodoxy in Hume's *History*.

Briefly, one could say that "natural religion" stands in opposition to "revealed religion"; its theologians are empirical, not metaphysical. Probably the most famous exponent of empirical theology in the eighteenth century was Bishop Joseph Butler (1692–1752),[22] whom David Hume greatly esteemed. In this essay, however, Hume is concerned to give a historical and psychological account of religion and is, by definition, on more dangerous ground than he would be if merely analyzing the postulates of natural religion. His introduction to the essay offers some consolation for the theist: "The whole frame of nature bespeaks an intelligent author; and no rational enquirer can, after serious reflection, suspend his belief a moment with regard to the primary principles of genuine Theism and Religion" (*Works*, IV, 309). Of course, a nature which only "bespeaks" an intelligent author is different from one which proves, indicates, suggests, substantiates, implies, or presupposes. The metaphor here hides more than it conveys, an ironic note which not even Hume's attacker, the Reverend William Warburton (1698–1779),[23] was thickheaded enough to miss when he remarked of Hume's essay that in it "He is establishing atheism; and in one single line of a long essay professes to believe in

[21] For a complete summary and analysis of the publication and difficulties of the *Four Dissertations,* see Ernest Campbell Mossner, "Hume's *Four Dissertations*: An Essay in Biography and Bibliography," *Modern Philology,* XLVIII, #1 (1950), 37–57.

[22] The best modern studies of Bishop Butler are Ernest Campbell Mossner's *Bishop Butler and the Age of Reason: A Study in the History of Thought,* and William J. Norton's *Bishop Butler, Moralist and Divine.*

[23] Warburton was one of Hume's most frequent critics and has the distinction of saying that the *Enquiry concerning Human Understanding* was eclipsed by Conyers Middleton's *Free Enquiry into the Miraculous Powers,* published the same year. Hume's feelings about Middleton's book are reported in his autobiography: "On my return from Italy, I had the Mortification to find all England in a Ferment on account of Dr. Middletons Free Enquiry; while my Performance was entirely overlooked and neglected." He later says that he "found by Dr. Warburtons Railing that the Books were beginning to be esteemed in good Company."

Christianity."[24] At best, Hume's admission above would imply Deism, certainly not the Christian principles so dear to Warburton. As for those "primary principles of genuine Theism and Religion," Hume never specifies them. After that guarded introduction, the essay itself makes a trenchant analysis of the origin of religion, leaving the reader with one primary impression: that man's intelligence grows in inverse proportion to his religious sentiment.

That seemingly apologetic introduction might catch the unwary believer off guard, and while he is examining the text and the religious attitude of the author, he could conceivably miss some of the other ironic thrusts at the theist in the essay. For example, in Section Fifteen, "General Corollary," Hume is making a list of some of the paradoxes or anomalies of religious behavior, to wit: "No theological absurdities so glaring that they have not, sometimes, been embraced by men of the greatest and most cultivated understanding. No religious precepts so rigorous that they have not been adopted by the most voluptuous and most abandoned of men" (*Works*, IV, 362–363). The order of the second sentence is somewhat reversed, for ordinarily a writer would point out that men who pretended to be religious actually engaged in reprehensible acts. Hume makes no assumption that these men are actually religious, but implies that religious principles are not so sacrosanct as to prevent a debauched person from adopting them. This implied insult is followed with a questionable compliment to the general value of religion: "*Ignorance is the mother of Devotion*: A maxim that is proverbial, and confirmed by general experience. Look out for a people, entirely destitute of religion: If you find them at all, be assured, that they are but a few degrees removed from brutes" (*Works*, IV, 363).[25] Hume leaves the implications to be derived by

---

24 *A Selection from Unpublished works of the Right Reverend William Warburton*, ed. by Francis Kilvert, pp. 309–310; cited in Mossner's article "Hume's *Four Dissertations*."

25 The same phrase occurs in Bernard Mandeville's short essay of 1714, *An Enquiry into the Origin of Moral Virtue*. Speaking of alleged altruists, Mandeville says, "those who wanted a sufficient Stock of either Pride or Resolution to buoy them up in mortifying of what was dearest to them, follow'd the sensual dictates of Nature, would yet be asham'd of confessing themselves to be those despicable Wretches, and were generally reckon'd to be so little remov'd from Brutes . . ." (*The Fable of the Bees*, ed. by F. B. Kaye, I, 45).

his readers; and the implications are vague, because this particular set of contrasts between what men say and what they do is not exactly in line with those which preceded it. A different kind of logic organizes the last quotation, and by summarizing the logic that makes up the irony in this passage, we can see its difference from the others in the series. First, the generalization: ignorance spawns devotion; and, of course, devotion is generally thought to be a component of religion. Nonreligious people are but a *few degrees removed* from the brutes. So far, so good. But nonreligious people are not necessarily ignorant. If they are not ignorant, they must be intelligent; if they are intelligent, they cannot be brutes. But they can be intelligent and be also a *few degrees removed* from the brutes. And who are those brutes? Why those very ones we thought we were admiring—the religionists. This reasoning should not make the logician blanch with horror, for it is not only in accord with Hume's feelings about the religionists, it is also logical. After all, nonreligious people, goes the postulate, can be intelligent, and intelligent people cannot be brutes. They can, however, be a few degrees removed from brutes, who are hardly to be considered intelligent. Moreover, what would be the logical corollary to the proposition that ignorance is the mother of devotion? The implied antithesis is that intelligence would be the mother of scepticism, a point of view quite in accord with the tone and procedure of the entire essay. Since the intelligent by definition cannot be brutes, that leaves only one other species in this series of propositions to whom the term can be applied, the religionists. They are the alternative to the sceptics in every other part of the logic that organizes the above quotation, and they must be so here.

In this instance we do not necessarily need Hume's opinions on religion to corroborate the ironic interpretation; it is in the words themselves. The faithful, reading the passage, might be jarred to discover that ignorance is the mother of devotion, especially if they stopped to consider the logical antithesis of that statement. Or, they might very well be curious about the paternity of devotion, since Hume was not given to careless use of metaphors. They would then be reassured to learn that nonreligious people were only a few steps removed from the brutes. Without bothering to follow out the logical implications of the passage, they miss the insults to their position. All of which proves, I suppose, that logicians make good ironists.

Like most good ironists, Hume recognized that irony is a reproduction of life; one of the functions of the ironists is to point out, sometimes with comment, sometimes not, the various manifestations of irony in life. The series of contrasting descriptions that close the "Natural History of Religion" are not only cast in an ironic mode, but they point up the irony that exists as a disparity between men's words and men's deeds. Consider, for example, the following passage:

What so pure as some of the morals, included in some theological systems? What so corrupt as some of the practices, to which these systems give rise?

The comfortable views, exhibited by the belief of futurity, are ravishing and delightful. But how quickly vanish on the appearance of its terrors, which keep a more firm and durable possession of the human mind? (*Works*, IV, 363)

Hume is both the writer of irony here and the observer of irony in life. He sees how absurd it is for men to have a warmhearted notion of immortality when they respond to the pressures of life as if they had nothing to expect beyond the grave. Perceiving the irony in life—and being able to tolerate if not enjoy it—is more a characteristic of the eighteenth century than our own. In a world not threatened by destruction from thermonuclear bombs, it was a little easier to be amused by the ironies of life, since one of the ironies of life did not include the overnight destruction of man by his own hand. The disparity between man's words and deeds was not so bothersome, although it perhaps should have been. For Hume, an allusion to one of the ironies of life was sufficient to delineate, as acutely as need be, man's lack of faith in that which he believed he had the most faith in. The irony, as Hume saw it, proceeded from a rational belief that one's irrational belief in futurity might after all be true. The recognition of this sort of irony in life, for a man studying the science of human nature, was as important as castigating life for being something less than it ought to be.

The recognition of irony by an author as a reproduction of life, and his subsequent allusion to it, raise an interesting problem: Must the author's perception of this irony in life strike a similar nerve in his readers so that the reader will understand the author's point? The answer is not a simple yes or no because of the various levels of meaning on which irony operates. The examples from Hume that we have just noted have a primary level of meaning which is supplemented by one's awareness of the other levels of meaning. It is the sort of irony which calls on the reader to use his intelligence to recognize the implications of the author and to seek them out himself; in other words, the reader adds much of the ironic tone by perceiving the author's purpose in pointing out the ironic in life. The method in Hume is excellent. The series of short, clipped contrasts that he enumerates are poignant in the simplicity with which they sketch the failure of man's behavior to measure up to his ideals. The method dramatizes the irony inherent in some given condition of life and places it in the proper perspective for the reader's judgment. This irony is almost the last word in artistic economy because it relies on the reader to do so much—but it gives him all the materials he needs.

In order that we may not mistake the subtlety of Hume's thought and his ironic mode, it is helpful to consider his correspondence during this period. In his younger years Hume was apt to be reserved and distant with all but the closest of friends; as he grew older he occasionally turned this reserve into an irony for criticism of importunate correspondents. One of his more or less friendly antagonists was Thomas Reid (1710–1796),[26] author of *An Inquiry into the Human Mind on the Principles of Common Sense* (1764), *Essays on the Intellectual Powers of Man* (1785), and *Essays on the Active Powers of Man* (1788). To judge from what Reid has to say of the *Treatise* in *An Inquiry into the Human Mind,* he considered part of Hume's works to be ironic, although not the same passages we have considered. In

---

[26] Despite his shortcomings, Reid was Hume's most important philosophical antagonist in Scotland. He taught philosophy at Aberdeen and succeeded Adam Smith in 1764 as Professor of Moral Philosophy at Glasgow. As a member of the "common sense" school, Reid militated against the paradoxes of perception discovered by Berkeley and Hume; he insisted on a distinction between perception and sensation, the latter being the occasion of the former. Reid is generally conceded to be the initiator of realism in Western philosophy. Dugald Stewart's *Biographical Memoirs of Smith, Robertson, and Reid* contains some useful commentary; see, also, A. C. Fraser, *Thomas Reid.*

a work that generally abuses Hume, Reid says, in his first mention of Hume:

It seems to be a peculiar strain of humour in this author, to set out in his introduction by promising, with a grave face, no less than a complete system of the sciences, upon a foundation entirely new—to wit, that of human nature—when the intention of the whole work [the *Treatise*] is to shew, that there is neither human nature nor science in the world. It may perhaps be unreasonable to complain of this conduct in an author who neither believes his own existence nor that of his reader; and therefore could not mean to disappoint him, or laugh at his credulity. Yet I cannot imagine that the author of the "Treatise of Human Nature" is so sceptical as to plead this apology. He believed, against his principles, that he should be read, and that he should retain his personal identity, till he reaped the honour and reputation justly due to his metaphysical *acumen*.[27]

Small wonder, then, that Hume did not respond favorably to Reid's work, and wrote him the following letter, which was solicited by Reid through the intermediacy of Hugh Blair, about the manuscript of the *Inquiry into the Human Mind*:

By Dr [Hugh] Blair's means I have been favoured with the perusal of your performance, which I have read with great pleasure and attention. It is certainly very rare, that a piece so deeply philosophical is wrote with so much spirit, and affords so much entertainment to the reader; tho I must still regret the disadvantages under which I read it, as I never had the whole performance at once before me, and could not be able fully to compare one part with another. To this reason, chiefly, I ascribe some obscurities, which, in spite of your short analysis or abstract, still seem to hang over your system. For I must do you the justice to own, that when I enter into your ideas, no man appears to express himself with greater perspicuity than you do; a talent which, above all others, is requisite in that species of literature which you have cultivated. There are some objections, which I would willingly propose, to the chapter 'Of Sight,' did I not suspect that they proceed from my not sufficiently understanding it; and I am the more confirmed in this suspicion, as Dr Blair tells me, that the former objections I made, had been derived chiefly from that cause. I shall therefore forbear till the whole can be before me, and shall not at present propose any farther difficulties to your reasonings. I shall only say, that if you have been able to clear up these ab-

[27] Thomas Reid, *Works*, ed. by Sir William Hamilton, Bart., I, 102.

struse and important subjects, instead of being mortified, I shall be so vain as to pretend to a share of the praise; and shall think that my errors, by having at least some coherence, had led you to make a more strict review of my principles, which were the common ones, and to perceive their futility.

As I was desirous to be of some use to you, I kept a watchful eye all along over your style; but it is really so correct, and so good English, that I found not any thing worth the remarking. There is only one passage in this chapter, where you make use of the phrase, *hinder to do*, instead of *hinder from doing*, which is the English one; but I could not find the passage when I sought for it. You may judge how unexceptionable the whole appeared to me, when I could remark so small a blemish. I beg my compliments to my friendly adversaries, Dr Campbell and Dr Gerard, and also to Dr Gregory, whom I suspect to be of the same disposition, tho he has not openly declared himself such. [28] (*HL*, I, 375–376)

Reid's failure to perceive the irony of Hume's remarks is ample testimony to his perspicacity. Hume would not have limited himself to the correction of one Scotticism, but Reid had so completely misunderstood

---

[28] George Campbell (1719–1796), Principal of Marischal College, Aberdeen, from 1759; D.D., 1764; Professor of Divinity, Marischal College, 1771; and author of *Dissertation on Miracles* (1762), which Hume read, and *Philosophy of Rhetoric* (1776). Alexander Gerard (1728–1795), also Professor of Divinity at Marischal College. Hume read and perhaps sponsored publication of Gerard's *An Essay on Taste* (1759), submitted to the Edinburgh Society in 1756; it was awarded the prize for the best essay on taste by a committee of which Hume was a member. Hume's own essay "Of the Standard of Taste" appeared in 1757 in the *Four Dissertations*. (See Ralph Cohen, "David Hume's Experimental Method and the Theory of Taste," *Journal of English Literary History*, XXV, #4 [1958], 270–289.) John Gregory (1725–1773) was Reid's cousin and Professor of the Practice of Physic in Edinburgh in 1766. His letters to Reid abuse Hume; for example: "It has been said here that you had written with great heat and asperity against Mr. Hume, because you differed from him about some metaphysical subtleties, of no material consequence to mankind. This is alleged by those who never read your book, and seem never to have read Mr. Hume's. You write with warmth against him, because he has endeavoured to invalidate every argument brought to prove the existence of a Supreme Being; because he has endeavoured to invalidate every argument in favour of a future state of existence; and because he has endeavoured to destroy the distinction between moral good and evil. You do not treat him with severity, because he is a bad metaphysician, but because he has expressly applied his metaphysics to the above unworthy purposes." Quoted from Sir William Forbes, *An Account of the Life and Writings of James Beattie, LL.D.*, I, 189–190.

the *Treatise* that Hume gave him one of the most ironic deferences he accords to anyone in his letters.[29] In one sense, Hume is shielding himself against the bothersome impertinences of people such as Reid. Having told us in his autobiography that he had early resolved not to engage in literary squabbles, he needed some method for coming to grips with his critics. Even if he did not respond with an immediate pamphlet, it was psychologically necessary to answer them. On the occasions that he took the opportunity to write directly to a critic, he was always careful to respond in the most gentlemanly fashion, or at least to give that impression to his critic. Reid missed the irony entirely, for he replied to Hume as follows:

Your system appears to me not onely coherent in all its parts, but likeways justly deduced from principles commonly received among Philosophers: Principles, which I never thought of calling in question, untill the conclusions you draw from them in the Treatise of human Nature made me suspect them. If these principles are solid your system must stand; and whether they are or not, can better be judged after you have brought to Light the whole system that grows out of them, than when the greater part of it was wrapped up in clouds and darkness. I agree with you therefore that if this system shall ever be demolished, you have a just claim to a great share of the Praise, both because you have made it a distinct and determinate mark to be aimed at, and have furnished proper artillery for the purpose. . . .

Your friendly adversaries Drs Campbell & Gerard as well as Dr Gregory return their compliments to you respectfully. A little Philosophical Society here of which all the three are members [and of which Reid was the founder], is much indebted to you for its entertainment. Your company would, although we are all good Christians, be more acceptable than that of Saint Athanasius. And since we cannot have you upon the bench, you are brought oftener than any other man to the bar, accused and defended with great zeal but without bitterness. If you write no more in morals politicks or metaphysicks, I am affraid we shall be at a loss for subjects. (*HL*, I, 376 n.– 377 n.)

Since the assumption that Hume was zealous for public acclaim and was bitterly disappointed when he failed, initially, to achieve it is mistaken, one can imagine the personal pleasure Hume gained from making his controlled response to a critic.

[29] See Mossner's *Life,* p. 299.

Ironic praise for an adversary's misunderstandings of one's philosophy marks Hume as a wit; it also indicates an emphasis on human failings that becomes more common in his last writings. Some of the good nature of his irony begins to disappear; he becomes caustic. Was it the disappointment of a young man who, thinking that he had arrived at a "true system" of human nature, was dismayed at his failure to reform the world? The irony is partially a reflection of disappointment. The greater emphasis, however, is on the hypocrisy and egotism of mankind, whose actual virtues are few but whose proclamations are many. Man is not what he seems to be, nor is he so glorious a creature as he pretends. Hume argues, by implication, that man must cease to regard himself as the best of all possible creatures in the second-best (heaven being first) of all possible worlds. Until he learns to cope with the actual state of human nature, and not an idealized, hypostatized state, he will forever commit barbarities, ill judgments, and stupidities.

Correspondence with someone like Thomas Reid was a dead-end street, since Reid had nothing to offer Hume. But his other correspondents were far from bleak, particularly a young French admirer, the Comtesse de Boufflers. Their friendship began with a letter from her, praising Hume's first volumes of the *History of England,* and they developed an amiable correspondence, although they did not meet until autumn 1763, when Hume visited France. In preparation for this visit, Hume wrote her, in September 1763, in a mood of good nature and irony:

But I now find, after . . . repeated applications have again embarked me in the world, that it is better for a man to keep in the midst of society; and I am particularly pleased with a scene of life, which will approach me near to your Ladyship, and give me an opportunity of cultivating the friendship of a person so much esteemed and so universally celebrated. I now give you warning, Madam, that your declarations in my favour have been so frequent and public, both in France and England, that you are bound in honour to maintain them, and that you cannot with a good grace retract upon a personal acquaintance the advantageous terms in which you have so often been pleased to speak of me. There is only one circumstance which can possibly excuse your displeasure against me; if I should be wanting in my regard and attachment towards you; since such a conduct must prove me a man not to be bound either by merit or obligation. (*HL*, I, 402)

Hume concludes by saying that he looks forward to the opportunity of "throwing myself at your feet," a scene, considering Hume's bulk, that must have provided an image for contemplation.

While comfortable in the presence of the "weak, pious sex," Hume must have been a little overwhelmed at the written ardor of the Comtesse de Boufflers. Generally speaking, his letters to her are as restrained as hers are unrestrained. He was not prevented by any sense of false modesty, however, from expressing his affection for her, and there is no doubt that he was genuinely and sincerely attracted to her, if not actually in love, since it is evident that their friendship developed into something more than just Platonic.[30] One would not select any of Hume's letters for a volume of the "world's greatest love letters," although the level of expression in them is usually better than that of letters selected for such a volume. Hume did not want to overcommit himself, and he must have reserved his most heartfelt expressions for the Comtesse's ears. At the age of fifty-two, when he first met her, he was unlikely to behave with the ardor of a young man. He realized the impossibility of any permanent arrangement—the Comtesse was married but separated from her husband—and he conveyed this apprehension to her under the guise of irony so as not to offend her. Writing on 14 July 1764 he says:

I confess with shame, that I am but too subject to this sentiment [of diffidence and jealousy], even in friendship. I never doubt of my friend's probity or honour; but often of his attachment to me, and sometimes, as I have afterwards found, without reason. If such was my disposition even in youth, you may judge that, having arrived at a time of life when I can less expect to please, I must be more subject to inroads of suspicion. Common sense requires that I should keep at a distance from all attachments that can imply passion. But it must surely be the height of folly, to lay myself at the mercy of a person whose situation seems calculated to inspire doubt, and who, being so little at her own disposal, could not be able, even if willing, to seek such remedies as might appease that tormenting sentiment.

[30] See Mossner's *Life*, pp. 460–464.

Should I meet with one, in any future time, (for to be sure I know of none such at present) who was endowed with graces and charms beyond all expression, whose character and understanding were equally an object of esteem, as her person was of tenderness; I ought to fly her company, to avoid all connexion with her, even such as might bear the name of friendship; and to endeavour to forget her as soon as possible. I know not if it would be prudent even to bid her adieu: surely, it would be highly imprudent to receive from her any testimonies of friendship and regard. But who, in that situation, could have resolution to reject them? Who would not drink up the poison with joy and satisfaction? (*HL*, I, 451)

Yet Hume was not seeking an opportunity for breaking off their relationship, but simply noting that the Comtesse was not free. The irony about his putative behavior upon "accidentally" finding someone of mutual proclivities is adequate evidence about his attachment to her.

While she was married, Hume would not indulge himself in thoughts of marriage. As it happened, her husband died in October 1764, while Hume was in France; but he could not expect her attention to turn to him. In 1752, six years after her marriage to Edouard de Boufflers, she had become the mistress of Louis-Francois de Bourbon, Prince de Conti, and she remained so during her association with Hume. On the death of her husband she was determined to become the legal wife to the Prince de Conti, which would have made her the third lady of the land in rank (*Life,* pp. 458–470). Upon hearing from her of the death of her husband and knowing what social gains she hoped to make of his timely departure, Hume wrote, in a tone of resentful irony:

This late incident, which commonly is of such moment with your sex, seems so little to affect your situation either as to happiness or misery, that I might have spared you the trouble of receiving my compliments upon it: but being glad of taking any opportunity to express my most sincere wishes for your welfare, I would not neglect an occasion which custom has authorised.

Receive, then, with your usual, I cannot say, with your constant, goodness, the prayers of one of your most devoted friends and servants. I hope that every change of situation will turn out to your advantage. In vain would I assume somewhat of the dignity of anger, when you neglect me: I find that this wish still returns upon me with equal ardour.

I hear . . . that you are to be in Paris on Saturday. I shall be there about that day se'nnight: I hope that your etiquette, which allows you to receive relations and particular friends, opens a wide-enough door for my admission. (*HL*, I, 476)

Hume, then, was not incapable of severe irony with a woman whose affections for him were not stronger than her desire for titled eminence, when she had professed the contrary. That he was wounded is obvious, and that he resorted to irony in telling her so should tell us something about his character: that amidst all his philosophy he was still a man, a human being who could feel that he had been unfairly dealt with. Even in the course of one letter he could not be entirely vindictive. The last line in the letter is a humorous reference to his bulk, which at that time must have been nearly 250 pounds. But it also says that he is willing to continue their friendship. A man like, say, Rousseau would probably have written her in tones of vituperative scorn, but it was enough for Hume to tell her, in the best of ironic modes, that he knew she was glad to have her husband out of the way, a good enough reason to be apprehensive about marriage to her. Events following the death of her husband proved Hume correct, for the Comtesse de Boufflers was, to use an inelegant phrase, a "social climber." In this particular example, Hume's point could be more damagingly made by the use of irony than by specifically calling her attention to the fact that everyone knew she was not sorrowed by the death of her husband, since it gave her the chance she needed. Irony is one of the best methods for telling someone that his true nature has been perceived and that any attempt to feign a different attitude will collapse under the weight of its own deceit. By meaning the opposite of what his words say, Hume can effectively criticize the Comtesse's behavior.

One of the purposes, then, in Hume's ironic tone in his final correspondences with the Comtesse de Boufflers is serious: he hopes to correct errors in taste, judgment, and sensibility. He paid her the highest compliment he could pay to any woman, or to any person for that matter; he closed a letter written in July 1764 with the following: "Among other obligations, which I owe you, without number, you have saved me from a total indifference toward every thing in human life. I was falling very fast into that state of mind, and it is perhaps worse than even the inquietudes of the most unfortunate passion: how much, then, is it inferior to the sweetness of your commerce and friendship!" (*HL,* I, 457). The ambivalent position of the man in love is easily clear. He recognized her interest in social gain, which she preferred to the admittedly more romantic idyll of satisfaction in love, and he comments unfavorably on the false values to which mankind pays homage.

Human beings are always constructing value systems which they never measure up to, but which they are capable of achieving. Are human beings to be faulted because they are not worthy or do not have the qualities of excellence that are requisite for such awe-inspiring, perhaps highly constrictive ideals? Or are they to be faulted because they construct an ethic in which they have only the slightest belief and have not the slightest intention of living up to? Hume, I believe, was inclined to think that such people gave human beings more credit than they were due, since they had festooned mankind with ideals which in practice it consistently ignored and which in practice it did not really accept. The problem was not that the human race was so lowly and so incapable of, for want of a better word, grace that it could not measure up to the ideals articulated by its high priests of morality. The problem was instead that men believed in such ideals about as much as they believed there were men on the moon. They were capable of achieving the high moral principles developed by mankind, their ancestors, but in practice they acted as if an entirely different set of principles were guiding them. The words in the "ideals" were false, and the feelings behind them were false; Hume would have nothing to do with either.

Consequently, the purpose of the irony in examples like the ones we have examined is that of adjusting man to his nature, making him see that he is not really such an exalted creature as he thinks. A sceptic who was also a man of reason could not accept the notion that man really believed all the pieties and platitudes he articulated; nor could he believe that man was so brutish as to be incapable of maintaining excellent moral standards which did not contradict his actions. So Hume pointed out, sometimes with ironic bitterness, more often with ironic gentility, this disparity and hoped that by the use of reason as a guide to the passions man would go between the horns of what must have been an uncomfortable dilemma. That men have not done so is a commentary, and a regrettable one, on man's inhumanity to himself.

In this chapter, we have seen Hume at cross-purposes with himself, pleased on the one hand and irritated on the other. The very work whose popularity gave him much satisfaction, financial and philosophical, the *History of England,* was the same work which brought him to the attention of the Comtesse de Boufflers. But who could doubt that he would have felt his life more profitable and exciting if he had not met the Comtesse? Or that he regretted having written the *History of England* because it brought him to her attention? The pleasure of authorship and the pleasures of feminine companionship were not incompatible in the eighteenth century, and Hume thought it highly unfortunate that the Comtesse's reading of the *History* had not signalled the beginning of a companionship that would have given him as much pleasure as he would undoubtedly derive from the knowledge of his posthumous fame.

It is important that we count the ironic response at this period of Hume's life as uppermost in the development of his character. It was never to develop into the bitterness that Swift is often accused of, nor was it to lose sight of the object of all Hume's philosophy—human nature, to which he would now be inclined to append the word "intractable." The *Treatise* really was an attempt to introduce experimental reasoning into the science of human nature, more so than any of the works written after 1752. In the works of these later years human nature is the object of scrutiny and analysis, and Hume is often dramatizing the necessity of not just *introducing* experimental reasoning, but of *incorporating* it into every planned action of human nature. Irony not only lends itself well to the articulation of Hume's scepticism, it is about the only literary genre which offered him so many possibilities of service. The main stream of irony in the eighteenth century was found usually in satire or in examples which fitted Lord Chesterfield's definition, "saying directly the contrary of what you mean."[31] Hume frequently diverges from this stream to create a "cosmic irony" for the reader, so that events and people, not words, become ironic. It is, to be sure, a different kind of irony, yet one which the reader immediately perceives.

[31] Chesterfield, Philip Dormer Stanhope, Fourth Earl of, *Letters to his Son,* ed. by Charles Strachey, notes by Annette Calthrop, I, 36.

For Hume, it is probable that caricature, pasquinade, or burlesque simply were not subtle enough, that his irony had to be indirect, that in his culturally awkward position of religious sceptic his irony demanded a reader who could respond to a less visceral approach than that of Swift or Pope. But in choosing his events and people so as to suggest this cosmic irony, Hume offers the reader opportunity to participate in the ironic mode. The irony is not "greater" for that reason— no one is going to pretend that Hume and Swift or Hume and Pope share the same glories as ironists—but it does help to explain some of the pleasure we have in reading Hume. The departure from the norm is refreshing, if not rhetorically fascinating; and it was probably required by the kind of man Hume was and by the kind of environment he lived in. A parson perhaps could have written scathing irony about religion, but it would have been more acceptable than irony from a religious sceptic. So this period of intense literary activity in Hume's life reflects his attempt to make the most of what must be called his "mature" style. He directs the reader's attention toward the irony of people or events cast sometimes by fate, sometimes by choice, into a framework both meaningful and absurd at the same time. The finest product of this matured style incorporates all the various forms of the ironic mode, from "cosmic irony" to "saying directly the contrary of what you mean." The next chapter deals, in part, with the work, the *Dialogues concerning Natural Religion,* that was substantially Hume's last, written during the 1750's, revised off and on by Hume up to the last days of his life, and published posthumously.

4. The Culmination of a Literary Mode

"It is difficult to be more detached from Life than I am at present."

In the late summer of 1766 Hume left France and returned to Edinburgh with, as he said, the prospect of "burying myself in a philosophical Retreat." This commendable plan was disrupted by an invitation from Lord Hertford[1] to serve as Under-Secretary of State, Northern Department. Although Hume served well, he was involved in a number of altercations too complicated for summary here.[2] One of these, the Douglas Cause, involved his friend Andrew Stuart. The claimants in the Douglas Cause were (1) Archibald Steuart-Douglas, alleged son of Lady Jane Douglas, the sister of Archibald, the Marquess of Douglas, and (2) the Duke of Hamilton, the nearest male heir. Hamilton, to whom Andrew Stuart and Baron Mure of Caldwell were guardians, contended that Archibald Steuart-Douglas was not the lawful son, as indeed he was not, since he was "purchased" by Lady Jane in her fifty-first year from his French parents.[3] Initially, the Court of Sessions at Edinburgh decided in Hamilton's favor, but the House of Lords reversed the decision in 1769. Andrew Stuart was understandably disappointed and published in January 1773 *Letters of the Right Honourable Lord Mansfield from Andrew Stuart, Esq.* About those

---

[1] Francis Seymour Conway, Earl of Hertford (1718–1794). Hume served as his secretary on Lord Hertford's Embassy to Paris in 1763, which was one of the reasons for his visit to France; Mme. de Boufflers was the other. The complete story of Hume's service as Embassy Secretary can be found in *Life,* pp. 489–506.

[2] See *Life,* pp. 533–556 for a summary of these difficulties.

[3] See *Life,* p. 550.

Letters Hume wrote the following ironic paragraph to his friend
Stuart:

I am sorry to tell you, honoured Sir, that David Hume, whom perhaps
you look on as your Friend, goes about railing at you in every Company: Son
of a Whore and Son of a Bitch are the best Appellations he can afford you.
He says, that it is intolerable, that this damnd Fellow, who was bred to
nothing but drawing of Bonds and Leases, or at best Settlements and En-
tails, which are the sublime of his former Profession, shoud turn Author,
and at once surpass him and all his Brethren: I am told that he has engag'd
the Principal, who, I hear, has the same Opinion of your Performance, to
speak the same Lan[guage.] Such is the base Envy and Malignity of these
low Minds! (*HL,* II, 271)

Hume and several other friends of Stuart had sat in conference on the
Letters and had passed favorable judgment on the sentiments ex-
pressed. The irony is re-enforced by the signature, David Stuart-
Moncrief, a common acquaintance respected by neither Hume nor
Stuart.

This particular letter is evidence, if any be needed, of Hume's
firmly established penchant for irony even at this time of his life. For
the purposes of this chapter it is additionally important because Hume
spent some time during the last part of his life revising and polishing
the *Dialogues concerning Natural Religion.* Hume was less and less
inclined during this period to disguise his religious scepticism. But his
social intercourse was limited primarily to dear and lifelong friends in
Edinburgh, and there was little likelihood that they would disturb his
peace. His tranquillity was disturbed, however, by one James Beattie
(1735–1803), described by Hume in 1775 as "that bigotted silly
Fellow, Beattie." Beattie's most famous book, from which we have already quoted (Chapter One), was *An Essay on Truth,* and he attacked
both Hume's philosophical and religious positions. Hume was no doubt
angered by Beattie's stupidities, but he would probably take an ironic
pleasure from the remark of Beattie's biographer, Sir William Forbes:
"Dr. Campbell's prediction [that the *Dialogues* was "too dry, and too
metaphysical, to do much hurt"], as to the fate of this posthumous
work of Mr. Hume's, seems to have been completely verified; for the

'Dialogues concerning Natural Religion' are now never heard of."[4]

It is in this context of altercations and philosophical disturbances that we must consider Hume's last work, which presents the most substantial criticism of religion made in the eighteenth century. Indeed, it is not just a criticism, it is an actual contribution to the development of religious thought, for the demise of the argument from design led ultimately to the modern emphasis on faith as the starting point for all theological deduction. The *Dialogues* is an example of "creative scepticism."[5] It is helpful, then, to ascertain Hume's religious attitude, as expressed to clerical friends, and to know what was going through his mind as he revised the *Dialogues*. Hume was not afraid to let his real sentiments about religion be known, although he would address in 1761 his good friend, the Reverend Hugh Blair (1718–1800), minister of the Canongate Kirk in Edinburg, in an ironic vein:

I have perused the ingenious performance [George Campbell's *Dissertation on Miracles*, which attacked Hume], which you was so obliging as to put into my hands, with all the attention possible; tho not perhaps with all the seriousness and gravity which you have so frequently recommended to me. But the fault lies not in the piece, which is certainly very acute; but in the subject. I know you will say, it lies in neither, but in myself alone. If that be so, I am sorry to say that I believe it is incurable. (*HL*, I, 348–349)

Hume's relations with Campbell were relatively friendly, but part of the remainder of the letter to Blair is devoted to a criticism of Campbell's ideas. Finally, Hume, after mentioning that Campbell "denominated [him] an infidel writer, on account of ten or twelve pages which seem to him to have that tendency," has a request to make of Blair on the subject of the Christian religion:

---

[4] Forbes, *Life of Beattie*, II, 53, 53 n. Forbes' observation is not very learned, since the *Dialogues* had been reprinted as "third edition," in London in 1804. Its reproductions since then, especially in this century, are too numerous to catalogue.

[5] The subtitle of Margaret L. Wiley's book *The Subtle Knot: Creative Scepticism in Seventeenth-Century England,* which is one of several books and articles employing this concept in relation to Restoration and eighteenth-century literature. Professor Mossner has also used the term: "Hume and the Ancient-Modern Controversy, 1725–1752: A Study in Creative Scepticism," *University of Texas Studies in English,* XXVIII (1949), 139–153.

Whenever I have had the pleasure to be in your company, if the discourse turned upon any common subject of literature or reasoning, I always parted from you both entertained and instructed. But when the conversation was diverted by you from this channel towards the subject of your profession; tho I doubt not but your intentions were very friendly towards me, I own I never received the same satisfaction: I was apt to be tired, and you to be angry. I would therefore wish for the future, wherever my good fortune throws me in your way, that these topics should be forborne between us. I have, long since, done with all inquiries on such subjects, and am become incapable of instruction; tho I own no one is more capable of conveying it than yourself. (*HL*, I, 351)

Hume apparently did not fear to address himself directly to any religious problem, but he did not want to be proselytized. Nothing is particularly ironic in either of the above quotations, except in the tone of the first. They do tell us, however, that among his friends of the "Moderate" clergy he could discuss religious differences frankly and openly.

One of those friends of the clergy was the Reverend John Jardine (1715–1766), who could return Hume's ironic sallies in the same fashion that Hume made them. Unfortunately, only one complete letter from Hume to Jardine is extant, but it can give us an idea of the good-natured relationship between the two. In discussing some arguments about a professorship for Adam Ferguson (1723–1816), Hume closes by telling his friend that he hopes he "will second these arguments with all your usual eloquence, by which you so successfully confound the devices of Satan, and bring sinners to repentence." In closing, Hume refers to himself as "Your most obsequious humble servant" (*HL*, I, 287), a closing he would not use in earnest. In a letter to Blair he relates a story about himself which Blair may communicate to Jardine, saying this of his friend:

I hope it will refute all his idle Notions, that I have no turn for Gallantry & Gaiety, that I am on a bad footing with the Ladies, that my turn of Conversation can never be agreeable to them, that I never can have any Pretensions to their Favours &c &c &c. A Man in Vogue will always have something to pretend to with the fair Sex. (*HL*, I, 438)

This agreeable pleasantry inspired his friend Jardine to a letter whose irony must have been the delight of Hume. It argues a relationship between them in which the ironic thrust and good-natured raillery formed the basis for many delightful times together. Consider this excerpt from a long letter to Hume:

I have attempted 4 or 5 times to write to you, But this poor Church has for some time past been in such Danger, that I could never find time for it. She had imployed all my Thoughts & Care for these 12 months past. The Enemy had kindled such a flame that the old burning bush was like to have been consumed altogether. I know it will give you pleasure to hear, that my Endeavours to preserve her, have been crownd wt Successe. She begins to shine furth wt her antient Lustre, & will very soon be, not only fair as the Sun, but to all her Enemies, terrible as an Army wt Banners. Ever since you left us all your Brn in the Regency have been in a state of Persecution; but God be thanked, the Tables are changed. It is in our Power now to persecute, which like orthodox Churchmen we shall not fail to do wt the outmost Rigor.

I beg you will notify this Resolution of ours to the Archbishop of Paris & the other Leaders of the Gallican Church. This will tend much to remove their prejudices against an Union wt our Church which we suppose is already in great forwardness in consequence of your Labours among them; of which we hear every day most favourable accounts.

The Regency here are of opinion, that you ought not to be too rigorous in your Terms of Accomodation. Proceed on the plan of Compromise. E. G. Tell them, if they will give up the Worship of Images, they shall be left at full Liberty to persecute. If they will part wt four or five Sacraments we will give up as many Commands. And wt respect to the Sacrament of Matrimony particularly, if they will renounce that, the Clergy by way of Indemnification shall be allowed to commit Adultery as often as they see it for their Edification or Amusement. From these few hints, you will easily percieve, in what manner we wish this Treaty of Union between the two Churches may be carried on. . . .

If they insist on having a Long Creed or Confession of Faith, consisting of many articles, I have no objection to it, provided that each of those articles be expressed so as not to be understood, and will affoord sufficient Matter of altercation among the Learned.

You know that my admonitions heretofore have done you much good. You often stood in need of them, and I am sorry to observe from some Passages in your letters to the Brethrn here, you stand very much in need of them at present. I clearly perceive, tho' you dont seem to have the least apprehension of it yourself, that you are in great danger of being seduced to

the Commission of the Sin of Uncleannesse. An inordinate Love of the fair
Sex, as I have often told you with Tears, is one of those Sins, that always,
even from your earliest Years, did most easily beset you. This is your weak
Side, Satan has at last discovered it, & on this unguarded Quarter, he is now
making his assault. He makes love to you, by assuming the most ensnaring of
all Forms, viz That of a fine Lady. Believe me, all those fine Ladys of Wit &
Beauty, you speak of with so much Rapture, are all Devils. I dont say, that
they have that antient visible Symbol of the demoniacal presence, by which
Satan was discovered in former times, viz the Cloven foot; The Devil is
grown a great deal more cunning than he was in the Days of our Forefathers,
and therefore that this diabolical Mark, may be the better concealed, he has
placed it more out of Sight; but tho' it is not now so easily seen as it was, yet
it may be as easily felt, if you make diligent Search for it. I beseech you consider seriously, what Dishonour it will reflect on your Character as an apostle
sent from the purest Church on Earth to convert the idolatrous Papists, if it
shall hereafter appear that during the Course of your Mission, you have been
carrying on a criminal Correspondence with French Succuba's. The great Reformer Luther has written very learnedly on this Subject in his Book called
Table Talk. I desire you to peruse the Chapter on Incubus & Succuba. (*HL*,
II, 352–353)

This delightful letter only makes us wish that more of Hume's correspondence with Jardine were extant. I quote it primarily as evidence of
the continuous manifestations of irony among Hume's friends. Its presence among his clerical friends indicates that Hume's scepticism, con-
joined with their piety, was not so strong-willed that friendly relations
were impossible. Instead, I should imagine that handling each other's
religious sentiments ironically made their friendship much more bear-
able and substantial. It is refreshing to note in this letter that Jardine
could return Hume's raillery with the best sort of ironic jibes at an
institution frequently the subject of Hume's criticism. Jardine's ingenious use of sexual humor in warning his friend that Satan had
finally found a way to control him must have brought uproarious
laughter. Its importance here, however, is that Jardine seems to recognize some of the legitimacy of Hume's criticisms of the church, and
he, following Hume's example, can treat them ironically. It is a clue
that suggests Hume's pronouncements upon the church and religion
in general were always tinged with irony and that his friends of the
cloth, recognizing this irony, were not likely to take seriously any

seeming professions of piety in his publications; and that they did recognize, however slightly, the force of Hume's arguments.

Irony in religion, I should argue, brings out the best in artistry, the best in scholarship, and the best in philosophy from David Hume. If this is true of some of the works we have already discussed, how much more true it must be of his finest work on religion, the *Dialogues concerning Natural Religion*. This is a book whose intellectual genealogy has yet to be fully studied,[6] but it is a book full of irony; the author frequently spoke about it in ironic terms while seeking for more than twenty years to have it published. Yet its tone and Hume's seemingly offhand treatment of it nonetheless portend a use of irony in discussing religious concepts on a scale quite unlike any of his previous writings on religion. It is one of his most carefully polished works, although it is only now achieving the reputation it deserves.

In order to keep in mind the background of the arguments, perhaps a preliminary summary would be helpful. The form is a dialogue with the following characters: Philo, the sceptic; Cleanthes, the empirical theologian who infers a theology from the order of nature; Demea, the rigidly orthodox, a priori theologian; and Pamphilus, the student narrator. The discussion is devoted to the source of religion and the analogy between the created world and the mind of a Deity. The identity of the various speakers in the *Dialogues* has been the subject of some conjecture and scholarship. Scholars will now usually agree that Philo represents Hume's general position, while Cleanthes represents Bishop Butler, or the "scientific" school of theologians, and Demea, perhaps Samuel Clarke.[7] Other identifications of the characters have been made, but the one of Hume as Philo is of primary importance.[8] It is from Philo that we hear arguments about the nature and being of a Deity which bear the Humean stamp.

---

[6] Books in which the *Dialogues concerning Natural Religion* has been discussed are countless, but the best is found in Norman Kemp Smith's introduction to his edition of the *Dialogues,* the text from which all quotations are taken. John Laird's, *Hume's Philosophy of Human Nature* also has a good discussion.

[7] See Ernest Campbell Mossner, "The Enigma of Hume," *Mind,* XLV (1936), 334–349.

[8] Early commentators, unlike some of their nineteenth-century and latter-day counterparts, were not fooled by the "victory" given to Cleanthes at the

In addition to this identification of the characters, considerable evidence exists that Hume modeled his *Dialogues* on Cicero's *De Natura Deorum*.[9] Ciceronian homologues should be considered when we are studying Hume's use of irony in the *Dialogues,* for they tell us about the characters' roles in the mechanics of the dialogue. For example, in Cicero's *De Natura Deorum* Pamphilus is mentioned as a certain disciple of Plato. In Hume's *Dialogues* the role of Pamphilus is that of minor narrator, and less than one per cent of the words come from him. As a strong antirationalist, Hume was not interested in promoting the Platonic view of life or nature, and much of his philosophy is an implicit, often explicit, attack on Platonism. When he assigns the role of minor narrator to a Platonist—giving him, in effect, a role greatly inferior to that he played in antiquity—we may suspect that something more than chance naming is at work. Add to this conjecture the knowledge that Hume's names for his characters have precise parallels in Cicero, as well as in Greek and Roman philosophy, and the probability increases that Pamphilus is a symbol for the Platonists, and that their reputation with Hume, to put it mildly, has waned. From that information, I would argue that one of the secondary purposes of irony in Hume's works is to make a wry suggestion about the lessened importance of the rationalistic position in the eighteenth century. It is, if you will, name calling at its most subtle and its very best. I say it is the best because of the economy it employs to achieve an important antirationalistic position. For Hume it was irony enough to give a Platonist an inferior role in his *Dialogues* and to let his readers infer from that his opinion of Platonism, or any other of the brand names on the shelf marked "Platonism."

---

conclusion of the *Dialogues.* See, for example, T. Hayter, *Remarks on Mr. Hume's Dialogues, concerning Natural Religion,* pp. 2–3: "The fact indeed indisputably is, that Philo, not Cleanthes, personates Mr. Hume. Cleanthes assumes at times . . . the tone of Demea: while Philo possesses in general the sole exclusive privilege of retailing the purport of Mr. Hume's former Philosophical productions.—Every remarkable trait and feature of those productions may be traced in the parts of the Dialogue assigned to Philo."

[9] See my two articles: "Empirical Theists in Cicero and Hume," *Texas Studies in Literature and Language,* V (1963), 255–264; and "Sceptics in Cicero and Hume," *The Journal of the History of Ideas,* XXV (1964), 97–106.

If Pamphilus is easily accounted for, the ending of Hume's *Dialogues,* which has often been cited as proof that Hume, after all, was a religious man, is apt to offer more pitfalls for the unwary. Let us look at that ending. Philo is speaking:

To be a philosophical sceptic is, in a man of letters, the first and most essential step towards being a sound, believing Christian; a proposition which I would willingly recommend to the attention of PAMPHILUS: And I hope CLEANTHES will forgive me for interposing so far in the education and instruction of his pupil.

CLEANTHES and PHILO pursued not this conversation much farther; and as nothing ever made greater impression on me, than all the reasonings of that day; so I confess, that, upon a serious review of the whole, I cannot but think, that PHILO's principles are more probable than DEMEA'S; but that those of CLEANTHES approach still nearer to the truth. (*Dialogues,* p. 228)

Aside from the irony of Philo's closing remark,[10] we may legitimately ask if Cleanthes really does get the best of the argument. If he does, then his is not the sort of argument—quantitatively or qualitatively— that most of us would want to underwrite. Even if Philo did accept the validity of Cleanthes' arguments (and he does not reject them *in toto*), the most elemental fact to remember about the exchange between Cleanthes and Philo is that Philo has approximately three times as much space as Cleanthes in the discussion. The proportions are as follows: Cleanthes, twenty-one per cent; Philo, sixty-seven per cent; and Demea, twelve per cent.[11] Quantitatively, we would hardly infer that Cleanthes had been the victor in the arguments, but, also, the quality of his reasoning is quite inferior to that of Philo, as Kemp Smith has argued. Even if the quantity were equal—or even the quality—it is still Pamphilus who makes that judgment. Pamphilus, the symbol of a school of philosophy whose ideas were philosophical anathema to Hume, would not be likely to let his sentiments fall in favor of the sceptic. Moreover, Cleanthes' views are much more empirically based than those of any

[10] Cf. Anthony Ashley Cooper, Third Earl of Shaftesbury, *Characteristics of Men, Manners, Opinions, Times,* II, 209: "I consider still that, in strictness, the Root of all is THEISM; and that to be a settled Christian, it is necessary to be first of all *a good* THEIST."

[11] Mossner in "The Enigma of Hume" makes the computations based on the page count given by J. Y. T. Greig in *David Hume,* pp. 236, 236 n.

Platonist, which re-enforces the ironic role played by Pamphilus. How much would an avowed antirationalist (Hume) value the judgment of a Platonist about the quality of a religious discussion?

The irony of Pamphilus' closing remark is more evident when we consider the arguments advanced by Philo against Cleanthes. How comforted would the devout be to read through the *Dialogues* only to discover that their cherished argument from design had been demolished? It is to be doubted that they would find much intellectual or emotional easement in the few words with which Hume so casually closes the discussion. That very casualness is what creates the irony: for it is nothing more than a condescending sop to the rigidly righteous, who, if they thought about the person speaking and about the superiority of Philo's reasoning, would realize the insult. Hume himself obviously did not think that Cleanthes had the better arguments, since he let a Platonist, a man for whom he had little philosophical or intellectual sympathy, pass judgment upon the discussion. To recognize, then, the irony of the ending of the *Dialogues,* the outside information which we require is knowledge of Hume's conviction that Platonist thinking was wrongheaded and misleading. Knowing this, we can question if he would, in earnest, permit a Platonist to pass unfavorable judgment on arguments he knew to be clearly superior to the ones favored by the Platonist. The closing of the *Dialogues,* therefore, is an example in which the words are inconsequential, since the technique and presentation suggest a larger meaning than a superficial reading would give. An ironic thrust at the pious, it is designed to tell the reader where the author stands, if the reader is willing to suspend judgment until he has some additional knowledge. Although not artistically necessary—Hume could have easily constructed an ending in which Philo's superiority was announced—it exhibits admirable artistic economy. The philosopher disposes of both the Platonist and the rigidly righteous at the same time, making the Platonist appear to be a fool for his incorrect judgment and mocking the rigidly righteous for not seeing the weaknesses of Cleanthes' arguments.

The *Dialogues* was not a book from which the pious or devout could take much comfort, although its appearance is deceiving. The title might lead one to believe it dealt with the naturalistic origins of religion; what actually occurs is different: a systematic attack on the argument from design and its related concepts. Not only that, but any supernatural, a priori arguments about the nature and being of God are discounted by Cleanthes, the empirical theologian whose naturalistic approach to religion is repugnant to Demea. Philo's approach is markedly superior to that of Cleanthes and is everywhere damaging to any defense of religion on naturalistic grounds.

In spite of the superiority of Philo's philosophical position, he professes belief in God and his goodness at various places in the *Dialogues*. Are we to take these professions seriously, or may we ignore them? For example, consider the opening paragraph, in which the reader is given the immutable "truth" on which the discussion is predicated:

> What truth so obvious, so certain, as the *being* of a God, which the most ignorant ages have acknowledged, for which the most refined geniuses have ambitiously striven to produce new proofs and arguments? What truth so important as this, which is the ground of all our hopes, the surest foundation of morality, the firmest support of society, and the only principle which ought never to be a moment absent from our thoughts and meditations? But in treating of this obvious and important truth; what obscure questions occur, concerning the *nature* of that divine Being; his attributes, his decrees, his plan of providence? (*Dialogues*, p. 128)

Why should the recommendation that the "most ignorant ages" have acknowledged the being of a God carry so much weight? Surely it would be a much better recommendation if the most *enlightened* ages had acknowledged his being. Even if the phrase is stylistically an antithetical balance to the one which follows, no violence to style would have been done if Hume had substituted "intelligent" for "ignorant." Knowing Hume as we do, we would probably be correct if we argued that this passage was qualified in a way calculated to hide its irony from the faithful, while the irony revealed the true importance of the words. It is only one word, but it gives us a clue to the second and much more important level of meaning that Hume is aiming at. By picking up this clue we can discover further evidence that the above passage is not an acquiescence to the rigidly righteous, but is instead a sly rebuke to them.

If this line of reasoning seems to be pushing a point too far, let us remember that these words come from our Platonist, Pamphilus. A

Platonist would probably want to start with the assumptions Pamphilus outlined; a sceptic would not be willing to take anything for granted. As a sceptic, Philo would not be likely to make the assertions Pamphilus does, but we would certainly have to reconsider the ending if he did close the *Dialogues* with the preceding quotation. We know, however, enough about Hume's opinion of Platonists to overlook any literal interpretation. Technically, the conduct of Pamphilus' arguments is ironic. A weak and (to Hume) philosophically ignominious character affirms what is indisputable; yet this supposedly indisputable ground is mangled beyond recognition. By the time the friendly discussion concludes, Hume has accomplished just the opposite of what Pamphilus expected, although, to judge from the final words of the *Dialogues,* Pamphilus was too dense to recognize it. Even as a Platonist, he is making some awkward concessions when he thinks that Cleanthes' arguments are more probable than Philo's. From the opening statement to the closing statement, much happens that would not sit well philosophically with a Platonist. Not even Cleanthes accepted the obvious certainty of the being of a God; yet Pamphilus, who at the beginning of the essay found that "truth" so obvious, thinks at the end that Cleanthes was the victor. The irony of this conclusion of affairs in the *Dialogues* is attributed, I think, to the skill with which Pamphilus' pretensions and presuppositions are deflated as the conversation progresses.

Assertions about the certainty of God's existence appear throughout the *Dialogues,* one of the most interesting ones coming in Part III:

By the whole tenor of your discourse, one would imagine that you were maintaining the being of a God, against the cavils of atheists and infidels; and were necessitated to become a champion for that fundamental principle of all religion. But this, I hope, is not by any means a question among us. No man; no man, at least, of common sense, I am persuaded, ever entertained a serious doubt with regard to a truth so certain and self-evident. The question is not concerning the *being* but the *nature* of *God*. This, I affirm, from the infirmities of human understanding, to be altogether incomprehensible and unknown to us. The essence of that supreme mind, his attributes, the manner of his existence, the very nature of his duration; these and every particular, which regards so divine a Being, are mysterious to men. Finite, weak, and blind creatures, we ought to humble ourselves in his august presence, and, conscious of our frailties, adore in silence his infinite perfections, which eye hath not seen, ear hath not heard, neither hath it entered into the heart of man to conceive them. They are covered in a deep cloud from human curiosity: It is profaneness to attempt penetrating through these sacred obscurities: And next to the impiety of denying his existence, is the temerity of prying into his nature and essence, decrees and attributes. (*Dialogues*, p. 141)

This extravagant statement, with its Biblical rhetoric, is neither from Philo nor Cleanthes, but from Demea, the incurable dogmatist who leaves the discusion when he sees it is not going his way. That alone would be sufficient to pass judgment upon the function of Demea: he is an object of satire. He is given the worst arguments, the most illiberal temper, and the least reasoning ability. When both Cleanthes and Philo insist on some sense impression of God before they could agree about his existence, Demea replies with this mumbo jumbo about a Deity eye has not seen, ear has not heard—in fact, a Deity not even conceived. If it is not possible to conceive God or his infinite perfections, how in the world can we be sure of his existence? Having no idea whatsoever of God and yet believing in him—or, better, it—is worse than having the wrong ideas about a God that might in fact exist. Even the rigidly righteous would not be attracted to this essentially irreligious position, since it is based on an obvious contradiction, a belief in something that cannot be conceived. The ironic mode is created both by the extravagant illogic and by the character of Demea, because both are considerably more than a stone's throw away from even the least empirical theologian. Hume certainly could not have embraced Demea's position, but he successfully caricatures a kind of unthinking religious fever that persists even to our own time.

The characters of Philo and Cleanthes are sufficiently well established in the *Dialogues* to prove that they would not make a statement anything like Demea's. If Philo did, however, make a concession to a theological position some difficult problems would arise, since it would not be in line with the reasoning he follows. Such an assertion from Philo about the existence of God does in fact appear almost immediately after Demea's statement:

After so great an authority, DEMEA, replied PHILO, as that which you have produced, and a thousand more, which you might produce, it would appear ridiculous in me to add my sentiment, or express my approbation of your doctrine. But surely, where reasonable men treat these subjects, the question can never be concerning the *being* but only the *nature* of the Deity. The former truth, as you well observe, is unquestionable and self-evident. Nothing exists without a cause; and the original cause of this universe (whatever it be) we call GOD; and piously ascribe to him every species of perfection. (*Dialogues*, p. 142)

Here we need to employ the sceptical approach that Philo himself has used throughout the *Dialogues* and ask just what "authority" Philo-Hume is referring to. The only "authority" that Demea has produced has been in the form of rhapsodies about the Deity, a priori propositions, and nonempirical reasoning. Since Philo does not accept "authority" of this type anywhere else in the *Dialogues,* it is curious that he would do so here. If the authority is uncertain, it is certain that Philo would appear something more than merely "ridiculous" if he approved of Demea's doctrine. Where Demea might interpret the word "ridiculous" to mean "useless," we may well take it literally. Philo-Hume has throughout the discussion carefully expunged any contradictions, a priori judgments, or rhapsodies about the perfection of a Deity who is essentially inconceivable. It is impossible to believe that he would now accept such illogical reasonings, when he has assiduously excluded them before. The word "ridiculous," then, is to be taken literally, a reversal of the usual ironic mode when the literal appearance of the word is not the actual meaning. But Philo-Hume means for Demea to interpret the word to mean "useless," as it would normally seem to in that context. Instead, it forms an ironic commentary on the profession of faith that we had from Demea, who has, apparently, been omitted from the realm of "reasonable men" mentioned in the same sentence.

Still, we might wonder about the value of Philo's words. I do not think they can be interpreted as a statement of faith, because of the inherent contradiction in them, a contradiction which, I feel sure, Hume put in for a specific purpose. Philo does agree that we never question the being of the Deity, only his nature. But we discover that the Deity is a Deity in name only, for the word "Deity" is merely a convenient name we ascribe to the original cause of the universe, *whatever it be.* (And it could very well have been a spider, as Philo argues later.) Those three words throw an entirely different light on the interpretation, for they make clear that Philo is not willing to agree that the Christian, anthropomorphic God was the first cause. To Demea the Deity is wonderful, supernatural, perfect, mysterious, all-knowing (although inconceivable by human beings), and infinite; to the laconic Philo it is nothing but a name given to the cause of the universe, and that cause could be, literally, anything under the sun. Philo later speculates about the universe's being a spider or a vegetable, suggestions not entirely in accord with man's usual notions about the Deity.

Finally, the last sentence of the quotation ("Nothing exists without a cause; and the original cause of this universe [whatever it be] we call God; and piously ascribe to him every species of perfection."), with its emphasis on piety, is an unfavorable comment on the habit of identifying all good with the Deity, whether there be any rationale for it or not. Hume's use of the word "pious" (or any of its forms) is almost invariably ironic, and we can imagine the wry smile on his lips as he penned the word. When no universal agreement on what was perfect and what was not could be had, any ascription of a certain perfection to the Deity was fraught with danger. These reasons alone would be sufficient for us to recognize the ironic intent of Philo's seeming agreement about the being of God. What good to a theist is an agreement about the being of God when the sceptic uses the word in an entirely different sense?

Another reason for thinking Hume ironic presents itself; in the passage immediately following, some Miltonian personal elements break in: "Whoever scruples this fundamental truth deserves every punishment, which can be inflicted among philosophers, to wit, the greatest ridicule, contempt, and disapprobation" (*Dialogues,* p. 142). Hume himself had suffered throughout his life from ridicule from the orthodox clergy, from the lunatic fringe, and from other types of Christian charity. The language here is completely ironic, for few men in the eighteenth century suffered as much social obloquy for their religious beliefs as did David Hume. Even the mere knowledge that he was writing a tract on "natural religion" was enough to provoke unfavorable comment and vituperative disapprobation from the lunatic and even the orthodox clergy. The superficial meaning of the words here is the exact contrary of what Hume means. He could hardly have been insensitive to the attack made upon his moral character by the pious, but he evidently could use their venom with a light heart when he needed to. Having the good fortune to realize his innate intellectual and moral superiority to them, he could admit some disturbance at their carpings, but he more frequently than not made the sort of mental adjustment that enabled him to turn their invective to irony. Consequently, he could use their attacks in an ironic mode and could achieve a greater effect by irony than they ever could by arguments *ad hominem*. If we consider the two preceding quotations together, the inescapable conclusion is that Hume is employing one of the ironist's favorite devices, that of blame-by-praise. By seeming to praise Demea and seeming to blame those of a sceptical turn of mind, he criticized the illiberal religionists who would have everything their way, or not at all.

Demea realizes later on that Philo is actually not in agreement with his basic principle, and that Philo will have nothing to do with a priori proofs of the existence of God. The existence of God, regardless of what the surface of Philo's words may have implied, is exactly the subject under question. The irony lies in Demea's misinterpretation of Philo's words and in Philo's skill at mocking the most revered concepts of the traditionalists while also undermining the arguments of the scientific theologian, Cleanthes. It is a two-pronged attack that admits much less than it actually seems to.

In view of the ironic ambiguity that afflicts any alleged confessions of faith in the *Dialogues,* we would naturally be on our guard when finding them. Some of these have been cited by nineteenth-century scholars to prove that Philo-Hume really accepted the notion of a Divine Being. A profession of faith which seems most obvious occurs toward the end of the *Dialogues,* in Part XII:

I must confess, replied PHILO, that I am less cautious on the subject of natural religion than on any other; both because I know that I can never, on that head, corrupt the principles of any man of common sense, and because no one, I am confident, in whose eyes I appear a man of common sense, will ever mistake my intentions. You, in particular, CLEANTHES, with whom I live in unreserved intimacy; you are sensible, that, notwithstanding the freedom of my conversation, and my love of singular arguments, no one has a deeper sense of religion impressed on his mind, or pays more profound adoration to the divine Being, as he discovers himself to reason, in the inexplicable contrivance and artifice of nature. A purpose, an intention, or design strikes everywhere the most careless, the most stupid thinker; and no man can be so hardened in absurd systems, as at all times to reject it. (*Dialogues*, p. 214)

Again, careful attention to the choice of words will reveal more than the seeming reassurance to be derived from a superficial reading. That Hume had a deep sense of the human value of religion impressed on his mind I do not question. But to have a deep sense of religion impressed on one's mind does not logically imply that one is deeply religious. Hume, like all good sceptics, was interested in examining religion for any truth he might find in it; his mind was far-ranging and not limited to dry abstractions from technical philosophy. The deep sense of religion that he had is one that questioned the truth of religious absolutes. Religious absolutes must also discover themselves to reason, a qualification to his profession that excludes Divine Beings who are the products of a priori theorizing. Already he has ruled out a considerable majority of the arguments advanced in favor of the existence of a Deity. One of Hume's modern admirers, Norman Kemp Smith, has remarked about this particular passage in his edition of the *Dialogues*:

Philo's terms, in the second of the above confessions of faith, are more "artfully" chosen than at first sight appears. The God here avowed is an object of adoration *transcending* our powers of comprehension; the "contrivance and artifice of nature" is *inexplicable*. Philo adds, indeed, the phrase *"as he discovers himself to reason"*; but only, as the sequel shows, in order to point out that the Deity thus revealed is not to be equated with the God of religion; and so to withdraw nearly all that he has seemed to allow.[12]

The procedure Kemp Smith describes is typically Humean; when the philosopher most seems to be assenting to a religious proposition, he qualifies it so stringently as to make the initial proposition meaningless. Moreover, Hume's personal sentiments are again in the open in the last line of the quotation ("A purpose, an intention, or design

[12] *Dialogues,* p. 70. For Hume's expression that the arguments are artfully chosen see *HL,* II, 334 and 334 n.

strikes everywhere the most careless, the most stupid thinker; and no man can be so hardened in absurd systems, as at all times to reject it."). Not only had Hume been accused of being a wicked, impious man, but his philosophy had been called stupid and careless by such small fry as James Beattie and James Oswald (*fl.* 1766), who precipitously got into print with answers to Hume, accusing him of indulging in absurd systems. Knowing all this, we would be rash to think that Hume would have the hero of his *Dialogues* castigate those who would question not only the nature but the being of the Deity. Hume had elsewhere criticized the notion of God's being, and it is unlikely that he would here condemn those who had done what he so honestly did. Since the argument that he imagined himself more as Philo than as any other of the characters in the *Dialogues* is as strong as it is, we would not expect him to indulge in hypocritical self-criticism. Only a self-effacing masochist, from which Hume was considerably removed, would be inclined to censure his own views with the very terms by which such parasites as Beattie had described him. He would not, as a matter of personal behavior, have written the above lines with a straight face, and he recognized the irony inherent in ostensibly calling himself by those epithets his malefactors had so gratuitously bestowed on him.

In addition to the personal elements in the quotation which hint to us that Hume is saying the opposite of what he means, one of the other characteristics of irony is also present—ambiguity. All is well, until that phrase "no man can be so hardened as at all times to reject it [design]." The implication is that even a man hardened in absurd systems can at some times accept the argument from design; that is, no one is so foolish as to be always convinced of the invalidity of the argument from design. If he is convinced of the invalidity of that argument, it means the argument is not absolute and immutable; if it were, we would instantly apprise its logical impeccability and unquestionable validity. Philo's phrase, however, implies that the argument from design is capable of being accepted at some times, rejected at others, which leads us to wonder about the immutability and perfection of a Deity whose being can be rejected at some times, accepted at others. A Deity whose attributes are so inconstant as this, whose design sometimes convinces, sometimes does not, is not the sort either

Demea or Cleanthes has in mind when using the term "God." Could they accept the being of a Deity who could be rejected or accepted willy-nilly? Hume knew that they would not, for permanence or immutability were two of the most highly touted absolutes of the Deity. The injection of some ambiguous allusion to part-time acceptance of this immutability, would vastly weaken any concession which seemed to come from Philo. It might serve the double purpose of convincing the faithful, while providing the doubters or sceptics—who were somehow more perspicacious than the theists—with a clue to Hume's real meaning: if the existence of God can be doubted for any considerable time, then it is an existence whose evidence is not enough to convince an empiricist.

Two considerations unite to apprise us of Hume's use of irony here: (1) the ambiguity of part of Philo's admission of "faith"; and (2) the out-of-character asperity by which he deprecates sceptics and doubters. While the second piece of information is not absolutely necessary to detect the ironic tone, it is an aid because we know that Hume himself unreservedly held nontheistic positions and was personally offended whenever called "careless" or "stupid thinker" as a result of the honesty of his doubts or convictions. Philo does not anywhere in the *Dialogues* employ the type of language used by Hume's detractors. As a reconstruction of the Humean philosophical viewpoint, Philo would probably not use such epithets to describe the range and line of his own arguments, unless he meant them ironically. No man is so contemptuous of his own deeply held convictions that he will call them stupid or careless just to placate some orthodoxy, without making at least a mental reservation and usually, as in the example from Hume, loading the concession with ambiguity.

It will readily be seen that I am applying a unitary judgment to Philo; that is, I am evaluating his position by the bulk and import of all that he says in the *Dialogues,* not by a few scattered lines of seeming piety. Naturally, other examples of Philo's professions of piety exist, although not quite so strong as the ones I have quoted. But the great bulk of his argument, as well as the passion, conviction, and enthusiasm with which he presents it, lead us to what should not be a surprising observation: that the ostensible professions of piety are strategic. Hume grants the first step because the second step cannot be made. Hence, the pledges of affirmation are ironic since Hume is assenting to a meaningless proposition. The articulation of a premise beyond which one cannot go is epistemologically pointless, and Hume is no more serious about these concessions to piety than Bishop Butler would have been in establishing a College of Atheism. The function of these seeming "concessions" is to supply the religionist with some warm sentiment to cling to; but if he examines that sentiment closely, he will discover that the warmth is artificial.

Thus, the professions of piety in Hume's *Dialogues* are strategically ironic and should not be taken seriously. We have, however, examined only isolated material, and not the *Dialogues* as a whole. As a unity we may well inquire whether it serves any of the functions of irony as we normally think of them. To answer this query, we might consider Hume's attitude toward his late work. (The autobiography is, in fact, his "last work," but it is never referred to as such.) Hume was aware that the subject under discusion and the method of handling it would not sit well with the vast majority of religious or rationalistic thinkers of his time, and that the ecclesiastical drummers would want it suppressed, burned, or in any manner kept from the populace—or even from less orthodox clergymen. Hume took a good-humored view of all this opposition, or so one would gather in a letter written in 1763 to Sir Gilbert Elliot (1722–1777), whose religion was somewhat more orthodox than Hume's:

> Is it not hard & tyrannical in you, more tyrannical than any Act of the Stuarts, not to allow me to publish my Dialogues? Pray, do you think a proper Dedication may atone for what is exceptional in them? I am much become of my friend, Corbyn Morrice's Mind, who says, that he writes all his books for the sake of the Dedications. (*NHL*, p. 71)

This good-natured raillery suggests the reaction Hume expected—and posthumously received—from the publication of his *Dialogues*. (It would be convenient to think that the word "Pray" has an especial irony, but it occurs too often in Hume's correspondence to assume that.) To the Reverend Hugh Blair (1718–1800), who also urged Hume not to publish the work, he wrote: "I have no present thoughts of publishing the work you mention; but when I do, I hope you have no objection of my dedicating it to you" (*NHL*, p. 72). The consternation of Blair, or even Elliot, at finding a notorious piece of scepticism dedicated to him is pleasant to imagine. More important, however, than our amusement is the information the above letters give us about Hume's attitude. I should imagine if he were making jests of this type with his clerical friends, he was probably relishing the prospect of horror from the religious right. They had to be on their toes against so formidable an adversary as Hume, and, to continue this improbable metaphor, I imagine many of them were floored with a knockout blow of whose efficacy they were sceptical.

What would appear as professions of faith in the *Dialogues,* then, are not concessions to the pious; loaded with ambiguity, they are instead ironic counterthrusts to those who would demand uniform faith and piety from all, under penalty of social obloquy or, sometimes, hanging. Hume would appear to yield to the demands of the pious and admit the existence of the sort of Deity in whom a belief was necessary. Faced with the prospect of making a living in a society whose views on religion were greatly at variance with his own, he had to be discreet and to mask his true feelings in irony; thus he deceived those who were stupid enough to be deceived. Working in this complex of social conditions, his irony had many functions.

The most obvious function, mentioned above, was that of self-protection, in spite of the fact that the *Dialogues* was published after his death. It was written during his lifetime and Hume contemplated publishing it for a number of years before his death. Under the guise of subtle irony he could, if you will, have his cake and eat it too. Although this irony afforded him some protection from the rigidly righteous, it also served a deeper purpose. It enabled him to use the very words of his critics in an ironic mode, which, as a result of that ironic mode, gave them back better than Hume had received from them. It was not only a personal triumph to use their own words against them, it was an artistic triumph; the criticism, instead of knocking Hume off the perch of scepticism, boomeranged. The clerics who were intelligent enough to perceive Hume's irony and appreciate it discovered an even more serious criticism of their dogmas than they had imagined. It was bad enough to have one's favorite arguments supporting the existence of God demolished, but it was even worse to have one's own words call attention to the vapidity of those arguments.

If the clerics recognized the justness of the criticism, they knew that
they would have to deal with Hume on philosophical grounds, where
he was apt to have the advantage. By dramatizing the illogic and invalidity of certain religious arguments, for example, the argument
from design, Hume made an attack on their position from which re-
covery, if possible was absolutely necessary if religion was to have any
intellectual importance. Consequently, an appeal to religious prejudice,
name calling, and atheist baiting had to be ruled out as answers to
Hume. The intelligent, moderate clergy recognized that he had
weakened any naturalistic argument about the being of God, that
what was thought to be an empirical certainty was an error in logic.
Too, they would see that his ironic professions of faith were themselves criticisms both of their theology and the social applications they
attempted to give it. They had to find some way of answering Hume
on his own ground, or they would become intellectually disrespectable.
Hence, another of the functions of Hume's religious irony was to
force the theologians to find an intelligent answer—if indeed there
was one—to his attack.

The delayed publication of the *Dialogues concerning Natural Religion* constitutes an irony in itself, although it is representative of the
concern—genuine and spurious—exhibited by Hume's acquaintances
and friends for the ultimate disposition of his immortal soul. Ordinarily worried about Hume's ironic treatment of and approach to
religion, Hume's friends became even more worried when Hume's
death was imminent. The demise of a man who had courted lightning
bolts from heaven all his life portended an event which, had some
former-day Barnum been around, would have resulted in speculation
about his destination that not even Hume, in another lifetime of scepticism, could have quashed. His friends did fear for his soul; his enemies
were probably less worried, since they figured he would get what he
deserved;[13] unless, of course, one of them hoped to increase his own

[13] A particularly interesting abuse of Hume is found in [Bishop George
Horne], *A Letter to Adam Smith LL.D. on the Life, Death, and Philosophy
of his Friend David Hume, Esq.,* "By One of the People called Christians."
John Wesley, in Sermon CXXII, "On the Deceitfulness of the Human Heart,"
said of Hume: "Did David Hume, lower, if possible, than either of the former

stature by bringing the great infidel to a death-bed conversion, so popular in Hume's day as well as our own. That desire, incidentally, was the hope of more than one preacher. Hume's death, however, was a triumph of reason and irony over superstition and fear. Nosey James Boswell called twice on the philosopher while he was dying, only to be treated—although he little realized it—with ironic good nature when he inquired about the possibility of life after death and the nature of purgatory. Boswell, although not a religious stalwart himself, hoped to bring the light to Hume, a feat which he accomplished posthumously; in a dream of 1784, eight years after Hume died, Hume's fidelity to the Christian religion was confirmed, at least to Boswell's satisfaction, if not to anyone else's.[14]

Boswell may have been satisfied several years later that Hume died a Christian; none of the clerics of his time, however, were successful in making a believer of Hume. He steadfastly resisted all pleas for conversion; he was angered when Mrs. Mure told him he should burn his "wee bookies." The agonies of hell so vividly described by many a preacher of Hume's day could usually be counted on to bring around any recalcitrant. Hume was not simply recalcitrant; he was unsure of the accuracy of the religionists' descriptions, especially since empirical proof was lacking. If anything was to be committed to the flames, it was not likely to be he, Hume thought. The flames, though, were the

---

[Lord C—— and Sir R——; otherwise unidentified], know the heart of man? No more than a worm or beetle does. After 'playing so idly with the darts of death,' do you now find it a laughing matter? What do you now think of Charon? Has he ferried you over Styx? At length has he taught you to know a little of your own heart! At length you know, it is a fearful thing to fall into the hands of the living God!" John Wesley, *Works*, VII, 342.

[14] See *Private Papers of James Boswell from Malahide Castle*, ed. by G. Scott and F. A. Pottle, XVI, 20–21. Boswell writes: "awaked after a very agreable dream that I had found a Diary kept by David Hume, from which it appeared that though his vanity made him publish treatises of skepticism and infidelity, he was in reality a Christian and a very pious Man. He had, I imagined, quieted his mind by thinking that whatever he might appear to the World to show his talents, his religion was between GOD and his own conscience. (I cannot be sure if this thought was in sleep.) I thought I read some beautiful passages in his Diary. I am not certain whether I had this dream thursday night or friday night. But after I awaked, it dwelt so upon my mind that I could not for some time perceive that it was only a fiction."

end envisioned for Hume by many people—unless he made the conversion they confidently (at first) expected. But the eighteenth-century Savonarolas were reckoning without the force and power of Hume's scepticism; the regrets he might have had about not professing faith —and I doubt that he had any—he kept to himself. He was an empiricist to the last, and his preparation for death was shot through with irony.

Preparation for death is probably no easy matter. For a young man it is not quite imaginable; "no young man believes he shall ever die," says Hazlitt. But for a man of Hume's age it was a task more readily faced, and he acknowledged in his letters to his friends that he was within a few days of his own death. He knew of his illness for several months, and he prepared for it as rationally as a man might perform a scientific experiment. There were no spectacles, no weepings, no cursings of fate, no recriminations, no lapses of sanity, no feverish prayers—nothing, in short, any different from the way his life had proceeded for sixty-five years. That alone should be sufficient testament to the triumph of reason over superstition. He let his clerical friends have their say, and he calmly ignored their advice. They may have been expecting a final admission from Hume, a hope that he would not spend eternity in purgatory; they thought they were in on a secret and that Hume would want to share it. But the "Age of Reason" had a man of integrity until his last breath. Although his "passions" might have suggested that some discreet prayers would have been the better part of discretion, reason was the guide to those passions, and reason was not apt to believe in the efficacy of death-bed conversions. When he died, he died quietly and without fanfare, as the irony of fate would have it.[15]

Literature is not the exclusive domain of irony. It is far-ranging and restless, unlikely to be confined within the relatively narrow bounds of literature. In our study of the use and function of irony in Hume's life and writings, we have seen it appear as a criticism of life (includ-

[15] The conclusion of Hume's autobiography may be taken as his final statement about the importance of his life: "I cannot say, there is no Vanity in making this funeral Oration of myself; but I hope it is not a misplac'd one; and this is a Matter of Fact which is easily cleared and ascertained."

ing religion, politics, and the "weak, pious sex"), as a recognition of the irony of life, and as a mimetic reproduction of life. Hume's reasons for using irony point to some new ideas about his life and thought that will be, I hope, helpful to the student of the history of ideas.

Hume was certainly no Swift in his mastery of the form of irony, and it is not the purpose of this book to contend that he is a sadly neglected ironist of the eighteenth century who learned much and taught much about irony in a literary age dominated by that form of expression. Hume was cognizant of his own literary limitations, but the talents he did have he strove to improve, as he says in his autobiography: "I resolved . . . to regard every object as contemptible, except the Improvement of my Talents in Literature." Irony as a device and as a perception of crosscurrents in human endeavor is not so much a literary form with him as a way of life. While he may write ironically of certain suggestions and certain imperfections of the human race, his greater interest lies in the irony of life, in those events which represent a conflict between appearance and reality, between words and deeds, between promise and performance.

Throughout our study we have noticed several examples of irony that are not literary. These were examples of Hume's perception of some of the phenomena in human nature that led men to do unreasonable things. Hume saw man dissociating himself from reality, fooling himself by thinking that A was not A (or thinking that the statement "A is not not A" was a great scientific truth) or that words were deeds. The gap between what men said and what men did puzzled him, but it amused him more than it distressed him. As far as he could see, no actual harm accrued to the person who finally convinced himself that A was not A, from the force of will rather than the force of logic. Hume himself was aware of these crosscurrents of motivation, of the irony of the alternatives chosen in life. In himself the logical processes of scepticism may have brought him to the brink of nihilism or solipsism, but human nature could not make the jump. Logically, Hume thought, it might be impossible for him to know the certainty of any event in the future, but he always acted as if many events were certain. The irony that resulted from this conflict between logical uncertainty and psychological certainty was not the source of gloom and doom. Instead, the philosopher enjoyed this irony of life, feeling that a life controlled and established by inexorable future events was a life too dull, literally, for contemplation.

But how did Hume *use* this perception of the irony of life in his writings? What is its guiding function? One of its possible uses, of course, is to call the attention of other intelligent human beings to the ironic doubleness in human life. Men may very well believe that their words represent their actual beliefs, but they do not recognize that their actions are considerably different from their words. If they could perceive the irony in their words and their actions, they could possibly make the necessary changes that would create harmony between their words and actions. Such a resolution of conflict would not always be possible in all manifestations of the conflict. In other circumstances the perception of the irony in life could function to remind man that, to paraphrase, amidst all his philosophy or religion, he must direct his efforts toward the improvement of human nature. If nothing else, perhaps man could see that any philosophy or religion was barren and useless unless it had some application to the better understanding of human nature. Finally, and most importantly, we see Hume's acceptance of an ironic doubleness in human life as something inherent and probably permanent in human nature. It was not necessary to explain away these ironies of life, but to accept them as part of living and to enjoy them as irony. If one tribe of people thought cows were sacred and another thought them useful only when fattened, slaughtered, and roasted, then, Hume suggested, man should recognize this difference as no more than that, not as a symptom of immorality or impiety. That men should fight wars over such puny differences both amused and distressed Hume; but when these differences occurred on a smaller scale, he was more amused than distressed.

Hume amused himself most frequently with ironic thrusts at and ironic parodies of religious fervor, of dogmatic arguments about the nature and being of God, and of pretensions to intelligence by religionists. To the intelligent man religion, if it restricted man's inquiries into human nature by binding him to superstition and unreasonable beliefs, could do more harm than good. To the ignorant man religion could do more good than harm, primarily if it forced upon the "vulgar" a set of morals that induced them to keep peace with their fellow men. The ignorant dogmatists of the religious right were a source of constant amusement to Hume; what distressed him was the intelligent theologian whose logic was more than slightly askew. But the religionist, the theologian, and the pietistic evangelist were all the objects of his irony. The intellectuals had their a priori theorizing subjected to acute empirical analysis followed by an ironic apology for any harm that may have been done to "true religion." The dogmatists or the zealous ecclesiastics had their ridiculous assertions solemnly accepted by a philosopher with tongue in cheek. To Hume it was a double pleasure to let the fanatics think he was assenting to their views, for it spared him the necessity of unpleasant vituperation and allowed him the satisfaction of knowing that they little realized just how adroitly their legs had been pulled. This ironic treatment of religion worked in several ways. He hoped that the intelligent theologians would see that his ironic criticism of their views was the result of his belief in the illogic by which such views were derived, not the simple-minded carpings of the village atheist. With the dogmatists irony effectively shielded him from "the slings and arrows of outrageous fortune." With his clerical friends irony was a way in which undesirable proselytizing could be avoided.

Hume's religious irony is quantitatively and qualitatively greater than any of his other uses of irony. It appears in the *Treatise of Human Nature,* in almost any of his essays, in the *History of England,* and most prominently in the *Dialogues concerning Natural Religion.* Religion, the subject of continued scrutiny throughout Hume's life, can be counted upon to bring a reaction from him more quickly than any other subject. In print his reaction to any religious provocation was frequently cast in an ironic mode, as we have seen in just a few of many possible examples. In private correspondence, especially to his close friends, he delighted in pricking bubbles blown out of their religious soap pipes. His friends could reciprocate, as Jardine did, with the sort of ability to make light of both Hume's achievements and their own. It would be hard to say which particular form of irony Hume enjoyed more, that in personal correspondence or that in his published writings. I should imagine that he enjoyed the published irony more, since it struck home so directly.

Even if his published religious irony was his favorite form, he was not unique in Restoration and eighteenth-century literature. Samuel Butler and Jonathan Swift, amidst a host of pious reformers, mocked religion with as great assiduity, though with different purpose, as Hume did. They, of course, worked from one spoke of the religious wheel, satirizing and pasquinading the rest of the wheel. Hume's approach differed from theirs in only one respect, but it is a significant one. To continue our metaphor, Hume worked from outside the wheel, lampooning all forms of religion, accepting none, favoring none. For that reason his ironic discussion or handling of religious problems was often resented much more than the irony of others. Thus, in this one respect he is unique as a religious ironist in the eighteenth century: a man with impressive intellectual credentials, with impeccable moral standards, with a benevolent disposition who nevertheless thought of religion only in terms that were epistemologically unacceptable to him at the least, totally unacceptable at the most.

This ironic method of handling religious concepts is more important when we remember Hume's beliefs in the efficacy of any religion were lost when he was a young man, before he was eighteen. He gave up his beliefs reluctantly, as we gather from this letter of 10 March 1751 to his friend Gilbert Elliott:

And tis not long ago that I burn'd an old Manuscript Book, wrote before I was twenty; which contain'd, Page after Page, the gradual Progress of my Thoughts on that head. It begun with an anxious Search after Arguments, to confirm the common Opinion: Doubts stole in, dissipated, return'd, were again dissipated, return'd again; and it was a perpetual Struggle of a restless Imagination against Inclination, perhaps against Reason. (*HL*, I, 154)

At approximately the same time that he was writing these manuscript notes, which he regrettably burned, his *Treatise* was taking shape, and its details had begun to fall in place; it was probably completed by the time he was twenty-five. Thus, it would be naïve to say that Hume's opposition to religion represented the reaction of immature thought to immutable precepts, since this early disposition only grew in scope as his years progressed.

Considering the extent and depth of his ironic treatment of religion along with his early loss of religious sentiment and subsequent organization of his thoughts into the unity that produced the *Treatise*, we may well wonder if there is not a causal relationship between the two. I think there is, and it is extremely useful to the student who wishes to study Hume's philosophy as a unity. The origin of his philosophy, considered on this ground, would be in his early religious scepticism and his lack of faith. Professor Norman Kemp Smith, in his excellent study of Hume's philosophy, has argued that the portions of the *Treatise* dealing with moral problems were conceived first, and that it was Hume's preoccupation with ethics that led him into other branches of philosophy. Although Kemp Smith produces no real evidence to prove that the last part of the *Treatise*, which deals with moral problems, was written first, he argues that moral problems interested Hume first and led him into his philosophy. Certainly no one would deny that Hume's insistence upon benevolence as the spring that activated human morality pervaded all of his life and thought. Professor Smith's view is, I think, generally correct, but only when supplemented by a knowledge of Hume's lack of religious beliefs. It was, in fact, dissatisfaction with the answers to moral problems offered by religion that led Hume to read the pagan philosophers in order to consolidate his views on ethics. Finding religion incapable of solving problems of knowledge and morality, he abjured it and sought a synthesis of morality and knowledge based upon empirical reasoning.

Religious irony plays a greater role in his writings than "moral irony" could ever hope to play. Not only is he more ironic in discussing religion, but religion was the first intellectual discipline he discarded. Discarding religion, which formed the strong support of morality for many a pious Scot of his time, led him, as a philosopher, to seek some more reasonable basis for morality, a basis that would introduce experimental reasoning into the science of human nature. As he sought this reasonable basis for morality, he became more and more convinced of the fraud perpetrated (at least on him) by religion when it claimed more efficacy, more judgment, and more morality than it had any good right to do. But he realized that it carried the weight of tradition, and even a very determined young man would not stamp it out overnight. Is it not just probable, then, that Hume found himself inclined to treat religion ironically whenever the subject came up, especially where any concesssions to superstition, miracles, a priori theorizing, or God's existence were concerned?

Since religion forms the core of one of his most important essays, "Of Miracles," and since the reasoning in that essay is so greatly similar to the reasoning he employed throughout his life, I should argue that lack of religious faith—a refusal to accept any proposition not supported by experience or by reasoning in the light of experience —was the actual source of all his philosophy. This argument is buttressed by reference to the citations of his invariable treatment of religion in ironic terms when it asks to be taken for a more serious enquiry than Hume gives it credit for being, that is, when it assumes a position as the ultimate source of all knowledge. Hume does take religious propositions seriously, as he does in the *Dialogues*, but only so long as they meet the exacting tests of logic and empiricism that he so rigorously applied to them. When they fail these tests and attempt to regain their dignity by shrouding themselves in mystery, supernaturalism, superstition, and synthetic a priori propositions—not to mention the evangelistic exhortations by less intelligent religionists—Hume feels, then, that they are properly the objects of raillery, irony, satire, or sarcasm.

Consequently, I think his use of religious irony is by far the most important, since it tells us something about the growth and structure of his ideas, or at least it does if the reasoning in the preceding arguments seems plausible. It is interesting to note that a philosophy which grew out of lack of religious faith finally gave to the philosopher the tranquillity of mind that is supposedly the haven offered to the sceptic by religion. Certainly I think Hume would have accepted the validity of any religious proposition based upon experience and reason, as indeed most of us would; but he found them only claiming to do so and claiming more jurisdiction in human affairs than the evidence warranted. As a result, religious propositions were subject to his sometimes good-natured, often philosophically damaging, irony.

The progress and unity of Hume's thought is clearly understood if we accept the notion that its beginning was fathered by religious scepticism. In view of the numerous manifestations of religious scepticism, usually cast in an ironic mode, in all of Hume's thought, our choices about the origin of his philosophy are but few. From the religious doubt comes a wish to strengthen a nontheological basis for ethics; the result is an operational ethics which emphasizes benevolence as the most praiseworthy sentiment to which human beings can aspire.[16] In other words, religious scepticism, leading to all other forms of scepticism, made necessary an ethical system that did not promise heavenly delights or hellish punishments. These sceptical principles were then articulated in many other forms, sometimes with irony added; but a scepticism which pushed religion to the brink of destruction and then "apologized" for captious arguments had ironic overtones more important than any other form of irony in Hume's life and writings.

Hume's position as an ironist is, in its most concrete form, not one which would permit an anthologist to print some of his essays in a collection of irony. Instead, his position is that of one who uses irony for special purposes: one time for raillery, one time for criticism, another time for perceiving the irony of life. The student of irony and the student of the history of ideas might learn from his use of irony its important place in his life. In one instance it provided him with a *modus vivendi* for getting along amiably with clerical friends and acquaintances. In another it amused him as a perception of the differences in men and of the various modes of behavior produced by the same stimulus. In still another it criticized philosophical, religious, or ethical opinions that were too uncritically held. Hume was incorporating into his modes of thinking and writing the ironic mode, a tradition so strong in his age that he could not have ignored it. Irony ranged into all of his works; it was the most fortuitous and ubiquitous method for expressing his ideas.

Hume's life as *le bon David* was itself an ironic commentary on the morality that held all doubters and sceptics and non-Christians as evil, pernicious men incapable of charity or benevolence. Men like Dr. Johnson were more obvious benevolists because of their piety and because they were addicted to pointing out their own benevolence. Hume, however, was the opposite, morally and intellectually, of that

---

[16] In revising the *Enquiry concerning the Principles of Morals* a few days before his death, Hume made this correction: "Upon the whole, then, it seems undeniable, *that* nothing can bestow more merit on any human creature than the sentiment of benevolence in an eminent degree; and *that* a *part*, at least, of its merit arises from its tendency to promote the interests of our species, and bestow happiness on human society." (*Works*, IV, 179; *ECPM*, p. 14). This quotation is suggested for Hume's epitaph by Professor Mossner in his *Life*, p. 608.

which tradition would have him be. One cannot completely doubt his appreciation of the ironic role he led: alleged because of his scepticism to be wanton and uncharitable, he was, in fact, a perfect, good-humored benevolist.

I have spoken of a serious purpose in his irony, seemingly contrasted to irony whose sole purpose is levity. By now, we should realize that that distinction is as artificial as the words which define it. Instead, the serious and the playful are co-ordinated in his ironic mode of life, with the levity serving the gravity more often than not. But if the gravity of the principles and men criticized by his irony had always maintained the upper hand, his life would have been a pretty grim business. Had he taken life all in a serious vein, he probably would have degenerated into the psychotic trauma characteristic of those who cannot adapt themselves to a hostile environment or even an unfamiliar environment. Had he considered all criticism of his philosophy as criticism of himself (committing in reverse the *ad hominem* fallacy), he would not have had the intellectual stamina to produce his *History*, the later essays, or the *Dialogues*.

Hume exemplifies, then, the irony of life carried to a high degree. The purpose of an ironic life is usually that of Hume: to give the person of greatly superior intelligence a way of handling the pygmies who taunt him. In an age or place in which the illiberal are ready to crucify the man who dares to criticize them all and to demolish their idols, irony is frequently the best method of keeping one's skin, while at the same time permitting posterity to see one's real meaning. Posterity can now bestow on Hume the recognition of an ironic mode of life and an ironic mode of thinking, artfully achieved and surpassingly executed.

Appendix A

A True

ACCOUNT

Of The

Behaviour and *Conduct*

Of

Archibald Stewart, *Esq*;

Late
Lord Provost of *Edinburgh*.
In a Letter to a Friend.

Non potuit mea mens, quin esset grata, teneri.
Sit, precor, officio non gravis ira pio.

Ovid.

LONDON:

Printed for M. Cooper, in *Pater-noster-Row*, M DCC XLVII.

[Price One Shilling.]

A
TRUE ACCOUNT
OF THE
BEHAVIOUR and CONDUCT
OF
ARCHIBALD STEWART, *Esq*;
LATE
LORD PROVOST of *Edinburgh*.

Sir,

You inform me that you had great Curiosity to be acquainted with all Provost *Stewart's* Story, and the Circumstances of his Conduct in *Edinburgh*, when that City was taken by the Rebels in 1745: And that having got Copies of the Informations for and against him, you had been frightened from the Perusal of them by the Sight of two such long Law Papers, which, [4] you imagined, must be full of Citations and technical Terms, and abstract Reasonings, of which you are wholly ignorant. But allow me to tell you, your Delicacy is very ill founded. I shall say nothing of the Information against him; and I doubt not, but, as it was drawn by a Lawyer of known Capacity, it is as good as the Subject would admit of. But the Information for him is really an extream good Paper, and worthy of your Perusal. And could you doubt of it, when you know the Importance of the Cause, the Expectations of the Publick, and above all, when you saw, at the Foot, the Gentleman's Name who composed it?[1]

You desire me to give you an Abstract of the Story, in more familiar Terms, and in a Form, which would give you less Trouble to comprehend it. I must own, I would not indulge your Laziness so far, at the Expence of my own, were it not that I had great Obligations to Mr. *Stewart*, as well as a great personal Regard for him; and am desirous of putting his Cause in a just Light to you, who [5] had once been so far seduced by Calumny and vulgar Reports, as to have entertained some Doubts of his Innocence.

Your former Prejudices are not at all surprizing. Whatever general Contempt we may entertain for popular Rumours, 'tis difficult, when they come full upon us, not to lend, at first, some Attention to them; and they fortify themselves with so many Stories, and such numerous Circumstances, that it becomes difficult, at last, not to give even some Credit to them. But here is

---

[1] *Mr.* Ferguson *of* Pitfour.

Mr. *Stewart's* Advantage, which he has now happily attained, after suffering the greatest Hardships, and after the most tedious Delays: He is placed before a Court of Judicature. His Calumniators must cease their furious Obloquy and loose Accusations, and hearken to the more sober Voice of his Prosecutors. These have reduced their Charge to Article and Proposition, which they are engaged to prove and defend. He has had an Opportunity to answer; and his Answer is so good, so solid, so convincing, that the good-natured Mob begin to retract their Calumnies; and even the furious Zealots confess with Regret, that he [6] has been so cunning and sagacious, as to screen himself from all legal Proof and Punishment: The utmost Confession, surely, you will ever expect from them.

As often as I heard this Subject handled in Conversation (and nothing else almost was talk'd of for some time) I desired only every zealous Declaimer to consider the Force of the Garrison which the Provost commanded, and the Strength of the Place he was to defend. These are surely very obvious Considerations, and yet few People ever entred into them, otherwise it were impossible for such ridiculous Calumnies to have made such strong and durable Impressions. Let us run over them a little, in order to set the Matter in a just Light. This may lead us into some general, as well as particular Topics, that may not be uninstructive or unentertaining.

The great Difference betwixt the State of this Island at present, and what it was a few Centuries ago, is obvious to every one. At that time, the whole Defence of both Kingdoms was trusted to the People; who, tho' they received no Pay, yet never [7] neglected the Use of Arms; tho' disperst in their own Houses, yet lived under a regular military Subordination to their Superiors and Chieftains; and tho' obliged to labour for their Subsistance, considered, all of them, their civil Occupations as a Drudgery they submited to from mere Necessity, but regarded their military Atchievements as the only Source of Honour and Glory. What Actions of desperate Valour have been performed by such Troops, and what well-disputed Fields they have fought, is known to every one that has the least Acquaintance with the History of this or of any other Nation. And the Behaviour of the present Highlander, who preserves but a small Part of these antient Institutions, may set the Matter still more strongly before us.

The Highlanders are altogether as ignorant of Discipline as the Low-Country Ploughmen, and know as little the Nature of Encampments, Marches, Ranks, Evolutions, Firing, and all the other Parts of military Exercise, which preserves Order in an Army, and render it so formidable. They advance to Battle in a confused Heap, which some People have [8] been pleased to call a Column: They can use no Weapon but the Broad-Sword, which gives not one Wound in ten that is mortal, and obliges each Combatant to occupy double the Ground that would suffice, did he employ the Pushing-Sword or the Bayonet. And they become weaker by their Victories; while they disperse to their Homes, in order to secure the Plunder they have acquired: But still, as long as they retain a devoted Obedience to their Chieftain, who is their Officer, and value themselves upon military Courage above all Endowments, they can never justly be regarded as a contemptible Enemy.

When Men have fallen into a more civilized Life, and have been allowed to addict themselves entirely to the Cultivation of Arts and Manufactures, the Habit of their Mind, still more than that of their Body, soon renders them entirely unfit for the Use of Arms, and gives a different Direction to their Ambition. Every Man is then desirous to excel his Neighbour in Riches or Address, and laugh at the Imputation of Cowardice or Effeminacy. But the barbarous Highlander, living chiefly by Pasturage, has Leisure to cultivate [9] the Ideas of military Honour; and hearing of nought else but the noble Exploits of his Tribe or Clan, and the renowned Heroes of his Lineage, he soon fancies that he himself is born a Hero as well as a Gentleman. The Songs recited at their Festivals, the Fables transmitted from their Ancestors, the continual Strain of their Conversation; all this nourishes their martial Spirit, and renders them, from their Cradle, compleat Soldiers in every thing but the Knowledge of Discipline.

In the antient Civil Wars of *Scotland*, we find that the Highland Families were always of little Weight on either Side, and that the Battles were decided entirely by the *Douglasses*, *Carrs*, *Humes*, and the other Low-Country Borderers; who, preserving the same Manners and Institutions with their Countrymen in the Mountains, had acquired a superior Address and Bravery, by their frequent Skirmishes and Battles with the *English*.

We also find, that when all the Highlanders joined to all the Lowlanders, much more numerous and brave than they, invaded *England*, under the legal Authority of their Prince or Sovereign, that Nation were so far [10] from being alarmed at the Storm, that it scarce sufficed to rouse them from their Indolence and Repose. The Militia of the Northern Counties was commonly strong enough to repel the Invaders; and the Inhabitants of *London*, when Battles were fought in *Northumberland*, or the Bishoprick of *Durham* (for our Ancestors seldom advanced farther) heard of these Combats with as great Security, as now they read of the Wars betwixt the *Persians* and the *Indians*. 'Twas only when an ambitious Prince, like *Edward* the First or Third, undertook the Conquest of *Scotland*, that the whole Force of *England* was mustered up against us.

But now, (how can we think of it without Shame and Indignation?) when not above a fifth Part of these miserable Highlanders (who are no braver than their Ancestors) rose in Rebellion, they trampled down the whole Low-Countries, who were generally averse to their Cause, and whose Ancestors could have dissipated twenty times the Force of such Barbarians: They advanced into the middle of *England*, without meeting any Resistance: They drew a prodigious Alarm [11] into the Capital itself, the greatest City in the Universe; they shook and rent the whole Fabrick of the Government, and the whole System of Credit on which it was built. And tho' there were three regular Armies in *England*, each of them much more numerous than they, they retreated back into their own Country; and still maintained their Ground. Nor can any reasonable Man doubt, that if these Armies had been removed, eight Millions of People must have been subdued and reduced to Slavery by five Thousand, the bravest, but still the most worthless amongst them.

I shall never forget the Conversation on these Events, I had at that time with a *Swiss* Gentleman, that could not sufficiently admire how so great a People, who really are Lords of the Ocean, and who boast of holding in their Hand the Ballance of Power in *Europe*, could be so impotent and defence-less against so mean a Foe, *Let those Highlanders*, says he, *have invaded my Country, and the Militia of three* Swiss *Parishes would have have repelled, what the whole Force of your three Kingdoms is scarce able to master.* And if we allow only [12] a Battalion to a Parish (which seems reasonable in so populous a Country, and where every Man is disciplined) we shall find that this Boast contains no Exaggeration, but a serious, and, to us, a very melancholy Truth.

Since then, the Disposition and Discipline of this Age and Nation is such; what reasonable Man could be surprized to hear, that the Rebels had become Masters of *Edinburgh*, while it was not defended, but deserted by its timid Inhabitants. Methinks, we should at first have expected that Event as firmly as that they would enter *Kelso, Penrith*, or any defenceless open Village that lay upon their Road, I might add *London* to the Number, and suppose only, that the Rebels had advanced from *Derby*, and that Lord *Stair*, instead of encamping on *Finchley* Common, had led his Army down to *Exeter* or *Plymouth*. Would my Lord Mayor, who commands near a Million[2] of People, have ventured to give them the smallest Opposition; or, like a *Drawcansir*, have stood alone in their way, armed with [13] his Mace

---

[2] Comprehending the City of *Westminister,* and Borough of *Southwark,* which are indeed more properly his Allies than Subjects.

and great Cap of Maintenance? For I take it for granted, that every Mortal, Citizen and Courtier, Laity and Clergy, Man and Woman, old and young, would have deserted him.

I wish his Majesty would be pleased to honour me with the Command of either of the *Highland* Battalions, and that I had some honest *Jesuitical* Clergymen to lay my Scruples; I should think it a very easy Exploit to march them from *Dover* to *Inverness*, rob the Bank of *England* in my way, and carry my Spoils, without Interruption, thro' the whole Nation; provided the Army were disposed to continue mere Spectators of my Prowess.

To tell the Truth, one of the Persons whom I should be the most sorry to meet with on my Road, would be Mr. *Stewart*. For by all that I can learn of his Conduct, he acted the Part of so vigilant, active, and even brave a Magistrate (so far as he was tried) that he might create me some Trouble: But still, if his Force was no greater than what it was during the last Rebellion, he would not be able to give me any great Interruption.

[14] Let us enumerate that Force, in order to judge the better of it, and determine whether it was likely to resist the Rebels. We shall surely find a List of Heroes equal to those of which *Homer* has given us a Catalogue, if not in his *Illiad*, at least in his *Batrachomyomachia*, or Battle of the Frogs and Mice.

There were of the Town Guards ninety six Men, augmented at that time to 126. These are rather elderly Men, but pretty well disciplined; and indeed, the only real Force the Provost was Master of. The rest were, in a Word, undisciplined *Britons*, which implies just as formidable an Idea as undisciplined *Romans*, or undisciplined *Indians*. They were nominally divided into the Trained-Bands, the *Edinburgh* Regiment, and the Volunteers. But this Division was really what the Schoolmen call a Distinction without a Difference. For with regard to military Prowess they were much the same.

As to the Trained-Bands,[3] in what Condition that formidable Body may be in at present, or might have been in, at the time of [15] the Rebellion, I cannot tell; but I remember, when I was a Boy, I had a very contemptible Idea of their Courage. For as they were usually drawn out on Birth Days, and marched up through the Main Street, it was very common for any of them, that was bolder than usual, and would give himself Airs before his Wife or Mistress, to fire his Piece, in the Street, without any Authority or Command from his Officers. But I always observed, that they shut their Eyes, before they ventured on this military Exploit; and I, who had at that

[3] These Trained-Bands are commonly about 1200 Men.

time been accustomed to fire at Rooks and Magpyes, was very much diverted with their Timorousness.⁴ However, I question not, but there are many very honest substantial Tradesmen amongst them, and as long as that is granted, I suppose they will allow any one to make as merry as he pleases with their military Character.

[16] His Majesty's Warrant to raise the *Edinburgh* Regiment was not delivered to the Provost, till the 9th of *September*, seven Days before the Rebels entered the Town. The oldest enlisted, therefore, were now Veteran Troops of seven days standing: The youngest not less than a Quarter of an Hour. Their Number might amount to about 300. I am told, that their Appearance resembled very much that of *Falstaff's* Tatterdemallion Company, which his Friend supposed he had levied by unloading the Gibbets and pressing the dead Bodies. But the merry Knight defended his Company, by saying, *Tut, mortal Men, mortal Men, good enough to toss, Food for Powder.* Tho' it is my humble Opinion, that had the Mortality of the Regiment abovementioned depended on their being Food for Powder, they would have deserved the Epithet of the *immortal Body*, as much as the King of *Persia's* Guards, who, as *Herodotus* tells us, were dignified with that Appellation. But not to be too hard upon our Countrymen, I shall allow, that notwithstanding their Poverty, they would have behaved as well as the Million Regiment of *London*, so called from the [17] Property of the Soldiers, which, it seems, amounted to that Sum.

The Volunteers, who come next, to the Number of 400, and close the Rear, the Post of Honour in all Retreats, will, perhaps, expect to be treated with greater Gravity and Respect: And no doubt they deserve it, were it only for their well meant Endeavours in Defence of their King and Country. As to their Discipline and Experience, it was much the same with that of the others. I need not add their Courage: For these are Points almost inseparable. Religious Zeal makes a mighty Addition to Discipline; but is of no Moment when alone. *Cromwell's* Enthusiasts conquered all the Nobility and Gentry of *England*; and at the Battle of *Dunkirk* struck the *French* and *Spaniards* with Admiration, even under a *Turenne* and a *Condé*. But their Brethren at *Bothwell-Bridge* fled before they came within Sight of the Enemy. Which of these Examples our Volunteers were most likely to imitate,

---

⁴ 'Tis true, their Fear was better grounded than I believe they themselves imagined, for their Arms are commonly so bad, that a very moderate Charge of Powder would have made them burst about their Ears. These were the Arms which the Provost so feloniously allowed to fall into the Hands of the Rebels.

I leave to their own Conscience to determine. A Friend of mine, who has a poetical Genius, has made a Description of their March from the *Lawn-Market*, to the *West-Port*, [18] when they went out to meet the Rebels; and has invented a very magnificent Simile to illustrate it. He compares it to the Course of the *Rhine*, which rolling pompously its Waves through fertile Fields, instead of augmenting in its Course, is continually drawn off by a thousand Canals, and, at last, becomes a small Rivulet, which loses itself in the Sand before it reaches the Ocean.

Such were the forces over whom the Provost had some Authority. His Auxiliaries were two Regiments of Dragoons, under Mr. *Fowke*, then a Brigadier General, now happily a Major General, in his Majesty's Service. Of what Importance these were to the Defence of the Town, shall be considered afterwards.

I remember *Cardinal de Retz* says, that a great Prince made very merry with the new levied Troops of *Paris*, during the Civil Wars; and when he mentioned the Defence that might be expected from the City against the King's Troops, usually called it, *La guerre des pots de chambre*, The War of the Chamber-pots. As it is well known, that a Cham- [19] ber-pot is a very formidable Machine in *Edinburgh*, I wonder it has not been comprized amongst Provost *Stewart's* Forces; at least, amongst his Auxiliaries, in Conjunction with the rest above mentioned.

Having thus given a faithful Account of the Garrison, let us now bestow some Considerations on the Place, the Defence of which was expected from Mr. *Stewart*, and which he is supposed to have lost by Negligence or bad Intentions. A weak or no Garrison, in a Place weakly fortified, or not fortified at all, must be the Consummation of all Weakness. We are forbid by Philosophy to seek for more Causes than are requisite to explain any Phaenomenon. And I think it will fairly be allowed, that if these two Circumstances are admitted, 'twill be quite superfluous to have recourse to a third, *viz.* a weak or a treacherous Governor, in order to account for the Surrender of the Place.

You know, that the City of *Edinburgh* is surrounded for the greatest part, by a plain Wall about twenty Foot high, where highest, and about two and a half or three Foot thick, [20] where thickest. It is not, in many Places flanked by any Bastions: It has not Strength or Thickness enough to bear Cannon. The Besieged would not even have room to handle or charge their Pieces; but must set up aloft as Marks to the Enemy, who can annoy them infinitely more, and receive less Harm from them, than if both stood in an open Field.

You know, that this Wall, tho' near two Miles in Length, surrounds not the whole Town, but is supplied on the North by a Lake, which is fordable in many Places.

You know, that this Wall, for a very considerable Space, is overlooked by Houses, which stand within five or six Paces of it, and which it was impossible to destroy because of their Number and Value.

The Town is supplied with Water entirely by Pipes. Its Bread is even, strictly speaking, its daily Bread. For the Bakers never have by them more Flower than serves them a Day, but bring it continually from their Milns on the Water of *Leith*, as Occasion requires.

[21] Besides, as happens in all Civil Wars, there were so many disaffected Persons in Town, that had it been held out but for three Hours (which indeed was impossible) it was justly feared, that it would have been set on fire from within, in order to facilitate the Entry of the Rebels; nay, it was easily possible for the Rebels themselves to set fire to it from without, and force it, by that means, to a speedy Surrender.

It is obvious to every one, however ignonorant [*sic*] of military Affairs, that any Governor who incloses himself in such a Place, fights with Disadvantage, and has infinitely better Chance for Success, if he fairly opens his Gates, and marches forth to combat his Enemy in an equal Battle. For not to insist on the other Disadvantages above mentioned, the Circuit of these Walls is too large to be guarded by any moderate Garrison; the Enemy can draw them together to any one Place by a false Alarm, in the Night, or even in the Day; while he breaks in at a distant Place, that is weakly defended, and the Garrison, entangled among the Houses and Garden- [22] Walls, must be cut in Pieces, almost without Resistance.

This Measure therefore, of meeting the Rebels before they reached *Edinburgh*, was very prudently resolved on by General *Guest*, on the 16th of *September*, when Intelligence was brought, that the Highlanders were approaching; and he ordered Brigadier *Fowke* to advance with his Dragoons to the *Colt-Bridge* for that Purpose; he also desired Mr. *Stewart* to join what Infantry he could to sustain the Dragoons. The Provost ordered upon this Duty all the Town Guard, and all the *Edinburgh* Regiment that were fit for Service. He had no Power to order the Volunteers out of Town: He only consented, that, as many as pleased, should be allowed to march out. But, it seems, they had as little Inclination to go, as he had Power to order them; a few of them made a faint Effort; but, 'tis said, met with Opposition from some of the *zealously affected*, who represented to them the infinite Value of their Lives, in comparison of those Ruffians, the Highlanders. This Opposition they were never able to overcome.

[23] Brigadier *Fowke* (whose Conduct in this whole Affair is too remarkable to be forgot[5]) tho' he had only two Regiments of Dragoons, and a very few Infantry, was still a formidable Enemy to the Rebels. For, as much as regular veteran Infantry are superior to Cavalry, as much are Cavalry, especially in an open Field, superior to an irregular Infantry, such as the Highlanders; who cannot keep their Ranks, wherein consists all the Force of Foot; who cannot fire regularly in Platoons; who know not the Use of the Bayonet, and whose sole Weapon is their Broad-Sword, in which a Horseman, by his very Situation, has an infinite Advantage above them. Or if it were too sanguine to hope for a Victory from such a Force as the Brigadier commanded, a leisurely and a regular Retreat might a [*sic*] least have been made, tho' he had advanced within a Musket Shot of the Enemy.

[24] But before the Rebels came within Sight of the King's Forces, before they came within three Miles distance of them, Orders were issued to the Dragoons to wheel; which they immediately did, with the greatest Order and Regularity imaginable. As 'tis known, nothing is more beautiful than the Evolutions and Motions of Cavalry, the Spectators stood in Expectation what fine warlike *Manoeuvre* this might terminate in; when new Orders were immediately issued to retreat. They immediately retreated, and began to march in the usual Pace of Cavalry. Orders were repeated, every Furlong, to quicken their Pace; and both Precept and Example concurring, they quickened it so well, that before they reached *Edinburgh*, they had come to a pretty smart Gallop. They passed, in an inexpressible Hurry and Confusion, through the narrow Lanes at *Barefoot's* Parks, in the Sight of all the North Part of the Town, to the infinite Joy of the Disaffected, and equal Grief and Consternation of all the other Inhabitants. They rushed like a Torrent down to *Leith*; where they endeavoured to draw Breath: But some unlucky Boy (I suppose a *Jacobite* in his Heart) calling to [25] them that the Highlanders were approaching, they immediately took to their Heels again, and galloped to *Prestonpans* about six Miles further. Here in a literal Sense, *Timor addidit alas,* their Fear added Wings; I mean to the Rebels. For otherwise, they could not possibly imagine, that these formidable Enemies could be within several Miles of them. But at *Prestonpans* the same Alarm was renewed, *The Philistines be upon thee,*

[5] Non ego te meis
Chartis inornatum fileri,
Totve tuos patiar labores
Impune, Lolli, carpere lividas
Obliviones: Est animus tibi
Rerumque prudens, &c. &c.   HORACE.

Sampson, they galloped to *Northberwick*; and being now about twenty Miles on the other Side of *Edinburgh,* they thought they might safely dismount from their Horses, and look out for Victuals. Accordingly, like the ancient *Grecian* Heroes, each of them began to kill and dress his Provisions. *Egit amor dapis atque pugnae*, they were actuated by the Desire of Supper and a Battle. The Sheep and Turkies of *Northberwick* paid for this warlike Disposition. But behold! the Uncertainty of human Happiness; when the Mutton was just ready to be put upon Table, they heard, or thought they heard, the same Cry of the Highlanders. Their Fear proved stronger than their Hunger; they again got on Horseback, but were informed time enough of the [26] Falseness of the Alarm, to prevent the spoiling of their Meal.

By such Rudiments as these the Dragoons were trained; till at last they became so perfect in their Lesson, that at the Battle of *Preston,* they could practise it of themselves; tho' even there the same good Example was not wanting.

I have seen an *Italian* Opera called *Caesare in Egitto,* or *Caesar in Egypt*; where in the first Scene *Caesar* is introduced in a great Hurry, giving Orders to this Soldiers, *Fugge, fugge: a'llo scampo.* Fly, fly: to your Heels. This is a Proof, that the Commander at the *Colt-Bridge* is not the first Heroe that gave such Orders to his Troops.

'Twas in Consideration of such great Example, I suppose, that he has been so honourably acquitted,[6] and since promoted; while Mr. *Stewart* has been imprisoned for fourteen Months, forced to give a Recognizance of 15000 £. for his Appearance, and three times, [27] in a manner, brought upon his Trial. So true the old Proverb, *That it is safer for one Man to steal a Horse, than for another to look over a Hedge.*

But Mr. *Stewart* asserts, very justly, that he neither stole the Horse, nor look'd over the Hedge. He neither incurred any real Guilt, nor gave the smallest Foundation for any such Suspicion; the only adviseable Expedient for saving the Town was tried; and failing, with such multiplied Circumstances of Terror and Consternation, it left him, if possible, in a worse Situation than before, by that Discouragement, with which it imprest everyone. The Volunteers, before that time, had thought fit of themselves to give up their Arms to the Castle; the *Edinburgh* Regiment had also given up their Arms: The Burghers or Trained-Bands, deserted by the regular Forces, refused to expose their Lives, when they understood, by repeated Threatnings from the Rebels, that every Man, who made any Resistance,

---

[6] Upon his Trial, he justified himself at Mr. *Stewart's* Expence, and threw much Blame upon the Provost.

should be put to Death. In short an universal Panic, and that not groundless, had seized the People. 'Tis what the bravest and best disciplined Forces have been subject [28] to, and what is, with great Difficulty, cured, by the most expert Commanders. But 'tis unavoidable in every undisciplined Multitude, and is there perfectly incurable.

What tho' some faint Glimpse of Hope was afforded, by the Intelligence received, towards the Evening of this fatal Day, that Sir *John Cope* with his Army had been seen at Sea, off *Dunbar*. This Succour was too distant to relieve them from an Enemy, who was at their Gates. And the Minds of Men were now unbent, and had, with great Reason, abandoned all Thoughts of Defence, which they could not resume again, in such immediate Danger, and without any probable or possible View of Success.

In this Confusion, when nobody did his Duty, when nobody but Mr. *Stewart* seemed to think he had now any Duty to do, the Town, always un-garrisoned, always unfortified, now in an universal Consternation, perhaps divided within itself, was entered without Resistance by the Rebels.

[29] I should think it an Affront on your Understanding to shew you more particularly how unavoidable this Event is to esteemed; and therefore having put this main Point in a just Light, I shall touch, tho' briefly, on the other Articles of Accusation. They are, I own, like the Provost's Forces, pretty numerous; but surely the most disorderly, undisciplined Rabble that ever were led into the Field. They are rather the Subject of Ridicule than of any serious Opposition. For Instance,

The Lord Justice Clerk, several of the Judges, along with the King's Council, gave it unanimously as their Opinion, that the levying of a Regi-ment, without his Majesty's Warrant, was illegal: His Majesty, when ap-plied to, confirmed that Doubt by granting that Warrant: And the plain Words of the Statute requires such an Authority; yet the raising a Doubt upon this Head is deemed a Crime; tho' that Doubt, or any other Doubt, were it ever so ill grounded, must be allowed intirely innocent.[7]

[30] The Provost also is said to have raised a Doubt about the Legality of inlisting the Volunteers. And indeed, this Case is so much alike, or so much the same with the other, of raising a Regiment, that no wonder such a Scruple did arise. But he took Care, immediately, to consult the Lord Ad-vocate; and he also took Care, immediately, to acquiesce in his Lordship's Judgment. Yet this is one Article of Charge against him.[8]

The Town-Council intrusted the Inspection and Care of the Work to a

---

[7] Article the 1st.
[8] Article the 2d.

Committee under another Person: The Works projected were all finished before the Arrival of the Rebels. Are you not surprized he must answer for them, as if they were unfinished; or, as if they had chiefly been put under his Direction?[9]

Some Zealots had proposed to set up Marks of Distinction, from mere Suspicion on several Citizens, who behaved themselves peaceably. The Provost rejected so imprudent, so pernicious a Measure. Is he therefore criminal?[10]

[31] He offered Pay and Victuals to some Volunteers, that came from the Country; need I repeat the Question, if this Proposal renders him criminal?[11]

A Gentleman, Mr. *Alves*, travelling on the Road towards *Edinburgh*, passes the Rebels; and the Duke of *Perth* gives him a threatning Message to deliver to the Provost: The Provost does not immediately commit him; both because it did not appear, that he was any way guilty, in relating to the Chief Magistrate, a Story in which he had been involuntarily engaged; and because there was Danger of spreading the Story the faster, and intimidating the Inhabitants, by such a Commitment. Hearing a few Hours afterwards, that the Gentleman had been so imprudent as to tell his Message to others, he immediately committed him. You are not surprized, I suppose, after what you have read above, to find, that this is an Article of Accusation.[12]

He is also charged with receiving a Petition from the Inhabitants, keeping a Meeting with [32] them, and hearing a Letter read from the Pretender's Son. The receiving the Petition was innocent, and also unavoidable, unless he had shut himself up in his Closet. The calling a Meeting of the Inhabitants at such a Juncture, would also have been innocent. But he called no such Meeting. The Inhabitants, under Terror of the approaching Danger, pressed in upon him wherever he went, and would have their Complaints and Remonstrances heard; and the Provost, so far from consenting to read the Letter, openly and strongly opposed it, and left the Company to avoid hearing it.[13] All these Facts are public and notorious.

On the 15th of *September,* the Provost was called in the Evening to Lord Justice Clerk's, where Lord Advocate, General *Guest,* Brigadier *Fowke,* and several other Officers, were present. A Proposal was there made, that

---

[9] Article the 3d.
[10] Article the 4th.
[11] Article the 5th.
[12] Article the 6th.
[13] Article the 7th.

the Dragoons should be brought into Town, with a View to give them some Rest and Refreshment, and have their Horses fed in the Streets. But upon Reflection it appeared, that the Avenues of the Town might be taken pos- [33] session of by the Rebels, and the Streets barricadoed, the Houses lined, and the Dragoons by that means fall into the Hands of the Enemy. This Proposal, therefore, was most justly rejected. Next Day, after the near Approach of the Rebels, after the Flight of the Dragoons, after the universal Consternation of all Ranks, Mr. *Stewart* refused to sign any Order to these Dragoons, over whom he had no Authority, to return and enter into the Town; tho' he promised them all Kind of good Reception and Entertainment, if they thought proper to come. When I find the Refusal to sign such an Order, stated as an Article of Accusation against the Provost, I cannot think but the Accuser, foreseeing the Circumstances of Merit, which the Accused would plead, laid immediate Claim to them as his own Right; like a prudent General, who takes Possession of those Eminences or strong Grounds, that may be of Service to the Enemy. This Observation is, indeed, applicable to almost all the Articles; there is scarce any of them but might be cited as a Proof of Mr. *Stewart's* Vigilance, Prudence, Activity, or Moderation.

[34] If the Volunteers, in the Hurry of so active a Day, as the 16th of *September*, waited some time for Orders, without receiving any; this is also made an Article of Charge.[14]

The 10th Article is of the same Force with all the rest; tho' I shall not tire either you or myself, by narrating or refuting it. I shall only add a few Words, with regard to the *Eleventh* Article, which charges him with allowing the City Arms to fall into the Hands of the Rebels; because some People think there is a Foundation for this Charge, tho' they frankly allow all the rest to be frivolous, and even ridiculous.

First, Without mentioning the Insignificancy of these Arms, Mr. *Stewart* pleads, with regard to this Article, and with regard to all Articles, that have been, or may ever be charged against him, that, tho' Chief Magistrate, and President of the Town-Council, he was really but one Member, and had but one Vote. The supreme Command was in [35] the Council. They were criminal, if there be any Crime. It is not, nor can it be pretended, that he, in this or any other Instance, opposed, or overruled, or contradicted their Determination.

Secondly, There had several Messages come from the Rebels, threatening Destruction, if the City either resisted or secreted their Arms. It is a Ques-

---

[14] Article the 9th.

tion whether the Magistrates, for the saving of a few rusty Arms, ought in Prudence to have run the Risque of having these Threats executed, considering the known Barbarity of the Clans, and the then unknown Moderation of their Chieftains. But it is no Question, however the Magistrates had determined, that the People would not have consented; and consequently, that the secreting these Arms was absolutely impracticable.

Thirdly, Mr. *Stewart* showed all along a particular Attention to keep Arms out of the Hands of the Rebels. When it was proposed, after the News arrived of Sir *John Cope*'s being seen off *Dunbar*, to desire back again from the Castle, the Arms which the [36] Volunteers and the *Edinburgh* Regiment had carried thither; the Provost, apprehensive of the Consequences, rejected the Proposal; till he should see, as he said, a better Disposition in the Inhabitants, to make use of Arms. And he even sent a Message to General *Guest* in the Castle, informing him of the Consternation of the Town, and the little Authority which the Magistrates had, to force the Trained-Bands to deliver up their Arms; and desiring, at the same time, the General to send down a Party to carry up the Arms, or use some other Expedient to that Purpose.

Fourthly, It is proper to consider, in this Case, the Uncertainty of the Situation to which the Magistrates and Council were reduced, during the last and most distressing Scene of this unlucky Affair: Sometimes terrified with the immediate Approach of the Rebels; at at [*sic*] other times, incouraged with some Prospect of Relief; even towards the End of this Period there were some Hopes of the Return of the Dragoons. Nor was that Expectation quite over in the Meeting of the Council; until they heard the Rebels had entered the [37] Town. Had the Dragoons returned to the City, and animated the People in its Defence, the Charge against the Provost then, would have been inverted, Why did he send up the Arms to the Castle? Why did he carry them out of the way, when they might be instantly wanted for the Defence of the Town, and the near Approach of the Rebels made a Moment's Delay of great Consequence? And the Citation might have been adduced, which has been misapplied in the present Case, *Quod puncto saepe temporis maximarum rerum occasiones amittuntur,* That Success in the greatest Affairs, frequently depends on a Moment.

But, *Fifthly,* what if Mr. *Stewart* should say (which indeed he has here no manner of Occasion for) that he was in the wrong, and that in the general Hurry and Consternation, it was difficult not to forget something. Would any Man lay this as a criminal Accusation against him. I grant, in War, it is never allowed a General to say, *Non cogitavi,* I did not think of it. *Marlborough* or *Eugene* might be ashamed of such an Excuse: But the Provost was bred to a different Profession. And [38] I dare affirm, that even these great Generals, had they been ingenuous, might, twenty times in their Lives, have made use of this Apology.

The *Twelfth*, and last Article is, if possible, still more extraordinary than all the rest. It makes the Provost the *Scape* Goat, and charges him with the Sins of the whole People; because the People want Charity, and judge him criminal, therefore he must really be so. You may read, indeed, in your *Machiavel*, that, by a very peculiar and very absurd Law in the Republick of *Florence*, wherever the popular Opinion condemned a Man, it was lawful for a certain Magistrate, called the *Gonfalioneré*, immediately to put him to death, without any Trial or Form of Process. I have no Intention to deny, that Mr. *Stewart* would have fared very ill, had he been in *Florence* two Years ago; and had the present Provost been *Gonfalionere*. Tho' now I believe he would have no Reluctance to submit himself to a popular Tribunal.

> [39] *The People's Voice is odd,*
> *It is, and it is not the Voice of God.*

But tho' popular Clamours are not here, as in *Florence*, authorized by Law, it is plain, that, in Practice, at least in Mr. *Stewart's* Case, they draw very terrible Consequences after them. He was sensible of the Disadvantage he lay under; yet this would not discourage him from attending his Duty in Parliament. He put himself into the Hands of his Enemies; for such the Ministry had become; nor need we be in the least surprized at it. He suffered a severe Confinement for some time; and tho' this was by Degrees remitted, yet still it continued a Confinement for fourteen Months, very grievous to any Man, and very prejudicial to a Man of Business.

I have been certainly informed, that, very often when the Ministry, in prosecution of their usual Lenity, was resolved to give Mr. *Stewart* his Liberty, their Hands were continually stopped by a fresh Cargo of Lies and [40] Calumnies imported to them from *Scotland*; and which it required some time to examine and discuss.

Bu [*sic*] when, at last, he got his Liberty, and had the Prospect of a fair Trial, this happy Time, which should put a Period to all his Sufferings, was continually protracted, in the most unaccountable Manner in the World. At the first Diet in *March*, he was put off till *June*, and afterwards till *August*. When every Thing was then ready for a Trial, the Prosecutor deserted the Diet, and Mr. *Stewart*, as well as the Public, imagined, that all was over, and that his Enemies, conscious of his Innocence, were to free him from all farther Prosecution. But he is again, it seems, to be brought on his Trial, with additional Expence, and Vexation and Trouble. How long this may yet last is uncertain; and 'tis evident any Man might be ruined by the Continuation and Repetition of such a Practice: For which, it seems, our Law provides no Remedy.

[41] All these vexatious Measures gave the more Indignation, when we consider against whom, and by whom, they are exercised. You are perfectly well acquainted with Mr. *Stewart*, and know him to be a good Magistrate, a good Friend, a good Companion, a fair Dealer: A Man in every Action of his Life, full of Humanity, Justice and Moderation.

The Government too, is surely the fullest of Mildness, Equity and Justice in the World. The present Instance is, I believe, the only one, in near sixty Years, of an innocent Man, that has ever lain under the least Oppression. If our Government is faulty in any thing, 'tis rather in the opposite Extreme; and the present Times show sufficient Examples of it.

The Town of Edinburgh *was lost*; a most unexpected, and most unaccountable Event surely! But what was it when the Battle of *Falkirk* was lost; when a numerous, a veteran and a brave Army fled before a Handful of Highlanders whom they had scarce seen? I never heard that the Author of that Cala- [42] mity has been punished, or even questioned, or has met with the smallest Discouragement; I mean, from the higher Powers. For I was very well diverted, t'other Day, by the Account of a Sarcasm, he met with from a private Hand, which was the severest in the World.

When the Army fled to *Linlithgow*, they immediately quartered themselves about in all the Houses, and even in the Palace, where there dwelt, at that time, a Lady noted for Wit and Beauty; who observing their disorderly Proceedings, was apprehensive they would fire the Palace. She immediately went to remonstrate to a certain great General, and was received *pro solitâ suâ humanitate*, with his usual Humanity. Finding her Remonstrances vain, she took her Leave in these Words, *To take care*, says she, *of the King's House, is your Concern: For my Part, I can run from Fire as fast as any of you.*

> So spoke the Cherub, and her grave Rebuke,
> Severe in youthful Beauty, added Grace
> Invincible. Abash'd the Devil stood, &c. &c.

[43] It would be cruel to mention the unfortunate Knight; and, I believe, since we live in an acquitting Age, every Body is glad he was acquitted. I have heard, that all the Winter after the Battle of *Preston*, he was carried about *London* in his Chair, with the Curtains drawn, to escape the Derision of the Mob; till the News of the Battle of *Falkirk* arrived, and then he pulled back the Curtains, and showed his Face and his red Ribbon to

all the World. Thus the Reputation which the Hero of the *Colt-Bridge* was the chief Cause of depriving him of, the Hero of *Falkirk*, in a great Measure, restored to him.

Saepe, premente Deo, fert Deus alter opem.

I need not insist on the Mayor of *Carlisle*, Mr. *Pattison* (not *Paterson*) who defended so gloriously a fortified Town against the Rebels.

I shall only say, If all these Enormities pass unpunished, and Mr. *Stewart* alone the Victim, there are some People, to make [44] Use of the Allusion of a witty Author, that resemble very much the Monster in *Rabelais*, that could swallow a Wind-mill every Morning to Breakfast, and was at last choaked with a Pound of Fresh-Butter hot from an Oven.

I am, &c.

October 20, 1747.

POSTSCRIPT

[45] I INTENDED to have sent this by ——— but not being able to meet him before he left this Country, I was obliged to keep it by me till this time, when I hear, to my great Satisfaction, that Mr. *Stewart* has been acquitted by the Jury *Nemine contradicente*, and that all the Facts contained in his Information, and in the foregoing Letter, were proved with an Evidence and Conviction, even beyond what he himself imagined. The Trial was the longest and most solemn that ever was known in this Country; and the Judges were even obliged, by Necessity, to break through an established Custom and Law, and adjourned the Court, on Account of the absolute Impossibility of supporting, without Interrup- [46] tion, the Fatigues of so long a Trial. Mr. *Stewart* intended to have abridged their Trouble, by resting his Defence intirely on the Pursuer's Evidence, without adducing a single Witness of his own: But he was overruled in this by his Council, who approved of the Confidence arising from Innocence, but still insisted upon having two Witnesses adduced, for all the principle Facts, upon which he grounded his Defence.

Several of the Jury had been Volunteers during the Rebellion, and all of them were particularly distinguished by their warm Zeal for the Government. As some People had been foolish enough to make this Trial a Party Business, all Mr. *Stewart's* Friends were alarmed, when they saw the Names of the Jury. For tho' they were sensible of the Probity of these Gentlemen, yet they dreaded their Prejudices, and were afraid, that Truth and Innocence would not obtain so full a Triumph (as they did afterwards) over Passion and Party-Zeal.

[47] I can assure you the King's Advocate did not want Keenness in this Affair, to give the mildest Appellation to his Conduct. And here I must inform you, that what I heard of his Speech suggested to me a Remark, which I had often made, to the Honour of our Age and Nation, in one Particular, above the antient Times of *Greece* and *Rome*. Mr. *Grant* was very copious in insisting on the Suspicions this Country lay under with Regard to *Jacobitism*, the apparent Diffidence the Ministry had shewn to trust us with the Trials of the Rebels, the strong Conviction every one in *England* had of Mr. *Stewart's* Guilt, and the great Scandal his Acquital would bring on the Country; to which he added, that a very slight Punishment was intended, a few Days Imprisonment, and a small Fine, which one so rich as Mr. *Stewart* could easily bear. But though you know that such extraneous and popular Topicks as these, are very usual in all the Poems and Epilogues of *Cicero*, and even of *Demosthenes*; yet I can assure you this Imitation of the an- [48] tient Orators was not at all approv'd of, either by the Jury or the By-standers.

You will be very much surprized, I suppose, to hear, that many of the *Whigs* have betrayed such a furious Zeal on this Occasion, that they are mortified, or rather indeed inraged to the last Degree, that an innocent Man has been found innocent: And this has given Occasion to the opposite Party, to make his Acquital a Matter of infinite Triumph and Rejoicing; as much almost as the Defeat of *Val*, or the Surprizal of *Bergen-op-zoom*, or any other publick Calamity, that has ever befallen us. Whatever opposes or disappoints the Government will always be, without Distinction, a great Satisfaction to them.

But I shall further explain to you the great Difference betwixt a political and a religious *Whig*, in order to account for these odd Transactions. The Idea I form of a political *Whig* is, that of a Man of Sense and Moderation, a Lover of Laws and Liberty, whose chief Regard to particular Princes and Families, is founded on a Regard to the publick Good: [49] The Leaders of this Party amongst us, are Men of great Worth; the President, for instance, and Lord Justice Clerk, especially the Former. I say, *especially the Former*: for tho' 'tis certain the Conduct of the Justice Clerk was altogether commendable, as far as the Circumstances and Situations, in which he was placed, would admit; yet that of the President has been so singularly good and great, as to be the Subject of Admiration, and even of Envy, if Virtue could ever excite that Passion.

The religious *Whigs* are a very different Set of Mortals, and in my Opinion, are much worse than the religious *Tories*; as the political *Tories* are inferior to the political *Whigs*. I know not how it happens, but it seems to me, that a Zeal for Bishops, and for the Book of Common-Prayer, tho' equally groundless, has never been able, when mixt up with Party Notions, to form so virulent and exalted a Poison in human Breasts, as the opposite Principles. Dissimulation, Hyprocrisy Violence, Calumny, Selfishness are, generally [50] speaking, the true and legitimate Offspring of this kind of Zeal.

This Species of *Whigs*, whatever they may imagine, form but the Fag-end of the Party, and are, at the Bottom, very heartily despised by their own Leaders. Once on a time, indeed, the Breech got over the Head; when *Cromwel, Ireton, Warriston,* &c. ruled our Councils and Armies; and then there was fine Work indeed. But ever since, though their Assistance has been taken at Elections, and they have been allowed, in Return, to rail and make a Noise as much as they please, they have had but little Influence on our publick Determinations; and long may it continue so.

These are Mr. *Stewart's* greatest, and indeed, only Enemies. The political *Whigs* are, many of them, his personal Friends; and all of them, are extremely pleased with his Acquital, because they believe, what is, indeed, undeniable, that it was founded on his Innocence. I am charitable enough to [51] suppose, that the Joy of many of the *Tories* flowed from the same Motive. And as to those, if there were any such, who had a different Motive, he will not, I believe, give them any Thanks for a Concern, which is more likely to hurt than to serve him.

Novem. 4, 1747:

FINIS.

Appendix B

PETITION

of the

GRAVE AND VENERABLE BELLMEN,

OR SEXTONS,

of the

CHURCH OF SCOTLAND

to the

HONOURABLE HOUSE OF COMMONS:

Most humbly sheweth,

THAT whereas the Reverend Clergy of the Church of Scotland, moved by a sincere regard to the glory of God, which has so conspicuously appeared in men of the sacred character, throughout all ages, have applied to Parliament for an augmentation of their stipends.

And whereas the learned body of Schoolmasters, incited by their pious example, and moved by the same regard to the glory of God, have also applied for an augmentation of their salaries,

[188] And whereas it has pleased the Divine Providence to bless both these applications with such assured prospect of success; it might appear strange, if the grave and venerable body of Bellmen, being also Ecclesiastical persons, though of an inferior character, should be so backward in this Holy cause, and so neglectful of the glory of God, even though called upon by the illustrious and edifying example of their superiors.

The grave and venerable Bellmen, therefore, of the Church of Scotland, having weighed these considerations, do now presume to lay their case before the Honourable House of Commons, not doubting but they will meet with the same kind reception which is indulged to the Reverend Clergy and Learned Schoolmasters.

The Venerable Bellmen beg leave to support the petition by the following reasons:—

That it can be proved demonstrably from Scripture and reason, that the cause of religion is as intimately and inseparably connected with the temporal interests and worldly grandeur of your Petitioners as with any of these ecclesiastics whatsoever.

That your Petitioners serve in the quality of grave-diggers, the great use and necessity of their order, in every well regulated commonwealth, has never been called in question by any just reasoner; an advantage they possess above their brethren, the Reverend Clergy.

That their usefulness is as extensive as it is great; for even those who neglect religion, or despise learning, must yet, sometime or other, stand [189] in need of the good offices of this grave and venerable order.

That it seems impossible the landed gentry can oppose the interests of your Petitioners; since by securing so perfectly as they have hitherto done, the persons of their fathers and elder brothers of the aforesaid gentry, your Petitioners next, after the physicians, are the persons in the world to whom the present proprietors of land are the most beholden.

That as your Petitioners are but half ecclesiastics, it may be expected they will not be altogether unreasonable nor exorbitant in their demands.

That the present poverty of your Petitioners in this kingdom is a scandal to all religion, it being easy to prove, that a modern Bellman is not more richly endowed than a primitive apostle, and consequently possesseth not the twentieth part of the revenues belonging to a Presbyterian Clergyman.

That whatever freedom the profane scoffers and freethinkers of the age may use with our Reverend Brethren the Clergy, the boldest of them trembles when he thinks of us; and that a simple reflection on us has reformed more lives than all the sermons in the world.

That the instrumental music alloted to your Petitioners being the only music of that kind left in our truly reformed churches, is a necessary prelude to the vocal music of the Schoolmaster and Minister, and is by many esteemed equally significant and melodious.

That your Petitioners trust the Honourable [190] House will not despise them on account of the present meanness of their condition; for having heard a learned man say, that the Cardinals who are now Princes, were once nothing but parish curates of Rome, your Petitioners observing the same laudable measures to be now prosecuted, despair not of being one day on a level with the nobility and gentry of these realms.

May it therefore please, &c &c.

A
LETTER
to a
MEMBER OF PARLIAMENT,
WITH THE FOREGOING PETITION

Buckhaven, 27th January, 1751.

HONOURED AND WORTHY SIR,

It having pleased the Lord to visit his sinful people of this Church with many and great tribulations, it was with consolation we saw a kind of *Pisgah* prospect opened to us of better days, by the application of the Reverend Ministers and Learned Schoolmasters for an augmentation of their stipends and salaries; and we, having no less zeal in our inferior station, for the same holy cause, have also [191] agreed upon an application for a like purpose; which I am empowered to transmit you by the conveyance commonly called by the profane, the *Post*. For I do not find there is any gospel name for it. If it seemeth good in your eyes, after communing with your heart in prayer, it would be a furtherance of this Godly work, if you would get printed in the great city a sufficient number of this *Petition*, and order one to be delivered to every Member of the House, on the great day of grace, whereon the Reverend Ministers are to present their *Petition*, it might, with Divine assistance, very much forward so good a work, and might be the cause, that both of them may meet with the same success, which I am sure both of them equally deserve.

Now, worthy and honourable Sir, if you will be the instrument of the *Lord* in this holy undertaking, I do hereby promise you in my own name, and in that of all my brethren, that he amongst us, whom the *Lord* will bless with the comfortable task of doing you the last service in our power, shall do it so carefully, that you never shall find reason to complain of.

I am,
Honoured and worthy sir,
Your Friend and Servant in the Lord,
ZOROBABEL M'GILCHRIST,
Bellman of Buckhaven.

AUTHORITIES CITED

WORKS OF DAVID HUME

Dialogues concerning Natural Religion, ed. with Introduction by Norman
Kemp Smith. 2nd. ed. New York: Social Sciences Publishers, 1948.
History of England. 6 vols. Boston: Aldine Book Publishing Co., *c.* 1900.
*History of England from the Invasion of Julius Caesar to the Revolution in
1688, The.* 8 vols. London, 1773.
Inquiry concerning the Principles of Morals, An, ed. by Charles W. Hendel.
New York: Liberal Arts Press, 1957.
Inquiry concerning Human Understanding, An, ed. by Charles W. Hendel.
New York: Liberal Arts Press, 1957.
Letters of David Hume, The, ed. by J. Y. T. Greig. 2 vols. Oxford: Claren-
don Press, 1932.
New Letters of David Hume, ed. by Raymond Klibansky and Ernest Camp-
bell Mossner. Oxford: Clarendon Press, 1954.
*Petition of the Grave and Venerable Bellmen, or Sextons, of the Church of
Scotland to the Honourable House of Commons,* anon. London, 1751.
Reprinted in *The Scotch Haggis.* Edinburgh, 1822.
Philosophical Works of David Hume, The, ed. by T. H. Green and T. H.
Grose. 4 vols. London: Longmans, Green, and Co., 1874–1875.
Treatise of Human Nature, A, ed. by L. A. Selby-Bigge. Oxford: Claren-
don Press, 1955.
True ACCOUNT *of the Behaviour and Conduct of Archibald Steward, Esq.;
Lord Provost of Edinburgh, In a Letter to a Friend, A.* London, 1748.

OTHER WORKS

Books:

Beattie, James. *An Essay on the Nature and Immutability of* TRUTH, *in
Opposition to Sophistry and Scepticism.* 5th. ed. London, 1774.
Becker, Carl L. *The Heavenly City of the Eighteenth-Century Philosophers.*
New Haven: Yale University Press, 1960.
Boswell, James. *Life of Johnson, ed.* by G. B. Hill, rev. and enlarged by
L. F. Powell. 6 vols. Oxford: Clarendon Press, 1934–1950.
———— *Private Papers of James Boswell from Malahide Castle,* ed. by F. A.
Pottle. 18 vols. New York: Privately Printed, 1928–1934.

Broad, C. D. *Five Types of Ethical Theory*. London: Routledge and Kegan Paul, Ltd., 1956.

Burton, John Hill. *Life and Correspondence of David Hume*. 2 vols. Edinburgh, 1846.

Campbell, George. *Dissertation on Miracles*. Edinburgh, 1762.

———— *Philosophy of Rhetoric*. Edinburgh, 1776.

Chesterfield, Philip Dormer Stanhope, Fourth Earl of. *Letters to his Son,* ed. by Charles Strachey, notes by Annette Calthrop. 2 vols. New York: G. P. Putnam's Sons, 1925.

Flew, Antony. *Hume's Philosophy of Belief: A Study of His First Inquiry*. New York: Humanities Press, 1961.

Forbes, Sir William. *An Account of the Life and Writings of James Beattie, LL.D*. 2 vols. Edinburgh, 1806.

Fraser, A. C. *Thomas Reid*. Edinburgh, 1898.

Gerard, Alexander. *An Essay on Taste*. Edinburgh, 1759.

Greig, J. Y. T. *David Hume*. London: J. Cape, 1931.

Hayter, T. *Remarks on Mr. Hume's Dialogues, concerning Natural Religion*. Cambridge, 1780.

Hendel, Charles William, Jr. *Studies in the Philosophy of David Hume*. Princeton: Princeton University Press, 1925. Republished in a revised and enlarged edition by the Liberal Arts Press (New York, 1963).

[Horne, Bishop George]. *A Letter to Adam Smith LL.D. on the Life, Death, and Philosophy of his Friend David Hume, Esq.,* "By One of the People Called Christians." Oxford, 1777.

Hutcheson, Francis. *Philosophiae Moralis Institutio Compendiaria*. Edinburgh, 1742.

Huxley, Thomas H. *Hume, With Helps to the Study of Berkeley*. New York, 1897.

Jessop, T. E. *Bibliography of David Hume and of Scottish Philosophy from Francis Hutcheson to Lord Balfour*. London: A. Brown and Sons, Ltd., 1938.

Kant, Immanuel. *Critique of Pure Reason,* tr. by Norman Kemp Smith. London: Macmillan and Co., Ltd., 1956.

———— *Prolegomena to Any Future Metaphysics,* ed. and trans. by Paul Carus. Chicago: Open Court Publishing Co., 1949.

Knox, Norman. *The Word* IRONY *and its Context, 1500–1755*. Durham: Duke University Press, 1961.

Laird, John. *Hume's Philosophy of Human Nature*. London: Methuen and Co., Ltd., 1932.

Leroy, André-Louis. *David Hume*. Paris: Presses Universitaires de France, 1953.

——— *La Critique et la Religion chez David Hume*. Paris: F. Alcan, 1930.

Lucas, F. L. *The Art of Living: Four Eighteenth-Century Minds*. New York: Macmillan Co., 1961.

Mandeville, Bernard. *The Fable of the Bees,* ed. by F. B. Kaye. 2 vols. Oxford: Clarendon Press, 1924.

Mossner, Ernest Campbell. *Bishop Butler and the Age of Reason: A Study in the History of Thought*. New York: Macmillan Co., 1936.

——— *Forgotten Hume: Le bon David, The*. New York: Columbia University Press, 1943.

——— *Life of David Hume, The*. Austin: University of Texas Press, 1954.

Norton, William J. *Bishop Butler, Moralist and Divine*. New Brunswick: Rutgers University Press, 1940.

Parkin, Rebecca Price. *The Poetic Workmanship of Alexander Pope*. Minneapolis: University of Minnesota Press, 1955.

Popper, Karl. *The Open Society and Its Enemies*. Princeton: Princeton University Press, 1950.

Reid, Thomas. *Works,* ed. by Sir William Hamilton, Bart. 2 vols., 7th ed. Edinburgh, 1852.

Robbins, Caroline. *The Eighteenth-Century Commonwealthman*. Cambridge: Harvard University Press, 1959.

Rotwein, Eugene. *David Hume: Writings on Economics*. Edinburgh: Nelson, 1955.

Shaftesbury, Anthony Ashley Cooper, Third Earl of. *Characteristics of Men, Manners, Opinions, Times*. 3 vols. Birmingham, 1723.

Smith, Norman Kemp. *The Philosophy of David Hume: A Critical Study of its Origins and Central Doctrines*. London: Macmillan and Co., Ltd., 1949.

Standard Reference Work for the Home, School, and Library, The, Vol. IV. Minneapolis and Chicago: Standard Education Society, 1922.

Stephen, Sir Leslie. *English Thought in the Eighteenth Century*. 2 vols. New York: Harbinger Books, 1962.

Stewart, Dugald. *Biographical Memoirs of Smith, Robertson, and Reid*. Edinburgh, 1811.

Warburton, William. *A Selection from Unpublished works of the Right Reverend William Warburton,* ed. by Francis Kilvert. London, 1841.

Wesley, John. *Works*. 15 vols. London, 1872.

Wiley, Margaret L. *The Subtle Knot: Creative Scepticism in Seventeenth-Century England*. London: George Allen and Unwin, 1952.

Articles:

Cohen, Ralph. "David Hume's Experimental Method and the Theory of Taste," *Journal of English Literary History*, XXV, #4 (1958), 270–289.

Davies, Godfrey. "Hume's History of the Reign of James I" in *Elizabethan and Jacobean Studies Presented to F. P. Wilson*. Oxford: Clarendon Press, 1959. Pp. 231–249.

Horn, David B. "Hume as Historian" in *A Record of the Commemoration Published as a Supplement to the University Gazette*. Edinburgh: University Press, 1961. Pp. 25–28.

Mossner, Ernest Campbell. "An Apology for David Hume, Historian," *PMLA*, LVI (1941), 657–690.

———— "David Hume's 'An Historical Essay on Chivalry and modern Honour'," *Modern Philology*, XLV (1947), 54–60.

———— "The Enigma of Hume," *Mind*, XLV (1936), 334–349.

———— "Hume and the Ancient Modern Controversy, 1725–1752: A Study in Creative Scepticism," *University of Texas Studies in English*, XXVIII (1949), 139–153.

———— and Harry Ransom, "Hume and the 'Conspiracy of the Booksellers': The Publication and Early Fortunes of the *History of England*," *University of Texas Studies in English*, XXIX (1950), 162–182.

———— "Hume's *Four Dissertations*: An Essay in Biography and Bibliography," *Modern Philology*, XLVIII, #1 (1950), 37–57.

———— ed., "New Hume Letters to Lord Elibank," *Texas Studies in Literature and Language*, IV (1962), 431–460.

———— "Philosophy and Biography: The Case of David Hume," *Philosophical Review*, LIX (1950), 184–201.

———— "Was Hume a Tory Historian? Facts and Reconsiderations," *The Journal of the History of Ideas*, II (1941), 225–236.

Pomeroy, Ralph S. "Hume on the Testimony for Miracles," *Speech Monographs*, XXIX (1962), 1–12.

Price, John V. "Empirical Theists in Cicero and Hume," *Texas Studies in Literature and Language*, V (1963), 255–264.

———— "Sceptics in Cicero and Hume," *The Journal of the History of Ideas*, XXV (1964), 97–106.

Randall, John H., Jr. "David Hume: Radical Empiricist and Pragmatist," in *Freedom and Experience: Essays Presented to Horace M. Kallen*, ed. by Sidney Hook and Milton R. Konvitz. Ithaca: Cornell University Press, 1947. Pp. 289–312.

INDEX

Abercromby, James: letter to, 43, 45
Absalom and Achitophel: 3
Account of Stewart. SEE Hume, works of
Addison, Mr.: 79 n.
Advocate's Library: 75
ambiguity: in irony, 7, 56, 136, 138, 139, 141
Annandale, 3rd Marquess of: 36
anthropomorphism: validity of, 135
argument, from design: 123, 130–131, 138–139, 142
atheism: Hume accused of, 30, 77, 83–84, 106–107; Hume on, 59–60; mentioned, 140
Athens, Greece: 80
Augustan Age: Hume and 3, 4–5; characteristics of, 4
authority, concept of: in marriage, 14–15; and Deity, 134–135; mentioned, 31, 49
Aylesbury, Robert of: 100

Balfour, Arthur, 1st Earl of: 76 n.
Barebone, . . . (*History*): 85
Batrachomyomachia: 39
Beattie, James: on Hume's philosophy, 5, 30 n., 122, 138; mentioned, 75 n., 112 n., 123 n. SEE ALSO *Essay on Truth*
Bellmen's Petition. SEE Hume, works of
benevolence: of Hume, 64, 149; as basis for ethics, 65 and n.
Berkeley, Bishop George: 5, 9, 58, 110 n.
Blacklock, Thomas: sponsorship of, by Hume, 75 and n.
Blair, Hugh: and Hume's work, 34, 140–141; as intermediary for Reid, 111; Hume to, on religion, 123–124
"booksellers, conspiracy of": 79
Boswell, James: 29 n., 143 and n.
Boufflers, Comtesse de: affair of, with Hume, 16, 74, 114–118, 119; personality of, 17, 117; letters of, 114, 115; marriages of, 115, 116
British Museum: 79
Burns, Robert: irony of, 101–102
Butler, Bishop Joseph: philosophy of, 5, 28 n., 127; Hume's respect for, 26, 32, 106; mentioned, 18, 85, 140
Butler, Samuel: on religion, 148
Byron, George Gordon, Lord: 58

Caesar, Julius: 71

Caesar in Egypt (opera): 41

Campbell, George: on Hume, 122, 123; mentioned, 112 and n., 113. SEE ALSO *Dissertation on Miracles; Philosophy of Rhetoric*

Cartesianism: 6

Catholicism: 66, 88, 89, 91–92

Caulfield, James, Lord Charlemont: 16 n.

causation: types of, 28, 135; effect and, 57

Celts: 97

Characteristics . . . (Shaftesbury): 129 n.

Charles I: reign of, 77, 78, 79; religion under, 84, 86, 87–88; mentioned, 79 n.

chastity: in women, 9, 12, 13

Chesterfield, Philip Dormer Stanhope, 4th Earl of: 119 and n.

chivalry: 4 and n.

Christianity: aspects of: 21, 35, 56, 58, 135; Hume and, 88, 98, 123–124, 143, 151

Church of England: 86, 91

Church of Scotland: 62

church-state, relationship of: 90, 91–92, 98

Cicero, Marcus Tullius: 3, 128 and n. SEE ALSO *De Natura Deorum*

Clarke, Samuel: 127

classical virtue: 4

Cleanthes (*Dialogues*): description of, 127 and n.–128 n.; arguments of, 129–138 *passim*; mentioned, 136, 139

Clement VI, Pope: 100

Clephane, John: 61, 77

Coleridge, Samuel Taylor: on irony, 7

Commonwealth, the: 81, 83, 87

"conspiracy of the booksellers": 79

Conti, Prince de: 116

Cowley, Abraham: *Discourses* of, 83

Critique of Pure Reason: 27 n.

Cromwell, Oliver: Hume's on, 81, 82, 83; religion under, 84, 86

custom: truth and, 8; morality and, 69, 103

cynicism: Hume's, 29, 34

Dalrymple, Sir John: 79 n.

Deism: 107

Deity: as anthropomorphic, 58, 59, 88, 135; existence of, 127, 132–133, 134, 136, 137, 138–139, 146, 149; mentioned, 90. SEE ALSO God

Demea (*Dialogues*): description of, 127, 133; arguments of, 129, 131, 133–134, 135; mentioned, 128 n., 136, 139

De Natura Deorum: 128 and n.

design, argument from: 123, 130–131, 138–139, 142

Dialogue, A. SEE Hume, works of

Dialogues concerning National Religion. SEE Hume, works of

Discourses: 83
Dissertation on Miracles: 112 n., 123
dogmatism: reason and, 6, 52, 97; Hume's acceptance of, 6, 60, 66, 147; mentioned, 84
Don Juan: on Christianity, 58
Douglas, Archibald, Marquess of: 121
Douglas, Lady Jane: 121
Douglas Cause, the: 121
Druids: 97, 98
Dupe: 57, 94
D[uvernan], Countess of: 16 n.
Dysart, Mrs. Matthew: letter to, 70–71

Edinburgh: 36, 38, 39, 40, 61, 121
Edward I: 103
Eiron: 57, 94
Elibank, Lord Patrick Murray: 79 n.
Elizabeth I: religion under, 91, 92–93, 94; mentioned, 90
Elliot of Minto, Sir Gilbert: religion of, 140, 141; mentioned, 61, 74, 148
emotions: SEE passions
empiricism: Hume's, 27 and n., 37, 48, 72, 150; mentioned, 50, 67, 129, 133
England, Church of: 86, 91
Enquiry concerning Human Understanding. SEE Hume, works of
Enquiry concerning the Principles of Morals. SEE Hume, works of
entertainment: in literature, 97, 103–104
Epictetus of Hierapolis: 51
Epicurean: nature of, 22, 23–24; mentioned, 25
"Epicurean, The": 22, 23
Epicureanism: 23, 24, 25
epistemology: 8, 34, 50, 56
Essay on Criticism: 3
Essay on Man: 3, 103
Essay on Taste: 112 n.
Essay on Truth: 30 n., 75 n., 122
Essays, Moral and Political: 18, 33, 36
Essays and Treatises on Several Subjects: 21
ethics: as secular, 64–65, 67; relativism of, 68–69

Fable of the Bees: 107 n.
Fairfax, Sir Thomas: 81, 82
faith: as basis of religion, 28, 53; Hume's, 149
Falstaff, Sir John: 40
Ferguson, Adam: 124
Flew, Professor Antony: 47
Four Dissertations: 74, 105, 106 n.
Fowke, Brigadier-General: 41–42

Fraser, James: as Jacobite, 43, 44, 45; mentioned, 53 n.
Free Enquiry into the Miraculous Powers: 106 n.

Galileo: 81
George I: 79 n.
George II: 79 n.
Gerard, Alexander: 112 and n., 113
God: existence of, 21, 28, 131–142 *passim*, 146, 149; ways of, 48, 88. SEE ALSO
    Deity
Godfrey, Sir Edmunsbury: 89
Goldsmith, Oliver: 79 n.
Gothic era: 3–4
Gregory, John: 112 and n., 113
Gulliver's Travels: influence of, on Hume, 3, 30, 61; irony in, 61, 65, 66, 80

Hamilton, Gavin: 77
Hamilton, James George, Duke of: 121
Hazlitt, William: 144
Henry VII: laws under, 94, 95
Henry VIII: reign of, 95–96
Herodotus: 40
Herring, Thomas, Archbishop: 78
Hertford, Francis Seymour Conway, Earl of: 121
"Historical Essay on Chivalry and Modern Honour, An": 3, 13
history: writing of, 75, 80, 81
History of England. SEE Hume, works of
Hobbes, Thomas: and conformity, 4
Home, Alexander: 71
Home, John (David's brother): 62, 70
Homer: heroes of, 39
human nature: duplicity of, 10, 65, 109, 145; improvement of, 30, 114, 146;
    weaknesses of, 49, 59, 85, 90, 94, 104, 105; scepticism and, 58, 145; morality
    of, 66, 69, 118; science of, 72, 88, 109, 111 119, 149
Hume, David: environment of, 3–6, 72–73, 152; philosophy of, 4, 33, 34, 60,
    149–151; Comtesse de Boufflers and, 16, 74, 114–118, 119; correspondence
    of, 19, 33, 60, 70, 72, 99, 110; style of, 29, 38, 46, 90, 120; character of, 46,
    117, 119, 136, 148; politics and 71, 77, 78, 83; as historian, 75–76, 77, 80–81,
    83, 89, 95, 97, 98–99, 102; as Philo, 127–139 *passim*. SEE ALSO atheism;
    benevolence; philosopher; religion; scepticism; women
—, irony of: with clerical friends, 5–6, 123–124, 126, 147; tone of, 6, 7–8, 37,
    42, 46, 48, 49, 92, 101, 116, 117; use of, 7, 13, 16, 34, 38, 45–46, 65, 71, 72,
    80, 83, 87, 90, 92, 93–94, 110, 119, 122, 146; function and purpose of, 21,
    25, 29–30, 31, 35, 49, 52, 56, 58, 63–64, 103, 104–105, 109, 113, 117, 118,
    128, 141, 145, 146, 151, 152; characteristics of, 25, 29, 37, 40, 43, 63, 88, 89,
    145. SEE ALSO irony
—, works of:
Account of Stewart, urbanity of, 38; parodies in, 38–39, 39–41; ironic mode
    of, 42; mentioned, 36, 38 n., 43, 45

Bellman's Petition, parodies in, 62–63; mentioned, 53 n., 61 and n., 64

Dialogue, A, approach to ethics in, 67; irony of, 68–70, 90; mentioned, 70, 94

Dialogues concerning Natural Religion, revisions of, 120, 122; "creative scepticism" of, 123; speakers in, 127–128; irony in, 128, 129, 130–132, 134, 138–139, 147; argument from design in, 130–131; professions of faith in, 133, 134, 136–137; discussion of God in, 132–133, 135; mentioned, 26–27, 66, 105 n., 127 n., 150, 152

Enquiry concerning Human Understanding, irony in, 46, 48, 53–55, 57–59; on rationalism, 47–48; on value of passion, 51; scepticism in, 52; mentioned, 36, 60, 64, 70, 72, 106 n.

Enquiry concerning the Principles of Morals, Hume's opinion of 64; irony in, 65, 66–67; *Gulliver's Travels* and, 65–66; secularism of, 67; benevolence in, 151 n.; mentioned, 46, 47, 70, 72

"Epicurean, The," 22, 23

Essays, Moral and Political, 18, 33, 36

Essays and Treatises on Several Subjects, 21

Four Dissertations, 74, 105, 106 n.

"Historical Essay on Chivalry and modern Honour, An," 3, 13

History of England, reaction to, 75, 78–79, 114, 119; writing of, 76 and n., 79–80, 83, 89, 99–100, 152; irony in, 77, 81–103 *passim,* 147; on politics, 77, 92, 94–95, 98; on religion, 83–88, 89–90, 91–93, 98, 106; on human nature, 100–101, 103, 104–105; mentioned, 4 n., 21, 70, 74

My Own Life, on authors, 3; on women, 16; on finances, 33; on own works, 35, 46, 64, 77, 90, 97; on Charles I, 87; on self, 144, 145; mentioned, 113, 140

"Natural History of Religion, The," existence of God and, 106; on ignorance and devotion, 107; logic of, 108–109; mentioned, 105

"Of the Academic or Sceptical Philosophy" (*ECHU*), 59

"Of Chastity and Modesty" (*Treatise*), on women, 9–10, 11; irony in, 10–11, 13; on double standard, 11, 12–13

"Of Impudence and Modesty," 53 n.

"Of Love and Marriage," 13–14, 18

"Of Miracles" (*ECHU*), early version of, 26, 31–32; scepticism of, 52–53; irony of, 54–57, 91; logic in, 56; mentioned, 90, 150

"Of a Particular Providence and of a Future State" (*ECHU*), religious irony of, 57, 58; mentioned, 53

"Of the Passions," 105

"Of the Populousness of Antient Nations," 72, 80

"Of the Standard of Taste," 105

"Of Tragedy," 105

"On the Study of History," 80–81

"Petition" against James Fraser, 43–44, 45

"Platonist, The," 24

Political Discourses, 29 n., 70, 74

"Sceptic, The," 22

"Stoic, The," 22

Treatise of Human Nature, on life, 8–9, 34, 90, 119, 149; "recasting" of, 18,

22, 46–47; on religion, 26, 27–28, 36, 147; reaction to, 72, 103, 110, 113; mentioned, 33, 37
Hutcheson, Francis: 4 n., 9 n.
hypocrisy: reaction to, 13, 58

ignorance: merit of, 49–50, 107–108, 131; in Hume's time, 85, 100–101
Illiad: 39
Innys, the bookseller: 18
Inquiry into the Human Mind: critique of, 111–112
instruction: as esthetic principle, 89, 102, 103, 104
Interesting Anecdotes, . . . (Mr. Addison): 79 n.
irony: in Augustan Age, 4; "cosmic," 7, 102, 119, 120; ambiguity in, 7, 15, 37, 46, 56, 117, 136, 138, 139, 141; scepticism and, 7, 29, 49, 52, 92, 118, 119, 151; of life, 8, 18, 22, 55, 83, 109–110, 144–145, 145–146; good-natured, 17, 24, 28, 29, 35, 45, 114, 143; philosophical, 25–26, 48, 57; Socratic, 25, 50; religious, 26, 28, 31, 34–35, 57–58, 64, 84–89, 98, 104–105, 108, 120, 126, 127, 139, 142, 146–150; as a reversible vehicle, 37; both-and, 37 and n., 51; blame-by-praise, 37 and n., 41, 48, 114, 136; political, 38, 42, 71, 77, 78, 82, 98; ironist and, 73; historical, 80, 89, 93–94, 101, 102, 103. SEE ALSO Hume, irony of

Jacobites: 36, 39, 43, 45
James I: 77, 79 n., 84
Jardine, Reverend John: relationship of, with Hume, 124–127
Johnson, Dr. Samuel: on Hume, 29 n., 79 n.; mentioned, 102
justice: concept of, 65

Kames, Henry Home, Lord: as farmer, 19; relationship of, with Hume, 31–33, 34; mentioned, 18, 27
Kant, Immanuel: 27 n., 30 n.
knowledge. SEE epistemology

Laud, Bishop William: 86, 87
Locke, John: 5, 9, 58
Louis, of Spain, Prince: 100
Luther, Martin: 126

Madison, James: 92
Mandeville, Bernard: 107 n.
Marchmont Hugh, Earl of: 60
marriage: authority in, 14–15; Hume and, 16, 60–61
Mary I: 91
man: nature and, 5, 83, 118; woman and, 9–10, 11–12, 13–17; reality and, 34, 54, 145, 146. SEE ALSO human nature
Middle Ages: 97
Middleton, Conyers: 106 n.

Millar, Andrew: 78, 105
Milton, John: 6, 135
miracles: theories on, 31, 53, 149; testimony and, 54–55, 56. SEE ALSO Hume, "Of Miracles"
Modest Proposal, A: 3, 52, 53 n.
morality, sexual: double standard and, 10–11; hypocrisy of, 12; Hume's attitude towards, 17
Morrice, Corbyn: 140
Mossner, Ernest Campbell: 38, 43, 72
Mure, Katherine: 21, 143
Mure, William: relationship of, with Hume, 19–21; mentioned, 61, 121
My Own Life. SEE Hume, works of

National Library of Scotland: 75 and n.
"Natural History of Religion, The." SEE Hume, works of
naturalism: Hume's, 59–60
nature: man's place in, 8–9; uniformity of, 59; mentioned, 96. SEE ALSO human nature
Newton, Sir Isaac: 70
nihilism: 145
Normandy, Duke of: 99, 100

Oates, Titus: 89
"Of the Academic or Sceptical Philosophy" (*ECHU*): 59
"Of Chastity and Modesty" (*Treatise*): 9–13
"Of Impudence and Modesty": 53 n.
"Of Love and Marriage": 13–14, 18
"Of Miracles." SEE Hume, works of
"Of a Particular Providence and of a Future State" (*ECHU*): 53, 57, 58
"Of the Passions": 105
"Of the Populousness of Antient Nations": 72, 80
"Of the Standard of Taste": 105
"Of Tragedy": 105
"On the Study of History": 80–81
opera, Italian: Hume on, 41
optimism: of eighteenth century, 103
Orde, Nancy: 16 n.
Oswald, James (of Dunniker): 46, 60
Oswald, James: 138

passions: reason and, 5–6, 17, 55, 72, 93–94, 118, 144; Hume and, 60, 117
Pamphilus (*Dialogues*): description of, 127; as Platonist, 128–132 *passim*
"Petition" against James Fraser: 43–44, 45
Philo (*Dialogues*): description of, 127 and n.; as identified with Hume, 129–139 *passim*
philosopher: criticism of, 5, 10, 23, 24–25, 48, 49, 50–51; Hume as, 6, 33, 34, 60
Philosophiae Moralis Institutio Compendiaria: 4 n.

Philosophy of Rhetoric: 112 n.
Pimple, of Witham, Kill Sin: 85
Pistor (*History*): 93
Plato: on marriage, 15–16; rationalism of, 24, 50, 128
Platonism: criticism of, 50, 128–132
"Platonist, The": 24
Political Discourses: 29 n., 70, 74
Pope, Alexander: 29, 34, 103, 120. See also *Essay on Criticism; Essay on Man*
"Popish Plot": 89
Popper, Karl: 49
power: as struggle, 96–97
primogeniture: Hume on, 62–63
Pringle, Dr. John: 36
Prolegomena to any Future Metaphysics: 30 n.
Protestantism: 88, 91
Puritans: 90

Ramsay, Michael: letter to, 6–7
rationalism: irony and, 22, 57, 58; of Plato, 24, 50, 128; Hume and, 27, 48, 60, 102; mentioned 47, 52, 130. See also Platonism
reason: passions and, 5–6, 17, 55, 72, 93–94, 118, 144; scepticism and, 6, 31, 49, 118; in ethics, 27, 53, 67, 85, 103, 105; mentioned, 25, 90, 143
Reformation: 91
Reid, Thomas: on Hume's irony, 110–111, 112, 113; criticism of, 111–112, 112–113; mentioned, 114. See also *Inquiry into the Human Mind*
religion: Hume's contribution to, 26, 123; miracles and, 53, 54–55, 56; abuses in, 58, 84–86, 88; value of, 87, 107, 137; "natural," 88, 106, 127, 130, 131, 135, 136; Druid, 97, 98
Retz, Cardinal de: 40
Richard II: 102
Robertson, William: 79 n.
Roman History (Goldsmith): 79 n.
Rousseau, Jean-Jacques: 117
Russell, Bertrand: Hume compared to, 25, 29, 60; mentioned, 64, 82

St. Clair, Lt.-General James: 36, 43
sarcasm: 65, 150
satire: 4, 80, 150
Saxons: 97
Scapegoat: 57
"Sceptic, The": 22
scepticism: religion and, 4, 21, 26, 51, 60, 64, 86, 108, 122, 126–127, 141, 149–151; reason and, 6, 31, 49, 118; form of, 9, 22, 90, 123; irony and, 7, 29, 49, 62, 118, 119; human nature and, 58, 103, 145; mentioned, 63, 144
scholasticism: 57
Scotch Haggis, The: 61 n.
Scotland, Church of: 62

Scotland, literature of: 74, 75
Scots Magazine: 74
Scotticisms: 29 n., 74, 112
Selby-Bigge, L. A.: 72
self-deception: 88
self-love: 85
Shaftesbury, First Earl of: 89
Shaftesbury, Third Earl of: 129 n.
Shaw, George Bernard: 60
Shortest Way with Dissenters, The: 3
Smith, Adam: 95 and n., 110 n.
Smith, Norman Kemp: 129, 137, 149
Socrates: 50, 68
solipsism: 9, 145
Spectator: 3
Steuart-Douglas, Archibald: 121
Stewart, Archibald: Hume defends, 36–45 *passim*; trial of, 38
Stewart, Dugald: 110 n.
Stoicism: 51
Stone, George, Primate: 78
Strabo: 71
Strafford, Thomas, 1st Earl of: 78
"Stoic, The": 22
Stuart, Andrew: 121–122
Stuart, Prince Charles Edward: 38, 39
Stuart-Moncrief, David: 122
superstition: 98, 143–144, 149
Swift, Jonathan: on human nature, 29–30, 104; irony of, 34, 61, 80, 119, 148; Hume compared to, 45, 52, 119, 120, 145. SEE ALSO *Gulliver's Travels*; *Modest Proposal, A; Tale of a Tub, A*
Symposium (Plato): 15

Tacitus: 79 n.
Tale of a Tub, A: 3
Tatler: 3
testimony, human: Hume on, 53–55, 56
theism: 60, 80, 107, 135, 139
theology. SEE religion
Theory of Moral Sentiments: 95 n.
Thirty Years' War: 81
Toryism: 71, 77, 78, 83
Treatise of Human Nature. SEE Hume, works of
Trevor, of Norsham, . . . (*History*): 85

Unpopular Essays: 64

Vinnius: 3
Virgil: 3
Voet: 3

Wallace, Robert: 64
Walpole, Sir Robert: 20
Warburton, Reverend William: 28 n., 106–107
Wesley, John: 21, 142 n.–143 n.
Whiggism: 71, 77, 78, 83
William the Conqueror: 99, 100
witches: 21–22
Wolsey, Thomas: 96
women: chastity of, 9–10, 12, 13; double standard and, 10–11, 12, 13; marriage
    and, 14, 15; Hume and, 16–17, 60–61, 115, 117–118, 119, 124
Wordsworth, William: 24

Xenophon: 68

Yahoo: 32
Young Pretender: 38, 39